Barry Grantham

Barry Grantham is a performer, director and teacher of *Commedia* and related physical theatre. His background is professional theatre: his maternal grandfather was a music hall artiste and his father a classical actor, who first aroused an interest in the *Commedia dell'Arte* in his son. As a teenager, Barry worked as a mime and dancer, and went on to train with Idzikowski, a famous Harlequin with the Diaghilev company, and was coached in that role by him.

An early career working in almost every form of theatre, from the experimental fringe to the West End, and in films such as *The Red Shoes* and *Tales of Hoffman*, prepared Barry for a return to his first love, *Commedia dell'Arte*. In the 1970s, he began a series of workshops and performances at the Oval House Theatre and the City Lit, London, and formed the nucleus of the Intention Commedia Company, which has continued to give performances up to the present time.

He has performed and given masterclasses in Norway, Sweden, Holland, Germany and in Italy itself at the Teatro Municipale, Reggio Emilia. Recently he has performed at both Glyndebourne and the Royal Opera House, and is choreographer for Gifford's Circus. He currently writes, directs and appears as guest artiste with various companies while still running the Intention Commedia Company.

By the same author

PLAYING COMMEDIA
A Training Guide to Commedia Techniques

COMMEDIA PLAYS
Scenarios Scripts Lazzi

BARRY GRANTHAM

*Eight original plays
based on the different periods and styles
of the Commedia dell'Arte for performance,
workshop and training*

N H B

NICK HERN BOOKS
London
www.nickhernbooks.co.uk

A Nick Hern Book

Commedia Plays
first published in Great Britain in 2006
by Nick Hern Books Limited
14 Larden Road, London W3 7ST

Commedia Plays © 2006 Barry Grantham

Reprinted 2008

Barry Grantham has asserted his right to be
identified as the author of this work

Cover design: Ned Hoste/2H

Typeset by Country Setting, Kingsdown, Kent, CT14 8ES
Printed and bound in Great Britain by Cromwell Press,
Trowbridge

A CIP catalogue record for this book
is available from the British Library

ISBN 978 1 85459 871 4

CAUTION NOTE

In educational and workshop situations, groups are entitled
to perform these plays free of charge. If the plays are being performed
before a paying audience then a licence must be obtained.

Please contact the Performing Rights Manager, Nick Hern Books,
The Glasshouse, 49a Goldhawk Road, London W12 8QP,
fax +44 (0)20 8735 0250, *e-mail* info@nickhernbooks.demon.co.uk

Preface

My principle aim in writing this book was to provide a series of plays and sketches, inspired by the different periods and styles of the *Commedia dell'Arte,* suitable for performance or to be used as the basis for classroom and workshop study. For though improvisation is one of the distinguishing features of the genre, and the aim should always be to introduce as much improvisation and spontaneity into the performance as possible, a total lack of script presents, for many, an insuperable barrier to attaining a reasonable standard. Almost the only written play that gives a close approximation of 'Golden Age' *Commedia dell'Arte,* is Goldoni's *Servant of Two Masters,* and this was written as a protest at the low level to which, he believed, improvisation had sunk in around 1745. Though the play could not be bettered, alternatives and shorter vehicles should be available.

The techniques and performing disciplines of *Commedia dell'Arte,* together with an outline of its history and a detailed description of each of the Masks is given in my previous book, *Playing Commedia,*[1] but there remains this one major difficulty for companies, groups and individuals wishing to put these rules into practice, and that is the problem of improvising in an unknown idiom. And chances of getting to know the idiom are limited, because of the lack of models on which to base one's work (even in Italy it is not performed on a regular basis). Therefore in recent years, I have found that by initially working with a script, a grasp of *Commedia* can be achieved with greater certainty, and in a much shorter space of time, than attempting improvisation from the scenario alone. Once familiar with the idiom, greater improvisation can then be gradually introduced.

One should remember that at no time was *Commedia dell'Arte* totally spontaneous. The improvisation was laced with memorised speeches, rhymed couplets, witty sallies, exit lines, and above all, the rehearsed comic business we call *Lazzi.* To provide appropriate examples of these for insertion into the plays was my second preoccupation. In assembling

---

1. *Playing Commedia,* Barry Grantham, Nick Hern Books, 2000

this collection of comic business, drawn not only from the rather scarce *Commedia dell'Arte* accounts and illustrations, but also from traditions of pantomime, circus, music hall and early film, I realised that this part of the book was not merely an appendix to the plays, but a record of comic business that might be of value to directors, actors and performers, not necessarily involved with *Commedia*. I now feel that the plays are there as much to illustrate the use of *Lazzi*, as the *Lazzi* are there to augment the plays.

BARRY GRANTHAM

Acknowledgements

I would like to express my thanks to members of the Intention Company past and present, and to the many students especially of the Chalemie Summer Schools who first performed many of the plays.

To David Drummond of 'Pleasures of Past Times' for his valuable suggestions, to Nick Hern for his encouragement, to Jodi Gray for her enthusiasm and editing, and finally to my wife (and theatre partner), Joanie, for her support, criticisms and diligent proofreading.

Our thanks also

. . . to members of *The Intention Commedia Company*, including Miss Dawn Purkiss, Miss Joan Chorlton, Mr Anton Welbeck, Mr Richard Handley and Mr Grantham himself for posing for the photographs that illustrate this book.

Contents

Part One: The Plays

Fool's Gold
One-act play, with early Mask types but with *fin de siècle* 'Art House' influences   83

Harlequin Married
Mime play typical of Art Deco *Commedia dell'Arte* of the 1920s   99

The Haunting of Pantaloon – a Harlequinade
One-act play, based on the early Victorian 'spoken' style   109

The Duchess Mislaid
Large-scale two-act play, designed as a community project involving all the well-known Masks   129

Part Two: The Lazzi   207

Illustrations

How to Use This Book

Part One

Introductions

After the title page there follows the cast list and information on playing time, the period style, space required, etc. Then there is a short introduction for each play to establish its particular genre, period and source of its inspiration. There is a brief analysis of the characters and their traditions, and notes on costumes and settings. With certain of the smaller and less well-known Masks,[2] a brief description of their costume and characteristics may be given in the text before their first entrance. Costume and prop lists are not exhaustive, but there to give an indication of the production values involved.

Scenarios

Next, is the important scenario, which takes the form of the 'argumento' from which the *Commedia dell'Arte* actors would have constructed their entire performance. This gives the opportunity for more experienced performers to attempt scene-by-scene improvisation, which can later be compared against the written text and *Lazzi*.

Texts

However, the normal course will be for the text of the entire play to be given a company reading. The scripted scenes can then be rehearsed from the text in the usual manner. Where the physical actions or stylised business we term *Lazzi* are called for, a number in the text indicates where the appropriate description and instruction can be found in Part II. In cases where a *Lazzo* is very specific to a particular scenario, the description may be given within the text of the play itself.

The division of the script into scenes mirrors the scenario, and is there to help workshop and rehearsal. It does not imply any change of set or time, or an interruption in the flow of the performance.

---

2. In the *Commedia dell'Arte*, 'mask' can mean either the facemask itself or the character wearing it; in which case, here it is given a capital 'M'.

Part Two

The Lazzi for insertion into the text

Over sixty *Lazzi* are described in detail, most of which are applicable to specific scenes in one or more of the plays. They are listed alphabetically and cross-referenced to similar *Lazzi* under another name. The words of a particular scene would normally be learned, blocked and adequately rehearsed before working on the *Lazzi*, so that the characterisation and motivation can be carried through into the *Lazzi*, which should never become pure clowning. See further details in the introduction to Part II.

The Lazzi as workshop material

Alternatively, the *Lazzi* can also be used as workshop exercises, the students being divided into twos and threes to work on a *Lazzo*, with (or without) the help of the descriptions. The devising and performing of such *Lazzi* are an essential skill of the *Commedia* player, and as such should form at least one quarter of their training programme.

Either approach should inculcate a feeling for the special qualities of *Commedia* style in the performer, so that he or she can replace, extend or elaborate on the written text, varying it at each and every performance.

Studying Commedia

Of course the book as a whole may be studied by the interested reader, to whom it should give an insight into the many periods and styles of *Commedia dell'Arte*; its characters, plot constuctions, dialogue, and *Lazzi* in the absence of live performances.

Introduction

The very name *Commedia dell'Arte* presents a problem for those of us who want to press its claims as a major theatre force, as relevant today as it was at any time in its long history. It is a label so loaded with misconceptions, fallacious interpretations and divided opinions that I, along with many of my colleagues, prefer to use the shortened term of *Commedia*, except when referring to it in a strictly historical context.

This is not the place to offer a detailed definition of *Commedia*, and I hope and believe the following plays and *Lazzi*, in themselves, will define its scope, style, possibilities and limitations. However, there is part of the full term that I would like to dwell on briefly, and consider the significance of *'dell'Arte'*. Its meaning is something close to *'of the trade'*, which should bring to mind that whole world of medieval and Renaissance guilds, with their exclusivity, their secrets and their long apprenticeships. It is in the light of this, that I find that the translation of *Commedia dell'Arte*, as 'The Comedy of Skills', to be a most useful and pragmatic one. It is more rewarding to think of the *Commedia* as a trade, like that of any other artisan, rather than as an art form in itself; it being up to the individual performer to transform it into art, where he or she can. It is also the individual's responsibility to imbue these traditional skills, accumulated by its long line of practitioners, with vitality and the appearance of originality.

It should also be stressed that an understanding, training and knowledge of these traditions does not, and must not, mean that the possessor is dead to fresh influences. If we further consider comparison with any trade, such as that of the potter, the cabinet maker, the goldsmith or the builder, we see that skill handed down from master to apprentice does not preclude change, and in the past it has permitted major stylistic modification – from the Gothic to Renaissance, baroque, art nouveau and art deco. We can also realise that the 'new' is often brought into being by a return to fundamentals practised in an earlier period. So, in the same way, the theatre of the future may find renewal and inspiration, by a return to a form having affinities with the *Commedia dell'Arte*'s improvisation, stylisation, direct audience involvement, the use of multiple skills, and imagination replacing elaborate staging. There are indications that this indeed is taking place.

Commedia is about skill, which includes the elusive ability to improvise, but which must be supported by the detailed preparation of *Uscite, Chuisette, Consiglii,* and *Lazzi*.[3] If we take as an example the final scene from *The Path of True Love,* where the lover, Lelio, makes a formal proposal to Isabella, whilst still pursuing a duel with Captain Spavento, we will see that this would be impossible without pre-choreographing and considerable rehearsal. Some knowledge of stage fighting is required, and some familiarity with the films of Douglas Fairbanks and Errol Flynn to acquire the necessary panache, and/or Rostand's *Cyrano,* as an example of combining rhetoric with swordplay. In this way, not only is the actor exhibiting physical skill, but connecting to the whole tradition of European theatre culture. *Commedia* is a theatre of *Allusion* rather than *Illusion*; it takes delight in referring to things with which the audience must also be familiar, recognise, and willing to share a laugh about. As we share with the audience the whole joke, the whole game, the whole pretence, we also share with them a reverence for our mutual traditions.

There are individual introductions to each play, dealing with the specific aspects presented, although they are not hermetically sealed units and may bring up concepts, problems and opinions of more general interest or application. Likewise Part II, which is there in the first place to give *Lazzi* that are connected to a point in one or more of the plays, also includes variants and allied *Lazzi* that are not so specific.

When it comes to production, the aim should be to produce a viable piece of theatre inspired by the *Commedia dell'Arte,* featuring some of its eternal Masks and plot structure – a comedy to entertain today's audiences. It cannot, and we would not want it to be, an exact period re-creation; which would have to be in Italian, in accents now forgotten. We might find the humour unacceptable and dialogue tedious. This brings us to the important consideration of anachronisms: to include anachronisms can often make a performance closer to the spirit of *Commedia dell'Arte* than a production which studiously avoids them. Much of the humour would have included topical and local reference; so to get a similar reaction from the spectators one would have to offer a contemporary alternative – the name of Barbarossa might be substituted

3. 'Exits', 'Closings', 'Counsellings' and 'Comic Business' (plural form).

with that of Bin Laden. It is a matter of carefully judging the tone of the performance you want. All the plays given here are written in a style which, while not being archaic, avoids modernisms that would jar on the audience. Now you may want to do just that – jar or jolt the audience – and a production with such anachronisms could work well if that is your intention: Lelio drives a Lambretta, Brighella uses a chainsaw, and the Doctor sits at his door with a laptop. The choice is yours.

The choice of music is also open to personal preference, but the usual objective is to match the music to the period of the piece. For the earliest pieces – *Home from the Wars* and *Pantalone Goes A-Wooing* – there would be the raucous tones of the hurdy-gurdy, shawms, and bagpipe. In seventeenth-century plays, like *The Path of True Love*, the more dulcet tones of lute, recorder and harpsichord can be added. With the Harlequinade, we come to the mid-years of Victoria's reign, with its wealth of sentimental and comic melodies – played on portable instruments; fiddles, banjos and concertinas. A work like *The Duchess Mislaid*, relying on a more spectacular production and complicated scenery, could use recorded music along with other sound effects and theatrical lighting. Where there are musicians, they need to be on or near the stage, and their presence acknowledged – or if it is the actors themselves supplying the music so much the better. Those, as I said, are the usual objectives, but don't be afraid to blow the whole thing – tell the stories with rock music, laser lights, multi-screens and hip-hop dancing!

The approach to the lighting is very important (where the performance is not in the open air) and here we need to remember that through most of *Commedia* history, stage lighting, as we understand it, didn't exist. For most of the plays here, the lighting designer's scope has to be severely restricted. Both facemasks and comedy itself need a more or less continuous 'full up'. Full masks can often marry effectively with atmospheric lighting, but the *Commedia* 'speaking' half mask demands bright and clear illumination. There is some scope for lighting effects in *The Duchess Mislaid*, but always returning to a brighter stage for the comedy sequences. Not only does *Commedia* demand a bright stage, but the auditorium should not remain in total darkness either. *Commedia* cannot communicate with the 'black hole' facing the actors in a conventional present-day theatre. Bernard Shaw's axiom that 'the only Golden Rule is that there are no golden rules' is very true of *Commedia*; but if there were one, the above would be it.

When considering casting, there is a greater freedom in reference to age, gender and appearance than normally permitted in our television-dominated times. In addition to the cross-dressing demanded by the scenarios,[4] there is no reason why roles associated with a male or female gender – and not always the most obvious ones – should not be taken by their opposites. Often played by a woman, Pierrot is a Mask with an already large percentage of female in him, so we get little in the way of dramatic surprise. Now Brighella is different – he is macho, a streetwise bravo – so for a woman to play him may produce something interesting. In fact the best Brighella I ever worked with was a young Swedish girl whose offstage personality suggested none of the deviousness and covert violence she brought to the part and one of the best Italian Pantalones is a woman. Neither is there any rejection due to age, shape, size, colour or physical disability – a lame Captain and a Pantalone in a wheelchair could be wonderful.

4. *Lazzi of 'Cross-Dressing'*, No. 9, page 219

Part One
THE PLAYS

THE FALSE TURK
in Twelve Minutes

*One-act curtain raiser
in the style of the seventeenth-century
Commedia dell'Arte*

Cast

The Capo Comico – Company Manager
Pedrolino – Silent Zanni
Pantalone – Vecchio
Isabella – Innamorata
Flavio – Innamorato
Franceschina – Servetta
Arlecchino – Zanni

Source
Based on several seventeenth-century scenarios

Playing time
15 minutes including the Prologue

Stage requirements
Any interior or exterior space
Approx: 4 x 3 metres minimum

Costumes
Traditional *Commedia dell'Arte*
Turkish disguise for Flavio and Arlecchino

Props
Minimal

Music
Optional, including 'Eastern' for the entrance of the Turks

Introduction

The False Turk is a suitable introduction to the *Commedia dell'Arte* where either rehearsal or performance time is limited. It also gives the actors a chance to familiarise themselves with some of the principal Masks, with the 'Italianate' type of plot, which forms the basis of most extant scenarios, and the opportunity of playing some typical *Lazzi*. For actors unfamiliar with the style it doesn't present too steep a learning curve; and the Prologue with Capo Comico and Pedrolino (in this case the stupid pre-Pierrot) gives a chance for the type of mime/clowning with which most performers are familiar, before embarking on the less familiar *Commedia* genre.

The play itself is inspired by *I Finti Turchi*[5] and incidents to be found in several other early scenarios, but here in a vastly truncated form. In the Prologue the actors are seen briefly 'as themselves', and without their masks – a departure from the usual rule. This is done for two reasons; the dramatic one of providing an excuse for the drastic abridgement of the play, and the 'training' one of distinguishing between the naturalistic acting needed to represent 'The Players' and the bravura manner of *Commedia*.

The plot is a typical one: lovers parted by a tyrannical and avaricious father and the stratagems employed by the servants to bring the lovers together again and discomfort the offending parent. The characters are standard ones, and dressed traditionally. Pantalone wears his red pantaloons and jacket under his *zimarra*.[6] He has the brown mask with an aquiline nose and a straggly grey beard. He is irritable, threatening, aged but by no means weak.

Isabella appears at the very height of contemporary fashion (1670). She is beautiful, elegant, rebellious – her father's daughter. Flavio is handsome, well bred, and apparently somewhat inept until his change into the Turk proves another side to his nature.

---

5. *'Finto'* might more correctly be translated as 'fake' but this would give too much away.

6. Loose, full-length black coat.

Franceschina, here a serving woman of peasant stock, is old enough to comfort the motherless Isabella, but young enough to attract Arlecchino. Due to the extreme shortness of the play, a rounded portrayal of the characters is unlikely unless the actors have played them previously. This is particularly true of the mercurial Arlecchino. It is helpful if the actor portraying him keeps in mind Arlecchino's great devotion to his young master, Flavio, his malicious joy in playing on Pantalone's avarice, and his sense of involving the audience in the escapade.

The fact that the play itself must be completed in the twelve minutes shows the speed with which action and dialogue must be accomplished.

Scenario

Prologue

The Capo Comico, Pedrolino, Pantalone, Isabella, Flavio, Franceschina, Arlecchino.

The Capo Comico – the company manager – enters and announces the performance. No one appears, except the stupid and silent Pedrolino intent on sweeping the stage. The Capo Comico, in the hopes of filling the embarrassing stage-wait, asks him to entertain; the results give even greater embarrassment. The company, still not fully dressed and muttering among themselves drift in. Each actor is introduced by the Capo Comico, who then realises that the star performer,[7] Arlecchino, is not among them. They tell him that he is nowhere to be found. Each player in turn offers to take on the role, until Arlecchino himself appears and asks what play they are going to perform. *The False Turk* is chosen – a play that would normally take two hours. The Capo Comico tells them that it is much too late, in fact there are only twelve minutes left. At Arlecchino's suggestion, they offer to perform it in twelve minutes.

7. From around 1680, the role of Arlecchino had become the main attraction for the public, attaining something like star status, although his part in the play was only that of a lowly servant.

Scene 1

Pantalone, Isabella, Flavio, Franceschina, Arlecchino.

The cast announce *The False Turk in Twelve Minutes* in unison. Isabella tells us that she is in love with Flavio, and he confirms that the passion is mutual. Pantalone separates the lovers, informing us that he forbids the liaison. He also forbids that of his maidservant Franceschina with Flavio's man, Arlecchino. He orders Flavio to leave and never to see his daughter again.

A chance remark, that he will 'lose himself in the sands of the desert' from Flavio, and a fear from Isabella that her father might even force her 'to marry a Turk if he were rich enough', give Arlecchino and Franceschina the idea for a ploy to outwit Pantalone. Flavio leaves, and Franceschina advises Isabella to pretend to submit to Pantalone's will.

'His kingdoms stretch for more than a thousand camels'

Scene 2

Pantalone, Arlecchino, Isabella, Franceschina.

Arlecchino buttonholes Pantalone, telling him of a wealthy Turk who has come to the town looking for a wife, and wants to meet Isabella. At first Pantalone is reluctant, but is tempted by Arlecchino's tales of immeasurable riches.

Pantalone tells his daughter to prepare to receive a rich suitor. She refuses at first but is persuaded by Franceschina to pretend to submit.

Scene 3

Pantalone, Isabella, Flavio, Franceschina, Arlecchino.

Flavio, disguised as the Grand Turk, enters with Arlecchino as his Eunuch. He treats Isabella as if she were a slave girl for sale in the market, and says that he will take her. Arlecchino offers to 'buy' Franceschina.

Isabella, trying to fend off the Turk's advances, pulls on his beard and realises that this is Flavio. She consents to marry the 'Turk' as long as Pantalone will give his permission there and then . . . Franceschina also gets his blessing for her marriage to the 'Eunuch'.

The impostors reveal their true identities and Pantalone passes out as the story comes to an end. The company ask for applause for completing *The False Turk* in twelve minutes.

During the applause the Capo Comico enters with Pedrolino and 'presents' his company. They all exit, Pedrolino still with his broom, being the last on stage.

Finis.

Flavio and Arlecchino
return in disguise

The False Turk – in Twelve Minutes

Prologue

The Capo Comico, Pedrolino, Pantalone, Isabella, Flavio, Franceschina, Arlecchino.

The Capo Comico – the expansive actor-manager of the Commedia company – enters with a flourish, craves our attention, bows profusely and addresses the audience.

CAPO COMICO Gentlemen, ladies – your servant Francesco Gabrielli, manager of a renowned company of comedians, who have the honour of offering for your approbation one of their acclaimed comedies. Noble gentlemen, fair ladies. The famous Nessuni *Commedia* Company.

Nothing happens. The Capo Comico repeats the cue. Pedrolino puts a head out from behind a wing or curtain.

Pedrolino, come here at once. At once!

Pedrolino comes forward, sweeping the stage.

(*Sotto voce.*) Well, where are the company? Pantalone? Flavio? Isabella? Franceschina?

Pedrolino shakes his head and goes on sweeping.[8]

(*In his presenter's voice.*) Gentleman, ladies – the irrepressible Ped-ro-lino!

(*Sotto voce.*) Well, do something. Yes, you. Do some acrobatics, juggling. (*Pedrolino tries to do a trick but fails to pull it off.*) Well, dance. (*He stands as if he were preparing to do something.*) You're going to do something? I think you've already done something!

8. *Lazzi of 'Nothing will stop me'*, No. 46, page 255

Pedrolino suddenly takes up a 'listening pose', indicating that he can hear something.

Listen? Listen? I can't hear anything. (*Pedrolino takes a pose looking toward the players as they enter.*) Look? I can't see . . . Ah, there they are. Here they come!

The players wander in: Isabella and Franceschina, Flavio and Pantalone. They have not yet assumed the Masks (characters) they are to play. Pantalone has not yet put on his facemask, and the others are making final adjustments to their attire. They speak to one another in undertones expressing their dissatisfaction with how the company is run by the Capo Comico and annoyance at the non-appearance of their star player.

Distinguished spectators, the company have arrived. Allow me to present, Signor Pantalone di Bisognose. La Innamorata Isabella Biancholelli. La servetta, Franceschina. Our hero, Flavio dell Sarto –

As the manager calls each of them forward, they galvanise into action, bowing to the spectators. Pantalone will have donned his mask and the others completed their attire. The movements become stylised, precise, individualistic. Voices too will be distinctive and projected. They are in competition with each other for the attention and admiration of the audience.

– and where is Arlecchino?

The following section is in 'Player Mode' rather than 'Mask Mode'.

FLAVIO Last night he was very drunk and this morning nowhere to be found.

PANTALONE We can't play without an Arlecchino. I shall play Arlecchino.

Pantalone comes downstage centre and demonstrates the Arlecchino 'Attitudes',[9] which accompany the following verse:

Noble patrons, here you see,
Your slave, that knave of ribaldry,
Who'll every ploy and gambit try,
To make you laugh – until you cry!

9. *Lazzi of 'The Attitudes'*, No. 2, page 212

That well-loved Zanni from Bergamo,
The one, the only – Arlecchino!

ALL Ridiculous!

Isabella comes forward and offers herself for the role of Arlecchino, repeating the verse and 'Attitudes' to the same response from the rest of the cast.[10] Then Franceschina tries it and finally Flavio, who isn't even given time to give his rendition before they stop him with:

Ridiculous!

Pedrolino comes forward and is not to be prevented from presenting his silent version. The others just turn away which is why they don't observe the rapid entrance of Arlecchino, who stands mockingly just behind Pedrolino.

ARLECCHINO Ridiculous! (*He performs the verse and 'Attitudes' with flair and precision.*) So what are we playing?

PANTALONE *The False Turk.*

ARLECCHINO A very good choice. How long does it last?

PANTALONE Two hours.

CAPO COMICO But you have only twelve minutes left. (*Consulting a timepiece.*)

ARLECCHINO Very well, we'll do it in twelve minutes.

ALL *The False Turk?* In twelve minutes?

ARLECCHINO Why not?

Scene 1

Pantalone, Isabella, Flavio, Franceschina, Arlecchino.

The players form a line across the front of the stage, and perform a series of appropriate 'Attitudes'[11] as they enunciate the following in unison:

---

10. The '*Attitudes*' should be performed accurately, as each player's inappropriate character and costume will be sufficient to make them appear ridiculous.

11. *Lazzi of 'The Attitudes*', No. 2, page 212

ALL Signori. (*For example: Bow with right arm extended.*) Signore – (*Bow with left arm extended.*) – The False Turk (*Mime 'Beard'.*) in (*Mime 'Attend' by holding up one finger.*) Twelve (*Indicate twelve with fingers, 10 + 2.*) Minutes. (*Right arms held high.*)

They turn clockwise moving swiftly upstage. The Capo Comico comes forward and takes a fulsome bow and Pedrolino bows comically, still clutching his broom. Capo Comico grabs hold of him and marches him off the stage, their parts complete, until the curtain call.

The others now form a semicircle, from which they come forward in turn to lay the basics of the plot. From this point the cast are in 'Mask Mode': powerful, the tempo fast and the energy level high.

ISABELLA (*coming downstage centre*) Know then that I, Isabella, have given my heart to one, Flavio.

FLAVIO (*coming to join her*) And I, Flavio, ask her hand in marriage.

PANTALONE (*coming centre and parting them*) And I, Pantalone, father to Isabella, forbid it.[12] (*All three turn and walk upstage, Pantalone keeping the lovers apart.*)

FRANCESCHINA (*coming centre and indicating Arlecchino*) I, Franceschina, maid to Isabella, would pledge my troth with this wretch here.

ARLECCHINO (*coming to join her*) And this wretch here – Arlecchino, manservant to Flavio – would marry the wench but . . .

PANTALONE (*turning upstage and coming between them*) I forbid it. (*He pushes through them and they immediately embrace behind his back. He turns upstage and catches them.*) And I forbid that. (*He notices that Isabella and Flavio are also in each other's arms. He strides upstage and parts them.*) And certainly that! (*To Flavio.*) Get you from my house. (*Flavio strides towards the exit, stage left. Pantalone turns to Isabella.*) This Flavio is worthless. (*Aside.*) I should know, I ruined his father. (*To Isabella.*) You will marry a man of my choice.

The following section is an example of a specific Commedia mechanism in which the rest of the cast 'freeze' so the attention is drawn to a specific area of the stage.[13]

12. *Lazzi of 'Forbidding'*, No. 20, page 232
13. *Lazzi of 'Asides and Freezes'*, No. 1, page 211

FLAVIO (*to Arlecchino*) Arlecchino, my good friend and servant, I am banished. I will lose myself in the sands of the desert.

ARLECCHINO (*to audience*) Sands of the desert? There's a thought!!!

The 'Freeze' changes location, so the attention is on the new speakers.

ISABELLA Oh, Franceschina, my dear friend and servant, whom will my father force me to marry? An Ottoman Turk if he be rich enough! I will have none other than Flavio!

FRANCESCHINA (*to audience*) A Turk! There's a thought!!!

Franceschina and Arlecchino come downstage centre to conspire.[14]
Arlecchino then moves back left to 'clue in' Flavio by inaudible whispering.
Franceschina returns to Isabella.

FLAVIO (*aloud and across to Isabella*)
As I no longer hope to gain your hand.
I leave this moment for a far-off land.
To live, to die? I cannot tell.
Farewell forever, Isabella. (*He exits off left.*)

ISABELLA He's gone!
Not tempest wild nor raging sea,
Has cast my loved one far from me.
T'was my own father, sent him away,
To distant land, there to stay.
Thus all care and hope I lose,
No other lover would I choose,
Forever must I dwell in sorrow . . .

FRANCESCHINA Never fear, he'll be back – tomorrow. (*She tries to comfort Isabella.*)

PANTALONE He'd better not be. Pull yourself together, girl. I realise you've got to marry.

ISABELLA I will have no one but Flavio.

PANTALONE Don't worry, I'll soon find you someone more suitable . . . Yes, more suitable . . .

14. *Lazzi of 'Token Conspiring'*, No. 63, page 266

Pantalone moves away. Isabella weeps. Franceschina takes Isabella upstage to comfort her.

FRANCESCHINA He'll be back, he'll be back. (*They freeze.*)

Scene 2

Pantalone, Arlecchino, Isabella, Franceschina.

ARLECCHINO (*bringing Pantalone downstage centre*) There is a visitor in town – a Turk.

PANTALONE A Turk? I don't want any carpets.

ARLECCHINO No, he wants to meet your daughter.

PANTALONE My daughter doesn't want any carpets.

ARLECCHINO No, he wants to marry your daughter.

PANTALONE I'm not having my daughter marry a carpet-seller.

ARLECCHINO He's not a carpet-seller.

PANTALONE What's he selling then?

ARLECCHINO He's not selling – he wants to . . . er . . . buy.

PANTALONE Buy? Buy what?

ARLECCHINO Buy your daughter.

PANTALONE How dare you? Buy my daughter indeed!

ARLECCHINO He's a Sultan, looking for another sultana. He is rich beyond the dreams of Asia. His kingdoms stretch farther than a thousand camels, and his slaves are as the sands of the desert. His palaces are . . .

PANTALONE How dare you? (*Arlecchino mimes money.*[15]) How much? Well, if he's as rich as you say; my daughter might like a little Turkish Delight.

Arlecchino exits. Pantalone comes downstage and soliloquises.

15. *Lazzi of 'Money'*, No. 42, page 251

A Turk, eh? Rich beyond the dreams of Asia. That sounds suitable. What did he say? A thousand camels? Don't know where I'd keep the camels. But slaves are good – no salaries! (*Laughs and gets excited at the prospect.*)

A Turk, though? Well you can't say I'm prejudiced – Turk, Russian, Spaniard, Red Indian Chief; as long as he's got (*Mimes money.*) – even a Welshman. Not a Scot – he might be as 'careful' as I am. No, a Turk will be just fine.

(*To Isabella.*) Ah, Isabella, there you are. I think I've found you a new fiancé. What do you think of that? Aren't I a considerate father? You are to meet him today; so dry those tears – make yourself look your best. Franceschina, see that she . . . Well, you women know what to do.

ISABELLA I will not look my best. I will not marry some odious creature of your choosing, never, never, never!

PANTALONE You will do as I say . . .

ISABELLA Never!

In a rage Pantalone paces back and forth upstage while Franceschina and Isabella talk sotto voce downstage of him.

FRANCESCHINA I've never seen him so angry; you'll have to give in to him.

ISABELLA Never.

FRANCESCHINA Listen to me.

ISABELLA I will not listen – it's no good – I can be as adamant as he is.

FRANCESCHINA Just pretend.

ISABELLA Pretend?

FRANCESCHINA Pretend. Go on. Kneel. (*Isabella kneels before her father.*) Both knees.

ISABELLA (*on both her knees*) Not the foot on the hand bit? (*A traditional gesture of abject submission where the hand is placed palm up on the floor.*)

PANTALONE (*placing his foot – gently! – on Isabella's hand*) I see you submit. Now listen to what I have to say and don't interrupt.

ISABELLA Yes, Father.

PANTALONE Now you know that I have always had your best interests at heart?

ISABELLA Yes, Father.

PANTALONE And what I say is best?

ISABELLA Oh yes, Father.

PANTALONE Well, it's time you were married, my girl.

ISABELLA Oh no, Father.

PANTALONE Oh yes, daughter.

ISABELLA (*Franceschina gives her a nudge*) Yes, Father.

Pantalone is somewhat suspicious of her apparent submission but continues.

PANTALONE Well, there is a fine Eastern gentleman, of good address, whom I have chosen to be your husband. He will call within the hour, propose to you, and you will of course accept him.

ISABELLA Never!

PANTALONE What did you say?

ISABELLA (*Franceschina kicks Isabella covertly*) I said, 'I'd never do anything but obey my father in his every wish.'

PANTALONE What? You'll do as I say?

ISABELLA Of course, Father.

PANTALONE (*aside*) Strange. (*To Isabella.*) You're all right? Not ill or something? Well, that's settled. I am relieved. I think this may be him.

Scene 3

Pantalone, Isabella, Flavio, Franceschina, Arlecchino.

*Eastern music heard off (possibly provided by Arlecchino, with pipe and drum).
Then Flavio in disguise as the Grand Turk, with Arlecchino as his Eunuch,
enter and parade round the stage. They take up a position left of Isabella and
Pantalone.*

ARLECCHINO His magnificence Rancid Ben Bedouin, Caliph of
Kackerbad.

FLAVIO Your daughter? (*Circling round her as if assessing horseflesh.*) I make
no promises. (*Pinches her.*) Too thin! (*Holds her head to look into her
mouth.*) Good teeth.

ISABELLA (*to her father*) Are you going to let this barbarian insult me,
Father?

FLAVIO Ah, a fiery spirit, I like that.

*She grabs him by the false beard – on elastic. Flavio is revealed to her, and to
the audience – as if they didn't know! – but not of course to Pantalone.*

*Arlecchino has moved round, so as to be close to Franceschina, who, to her
discomfort, he is eyeing lecherously. He circles her in duplication of Flavio's
moves with Isabella.*

ARLECCHINO Your maidservant? Haven't you anything better to show
me? Oh well, suppose she'll do for a number-three wife.

FRANCESCHINA I'm not going to marry a Eu . . . (*Arlecchino takes hold
of her.*) You . . . !!!

FLAVIO And I'll take your daughter.

PANTALONE Oh no, you will not!!!

FLAVIO Why not? I'll make it legal. She will be my 145th wife.

PANTALONE Sir, this is too much. I am not prepared, even though you
are the richest man in the world, to see my daughter so abused.

ISABELLA Father, I'll marry him. I want to marry him.

PANTALONE You do? You do? Funny creatures, women. I'll never
understand them. Well, she must be better off than with that
weakling, Flavio. Very well, I give my consent.

ISABELLA So have we your solemn promise? I may marry this man? (*Making a point of indicating the man standing next to her.*)

FRANCESCHINA And master, have I your permission to marry this, er . . . Eunuch?

PANTALONE Oh, very well – I suppose he's better than that idiot, Arlecchino.

ISABELLA You won't change your mind?

PANTALONE I never change my mind.

ISABELLA Have we your permission, then? The play has only a few seconds left.

PANTALONE My consent and blessing on both the nuptials.

Flavio and Arlecchino take off their disguises. Pantalone swoons. Arlecchino comes downstage centre and addresses the audience. The others, including a recovering Pantalone, form a line either side of him.

ARLECCHINO As Pantalone faints away,
We must perforce conclude our play.
Censor our faults, but grant us that –

ALL (*using similar 'Attitudes' to the opening*) We played *The False Turk* in twelve minutes flat!

As they take their bows, the Capo Comico enters to present 'his' company. As they go, Pedrolino enters – still sweeping – and takes his bow.

Finis.

HOME FROM THE WARS

*Early Commedia dell'Arte sketch
in the style of Angelo Beolco*

Cast

Pulcinella – an ex-soldier
Rotalinda – his wife
Tortorina – an attractive neighbour
Cosimo – a very big man

Source
Early 'Street' *Commedia* in the style of Angelo Beolco

Playing time
15 minutes

Stage requirements
Ideally, a trestle stage with a back curtain,
otherwise any space with a central entrance

Costumes
Traditional early Pulcinella
Rotalinda and Tortorina: peasant dress of sixteenth-century Italy
Cosimo: Neopolitan Bravo

Props
Minimal

Music
Drum and any loud open-air instruments available

Introduction

Prior to the establishment of 'Golden Age' *Commedia*, with its humanist scenarios derived initially from Plautus and Menander, we have a number of examples of a more homespun style: no princesses, mad or otherwise, no exotic Turks, false or genuine, few doctors, lawyers or aristocratic merchants; more likely, butchers, porters, fishwives and peasant soldiers. Two actor/writers Angelo Beolco and Andrea Calmo created such fare for the Venetian populace in the early years of the sixteenth century, and in southern Italy the *Commedia dell'Arte* established a peasant style, robust and earthy, that was to feature the Neapolitan Pulcinella.

Of the present cast the only one likely to be familiar is Pulcinella. He is an interesting but difficult Mask to play, whose role in the South Italian *Commedia* is rather fluid, the character remaining consistent, but his trade or occupation varied. He has in common with his direct descendant, the British Punch,[16] a brutal and earthy nature.

At the opening of a typical *Commedia* play few, if any, of the Masks are married, though it is unlikely that all will remain single by the end of the piece. For one or more pairs of lovers, their delayed but inevitable conjoining is the very raison d'être of the performance. It is usual for a Zanni like Arlecchino to be finally tamed and tied by a nuptial knot to the Servetta, so that in later years the name of Harlequin is invariably paired with that of Columbine. But until the eighteenth century, when there was a move to give each Mask its female counterpart, most Masks remained resolutely bachelors. Both the Doctor and Pantalone are more likely to have had a wife, or be seeking one, than having one at the time of the play. The Captain may also seek a wife, but his attempts usually end in failure. There appear to be two notable exceptions; Burratino from *The Duchess Mislaid* is similar to Pulcinella. He is a Mask of many trades or professions and always seems a very married man. Pulcinella himself arrives on the scene well and truly wedded. In more than one scenario he disencumbers himself by the simple expedient of murdering her. His wife is most frequently given the name Rotalinda.

16. The main storyline used, even to this day, by Punch and Judy showmen is based on a Neapolitan *Commedia* scenario of the seventeenth century.

As Pulcinella is not unlike Mr Punch, Rotalinda in the sketch here is not unlike Judy.[17] Here at last we have a female comic character for whom a facemask is not only permissible but also mandatory.[18] There are no pictorial likenesses of Rotalinda, which leaves us free to invent one for her. The quintessential moment that should inspire us is just after her entrance, backwards on her knees. She turns to reveal a face so grotesque, worn and lugubrious in contrast to the expectations of her husband, and the prettiness of the neighbour, that it is usually greeted with laughter. Her costume is that of a Neapolitan peasant woman of the period.

Over the years Pulcinella's costume changed radically: here he should be in his earliest manifestation, which is the near-white loose trousers and collarless blouse, a low belt or rope below his large paunch. He has something of a hump on his back (but not stylised like Punch or the French Polichenelle). On his head, a white cap with the suggestion of his later sugarloaf. His mask is black or dark brown with a prominent Roman nose, and a forehead wrinkled, with a large wart.

The name Tortorina means 'little turtle dove'. This was historically the name of a Servetta, about which we know nothing, but one that implies her attractiveness and youth. Her costume is that of a peasant girl of the period. She would not normally be masked.

Cosimo is a Bravo (hired ruffian) or Zanni of preferably massive proportions. His costume is like that of a Zanni, but in aggressive Neapolitan colours. There is a version of the Zanni mask with a prominent nose (somewhat Captain-like) which suits him well.

The production is imagined as taking place on the trestle-type stage of the earliest days; a high platform (or cart) with a frame at the back from which hang a pair of curtains, providing a single central entrance. Pulcinella will arrive and depart through the audience. Rotalinda and Cosimo use the central parting. It can therefore be given in any space with or without rostra.

The piece belongs to the earliest period – the days in the marketplace, when the audience had to be gathered before the show could start – so would have started with as much noise and tub-thumping as could be mustered.

17. It is not known exactly how 'Judy' came by her name.

18. Our enthusiasm is spoilt a bit by the realisation that the part was most likely, and of course can still be, played by a man.

Scenario

Scene 1

Pulcinella.

Pulcinella enters and tells the audience that he has returned to his home-town after ten years away at the wars. He says how happy his pretty little wife will be to see him. He calls out her name, 'Rotalinda', to no response.

Scene 2

Pulcinella, Tortorina.

Tortorina, enters through centre curtains – she has just borrowed honey from her neighbour. Pulcinella mistakes her for his wife. She protests that she has never seen him before in her life. She exits and Pulcinella again calls for Rotalinda.

Scene 3

Pulcinella, Rotalinda.

Rotalinda now appears. At first they do not recognise each other. He asks after a pretty young girl called Rotalinda. She initially mistakes him for various tradesmen. When she at last realises who he is, she berates him as the villain who deserted her so long ago.

Disappointed in the change that the years have wrought, he none-theless thinks it worth putting up with her for the sake of a warm bed and a solid meal. He tries to convince her to take him back. She is reluctant, but in the end tells him that there is only one little thing stopping her. She calls out 'Cosimo'.

Scene 4

Pulcinella, Rotalinda, Cosimo.

Cosimo enters. He tells Pulcinella that Rotalinda is now *his* woman; this is *his* house; and the meal is for *him*! Pulcinella had better scram pretty quick, or he'll be torn to pieces. Cosimo and Rotalinda enter into the 'house'.

Scene 5

Pulcinella.

Alone, Pulcinella tells the audience he'll have to sign on again for the wars.

   Finis.

Pulcinella finds his wife again

Home from the Wars

Scene 1

Pulcinella.

Pulcinella is heard singing and punching out a rhythm on a tin pan hanging from his belt.[19] *He is at the end of a long and wearying solitary march, and his feet tramp heavily.*

PULCINELLA (*singing as he enters through the audience*)
> Down the long and dusty road,
> Comes a soldier with his load,
> Days are long, nights are worse,
> Empty belly, and empty purse,
> Returning home, home at last,
> Many a year and day have passed,
> Fighting the Turks, God knows what for,
> Home at last, home from the war . . .

He reaches the stage with the last lines of his song. He looks round wearily trying to identify his hometown, when he sees the audience and addresses them as citizens of Sarno.

Well, here we are in Sarno. Good old Sarno. Well, I think it's Sarno. Comes to something when you don't recognise your own hometown! So how are you, good people of Sarno? Gobstruck! Now I know I'm home. Wherever you travel, you'll never quite see that vacant look of staring stupidity, as you do with the people of Sarno. Oh, I'm not saying you are stupid; far from it. Under those masks of inanity, we – for I count myself of your number – are a people with a great talent and aptitude for . . . every kind of villainy and skulduggery.[20] So here I am, home from the wars. Ten long years

---

19. Musical accompaniment would be a bonus either from an external source or from the actor himself, if he is also a musician.

20. This is an example of memorised stock patter, inserted as required (also found in *Pantalone Goes A-Wooing*, Scene 2, page 43).

fighting the Turks; well, at first we fought the Turks, then we fought the Venetians, then the Papal States, then we fought each other. What? You don't believe I've been at the wars? What's that? Where are my war wounds? (*Ad lib.*) . . . And booty? Well, I did have booty, but I stopped at Fino and you know Fino; good wine, pretty women, and thieving cardsharpers.

So here I am, home to Sarno and my sweet little wife. How pleased she will be to see me, 'Come to my arms, Pulchi boy,' she'll say. Then it will be roast chicken, cool beer, and a warm bed, and a blissful sleep in the arms of my beloved. (*Calling.*) Rotalinda – my beloved – my sweet wifey! I'm home.

Scene 2

Pulcinella, Tortorina.

Ah, here she is. (*Tortorina appears through the centre.*) Didn't I tell you she was a beauty?

She has a distinctive sensual walk, rhythmic and almost stylised.[21]

TORTORINA Will you let me pass?

PULCINELLA Let you pass, my darling? It's me, Pulchi – I'm home. Don't you recognise me?

TORTORINA I've never seen you before in my life!

PULCINELLA I'm your husband. Don't you remember how fondly we said farewell, ten years ago?

TORTORINA Ten years ago?

PULCINELLA Ten years ago.

TORTORINA Ten years ago, I was eight years old, Sir. I live next door and just popped in to borrow a jar of honey. (*Exits through audience.*)

PULCINELLA Perhaps she'll be sweeter when she's had the honey. Still, it's nice to get to know the neighbours.

21. Like Marilyn Monroe in *Some like it Hot* (1959)

Scene 3

Pulcinella, Rotalinda.

(*Calling again.*) Rotalinda, my beloved, I'm home.

From behind the curtains Rotalinda is heard singing in a coarse and cracked voice. The curtains part and the rear end of Pulcinella's wife comes into view. It waggles from side to side as, on her knees, she energetically scrubs her 'front doorstep'. Pulcinella rubs his hands and paws the ground in a Lazzo of 'Lust'. [22] *He makes a dash for her and embraces her from behind.* [23]

ROTALINDA No milk today, thank you, Sid. [24]

PULCINELLA Sid? It's me, Pulchi. (*She turns to face him.*) I beg your pardon, madam, I thought you were my wife – a pretty young thing. She must have moved away. Her name was Rotalinda.

ROTALINDA I'm Rotalinda. Now be off with you, whoever you are. (*Pause.*) I seem to know your face. What's your name?

PULCINELLA Pulchi! Pulcinella!

ROTALINDA Oh yes, I remember. No, I don't want any knives sharpened just now. Call again next month.

PULCINELLA (*to audience*) Fancy that pretty young thing turning into . . . Well, at least it will be a meal and a warm bed for the night, and then who knows? I might get a little honey!!

ROTALINDA Wait a minute . . . I know you, you scoundrel, you beast, you forsaker, you breaker of women's hearts; you thief, you liar – you good-for-nothing!

PULCINELLA She recognises me! I'm home. (*He goes to embrace her, but she eludes his grasp and bars his way into the house.*) Well, let me in.

ROTALINDA Let you in my house after the way you've treated me?

PULCINELLA But I've been at the wars.

ROTALINDA At the whores? I bet you have.

22. *Lazzo of 'Lust'*, No. 37, page 247

23. *Lazzi of 'The Surprise Embrace'*, No. 59, page 263

24. The reference to 'a milkman named Sid' is an example of an intentional anachronism that will register with today's audience.

PULCINELLA Come, sweet wife; let me in – pretty Rotalinda, sweet thing. (*He woos her.*)

ROTALINDA (*she responds a little but is suspicious*) Have you got any money?

PULCINELLA Err. It's in the bank.

ROTALINDA In your imagination, I think.

PULCINELLA Take me back, Rotalinda. I'll be ever faithful to you, work hard, tend the garden, fetch and carry, feed the pig . . .

ROTALINDA Well, I would . . .

PULCINELLA You would?

ROTALINDA I might . . .

PULCINELLA You might?

ROTALINDA If it weren't for one little thing.

PULCINELLA And what would that be, my darling?

ROTALINDA (*calling off*) Cosimo!

Scene 4

Pulcinella, Rotalinda, Cosimo.

Enter the powerful and ferocious Cosimo.

PULCINELLA Ah, your 'Little Thing'!

COSIMO Are you bothering my wife?

PULCINELLA She's my wife.

COSIMO My wife, my woman, my home, my roast chicken, my cool beer. Now off with you, or I'll make mincemeat of you! [25]

They exit into the 'house'.

25. *Lazzi of 'Threats'*, No. 62, page 264

Scene 5

Pulcinella.

PULCINELLA Well, back to the wars, I suppose.

He leaves the stage to resume his journey. He picks up his song as he goes.

Finis.

Rotalinda sends Pulcinella packing

PANTALONE GOES A-WOOING

A one-act play set around c. 1580,
inspired by a contemporary painting

From the picture in the Drottningholm Theatre Museum, Sweden

Cast

Pantalone – an impoverished merchant
Arlecchino – a servant
Zanni – a second servant
Franceschina – a servetta (female servant)
La Donna Lucia – a wealthy widow

Source
Late sixteenth-century style, inspired by a well-known
painting in the Drottningholm Theatre Museum, Sweden

Playing time
40 minutes

Stage requirements
Approx: 5 square metres playing space
Optional: curtain set with a book-wing, with a 'practical'
upstairs window

Costumes
Duplicating the painting on which the play is based.
They are traditional for the period with Arlecchino
in his early, patched costume. Donna Lucia showing an
affluent lady of the late sixteenth century

Props
A horse blanket, a pair of horse's ears, a chamber pot, a bouquet
of wilting flowers, an edible leek, some 'horse droppings', etc.

Music
Mainly vocal effects. Additional music optional

Introduction

Pantalone Goes A-Wooing forms a bridge between the peasant-type play as we have in *Home from the Wars*, and the noble Italianate theme used in *The Path of True Love*. It is inspired by a famous and exceedingly instructive painting in the Drottningholm Theatre Museum, Sweden.

The picture was painted around 1580, which places the piece in the early years of the true *Commedia dell'Arte*. Pantalone is shown wearing the traditional red pantaloons and jacket. In this play he puts on his *zimarra* – the loose full coat, correctly black[26] (but in the painting a dark blue), when he starts his journey. He has a light brown mask and a virile and neatly pointed beard, suggesting that he is not entirely without aspirations of a progenitive nature.

The figure to his right holding a song sheet is the Zanni, garbed as usual in a loose, un-dyed, homespun suit with wide brimmed hat. He too has a beard and mask of muddy brown. Arlecchino's suit has the irregular patches of colour on off-white fabric as in his first incarnation. He wears a black mask and what appears to be a close-fitting red cap. He is also depicted here with horse's ears, which he will assume for part of the play. La Donna Lucia, whose head and shoulders appear at the window, is dressed at the height of fashion for the last years of the sixteenth century.

Only the face of a fifth character, presumably another Zanni, is visible from under the cloth on which Pantalone rides. This role has been omitted from the play in the interests of symmetry: Pantalone with two servants tends to work better than Pantalone with three.

Although the picture depicts an early style of performance, it is unlikely to be an open-air one. The dress worn by La Donna Lucia is either that of the aristocrat[27] who is performing the role, or one handed down to a principal actress of one of the better companies; no market troupe could have afforded such finery. There is also an elaboration on the

26. Black because of the sumptuary laws of Venice – even today all gondolas must be black.

27. There are many records of high-born persons appearing with professional actors at private performances.

early trestle stage; the back curtain is neatly pleated and there is a simple tower wing, to provide an upper window for La Donna Lucia. This is perhaps the earliest of similar two-storey constructions, that were to become very popular with the *Commedia dell'Arte* in the next century, but can be dispensed with for workshop and even performance. It works quite as well with Donna Lucia standing on nothing more elaborate than a bench or stool, and miming the presence of the window.

Another production from a similar scenario

The picture is valuable confirmation of the fundamental principles of *Commedia*. Here we have the inspiration for a very pure piece of theatre; the theatre of actuality, where the 'pretend' element is acknowledged and there is no attempt to create illusion. As is often the case with *Commedia*, there are various levels of 'pretend'. The players are pretending that they are the characters, who are pretending to go on a journey on a pretend horse. But in its way, Pantalone's poverty is so real that he is obliged to use his unpaid servants as his horse. The theme might be called 'Wit over Want'; there is an ever-present feeling of shortage and hunger. As well as being the actors playing the five Masks and telling the story of the wooing of the wealthy Donna Lucia, all are striving to entertain. This activity also springs from hunger – the piece must entertain or the actors won't eat – so they perform, as well as the comic *Lazzi*, music, song, dance and acrobatics. The basic tone of the entire play is one of skill, pace, power – in fact *Bravura*. This is not an easy play to perform, requiring a variety of skills and experience, if not in *Commedia*, then of similar physical theatre. The *Lazzi* require detailed rehearsal, as the performance requires familiarity with stage timing and audience handling.

A *Commedia dell'Arte* play is hardly complete without its Servetta, so she is introduced, be it only briefly, in the first scene. Here, she is called Franceschina, the solid, witty peasant woman of the Fossard engravings now stored in the Museum of Stockholm. The complaints from the male servants about her thinness may indicate just the opposite. The part can be taken by the actress playing La Donna if the cast is limited.

Scenario

Scene 1

Arlecchino, Pantalone, Zanni, Franceschina.

Arlecchino wanders onto the stage. He hears Pantalone's voice off, calling for him, and makes himself scarce, exiting in the opposite direction. Pantalone appears, calling for Arlecchino. He notices the audience and apologises for not having time to observe the usual pleasantries, as he must find Arlecchino immediately. He does make a few enquiries after the health of individual members of the audience and their families, while continuing to call for Arlecchino who has re-entered and played a '*Mimicking*' *Lazzo*.[28] On being discovered, they play the '*Here, here, then here*' *Lazzo*[29] together.

Pantalone tells Arlecchino that he now has no more money and must marry again. He asks for Zanni who enters and repeats the '*Here, here, then here*' *Lazzo* with Pantalone. Pantalone calls for Franceschina and tells her of his need to marry for money. He sends her to fetch his cloak, a bunch of flowers, and a horse blanket. ('*Nudge-nudge, wink-wink*' *Lazzo*.[30]) She returns with these. Pantalone dons the cloak, and Zanni,

28. *Lazzi of 'Mimicking'*, No. 40, page 249
29. *Lazzo of 'Here, here, then here'*, No. 28, page 239
30. *Lazzo of 'Nudge-nudge, wink-wink'*, No. 47, page 255

much alarmed, is required to cover himself with the blanket. He bends forward with his hands on Arlecchino's waist, assuming the body of the horse. Franceschina, familiar with the manoeuvre, gives Arlecchino a pair of horse's ears. She helps Pantalone onto Zanni's back, gives Pantalone the flowers, and waves to them as they set off – clip-clop, clip-clop!

Scene 2

Arlecchino, Pantalone, Zanni.

They circle the stage as horse and rider, jogging along, chanting and making appropriate actions and sounds (clip-clop). At last the horse stops and refuses to go further – Pantalone dismounts. Arlecchino separates but Zanni remains under the blanket. They do a *'Hunger' Lazzo*[31] and Zanni is revealed. They find themselves in Bergamo, and introduce themselves to the locals (the audience). Zanni explains the purpose of their visit and asks for help in locating La Donna Lucia – or any other suitable heiress in the vicinity. Zanni and Arlecchino go among the audience to make further enquiries, while Pantalone makes overtures to women in the front rows, asking after their financial status and willingness to be his bride. The servants return to the stage, Zanni brandishing a piece of paper which purports to give directions to find La Donna Lucia, who lives on the other side of town.

Scene 3

Arlecchino, Pantalone, Zanni.

The scene is entirely taken up with a *'Passeggiata'* (walking) *Lazzo*[32] in which they follow the written directions, miming the streets and buildings, turning corners, avoiding traffic, and asking help from invisible passers-by.

Scene 4

Arlecchino, Pantalone, Zanni, La Donna Lucia.

As they arrive at a small piazza, La Donna Lucia appears at her window (by carrying on and mounting her stool, unless there is practical scenery).

31. *Lazzi of 'Hunger'*, No. 30, page 240
32. *Lazzi of 'The Passeggiata'*, No. 49, page 256

She sings sweetly, welcoming the morn, which attracts their attention. They enquire if she is indeed La Donna Lucia – but are brusquely told to read the notice on her door. This says not only that here lives La Donna Lucia, but also that door-to-door salesmen, pedlars and other vagabonds are unwelcome. They try to assure her that they are none such, and explain the purpose of their visit. Pantalone advances and attempts to woo the unresponsive widow. When asked for her answer, she replies by emptying a chamber pot over the amorous Pantalone. Pantalone, insulted, is for giving up, but Zanni and Arlecchino remind him that they are destitute and another attempt should be made.

Pantalone asks Zanni to woo her on his behalf, so Zanni serenades her, extolling her beauty. She remains unimpressed and Arlecchino is pushed forward. Although he makes a hash of it, La Donna seems to show some interest and promises to come down. They are congratulating Pantalone when she appears before them. However, she has only disgust for the old man and is attracted to the youthful and athletic Arlecchino. She is willing to marry him, settling a large sum of money on him, so that they can live together without want. Arlecchino agrees, on the condition that the marriage take place back home in Venice, and that his friend Zanni and former master Pantalone be retained as their servants. Pantalone is put under the horse blanket, and Zanni assumes the horse's ears. Donna Lucia is helped by Arlecchino to get onto Pantalone's back and they start off for home – clip-clop.

Finis.

Pantalone Goes A-Wooing

Scene 1

Arlecchino, Pantalone, Zanni, Franceschina.

Arlecchino wanders on, but hearing Pantalone call him, makes off in the opposite direction.

PANTALONE (*calling from off*) Arlecchino! Arlecchino! (*Entering.*) Arlecchino! Where is that piece of rubbish?

(*To audience.*) Ah yes, good morning. Excuse me, no time for the usual pleasantries this morning.

Arlecchino has run on and hides behind Pantalone, 'Mimicking' his moves and words. [33]

How are you? How's your father? How's your mother-in-law? No time for all that – I must find Arlecchino. Arlecchino . . . (*Lazzo of 'Startling each other.'*[34]) Where have you been?

ARLECCHINO I've been here.

PANTALONE Before that? (*'Here, here, then here' Lazzo'.*[35]) . . . and before that?

ARLECCHINO I went to the kitchen to get something to eat. But there was nothing in the kitchen except Franceschina; I would have eaten her but she's got too thin. So I went to the pantry. But there was nothing in the pantry, so I went back to bed and dreamt of sausages until you woke me up so rudely . . .

PANTALONE Now listen carefully – I have no money.

ARLECCHINO No money? (*'Money' Lazzo.*[36])

33. *Lazzi of 'Mimicking'*, No. 40, page 249
34. *Lazzo of 'Startling each other'*, No. 58, page 262
35. *Lazzo of 'Here, here, then here'*, No. 28, page 239
36. *Lazzi of 'Money'*, No. 42, page 251

PANTALONE So, I will have to marry again.

ARLECCHINO I didn't know you ever were married.

PANTALONE Well, what about my son, Lelio?

ARLECCHINO I thought he was a b . . .

Pantalone gags Arlecchino.

PANTALONE Yes, then I married for Love . . . (*Brief sentimental dance.*[37]) But now I must marry for Money! (*Dance changes rhythm.*)

ARLECCHINO I'll be the best man – I'll be the only man. (*Rude gesture.*)

PANTALONE Fetch me Franceschina.

ARLECCHINO You're going to marry Franceschina?

PANTALONE Of course I'm not going to marry Franceschina; she hasn't got any money.

ARLECCHINO You're not going to eat her, are you?

Pantalone knocks Arlecchino about. Franceschina enters, startling Pantalone by suddenly appearing by his side.[38]

PANTALONE Ah, Franceschina, I want you to know I haven't got any money.

FRANCESCHINA What about the fifty lire in the little box hidden on top of the wardrobe?

PANTALONE What do you know about that? That's my savings for my old age.

FRANCESCHINA (*aside*) I wonder when that will be?

PANTALONE I therefore propose to propose to the wealthy Donna Lucia, who lives in Bergamo. Fetch me my Sunday cloak – I must look my best for La Donna Lucia. A bouquet of flowers, my travelling bag . . . and a horse blanket.

FRANCESCHINA A horse blanket?

---

37. *Lazzi of 'The Dance of Glee'*, No. 10, page 220
38. *Lazzo of 'Startling each other'*, No. 58, page 262

PANTALONE That's what I said.

FRANCESCHINA Ah, I see – a horse blanket! (*'Nudge-nudge, wink-wink' Lazzo.*[39])

PANTALONE And Arlecchino, bring Zanni to me. (*'Startling' Lazzo again*[40] – *Zanni is already there.*) Where have you been?

ZANNI I've been here.

PANTALONE Before that?

ZANNI Here. (*'Here, here, then here' Lazzo.*[41])

PANTALONE Yes, yes . . . But before that?

ZANNI I went to the kitchen to get something to eat. But there was nothing in the kitchen except Franceschina; I would have eaten her, but she's got too thin. So I went to the pantry. But there was nothing in the pantry, so I went back to bed and dreamt of sausages, until you woke me up . . .

PANTALONE (*to audience*) Have you followed the plan so far? I mean, do you appreciate the situation as it stands at the moment? I am going to propose to La Donna Lucia, whom I understand is very wealthy, and if she accepts me all my money worries are over. And why should she not? Am I not in my prime? La Donna Lucia lives in Bergamo, some miles from here – so I will need a horse.

Franceschina enters with the cloak, travelling bag, blanket, a bunch of flowers and (hidden about her) a pair of prop horse's ears. Pantalone puts on the cloak and puts the travelling bag over his shoulder. The blanket is handed to Zanni.

ZANNI What's this?

PANTALONE It's a horse blanket – put it on. (*Zanni puts the blanket over his shoulders. To Zanni.*) Well, bend over then.

ARLECCHINO (*to audience*) Oh, I know what we're in for; just you watch.

39. *Lazzo of 'Nudge-nudge, wink-wink'*, No. 47, page 255
40. *Lazzo of 'Startling each other'*, No. 58, page 262
41. *Lazzo of 'Here, here, then here'*, No. 28, page 239

Arlecchino puts on the horse's ears handed to him by Franceschina. Zanni leans forward, puts his hands on Arlecchino's waist and they form the 'horse'. Franceschina helps Pantalone onto Zanni's back. They start off. Franceschina waves goodbye.

Scene 2

Arlecchino, Pantalone, Zanni.

The 'horse' and rider circle the stage area to represent a long journey. This is a Lazzo requiring precise rehearsal.[42] *Arlecchino and Zanni create the rhythm with the tramp of their feet and by chanting as follows:*

ARLECCHINO (*chants*) Clip –
ZANNI (*responds*)　　　　　 – clop.
ARLECCHINO (*chants*) Clip –
ZANNI (*responds*)　　　　　 – clop.
ARLECCHINO (*chants*) Clip –
ZANNI (*responds*)　　　　　 – clop.
TOGETHER Cliperty-cloperty.

> *Repeat ad lib. Pantalone helps to promote the impression of travelling by acknowledging passers-by, reacting to different landscapes and miming weather and temperature variations. Pantalone starts to sing along.*

ARLECCHINO (*chants*) Clip –
ZANNI (*responds*)　　　　　 – clop.
ARLECCHINO (*chants*) Clip –
ZANNI (*responds*)　　　　　 – clop.
PANTALONE Here rides a suitor in his prime
ARLECCHINO (*chants*) Clip –
ZANNI (*responds*)　　　　　 – clop.
ARLECCHINO (*chants*) Clip –
ZANNI (*responds*)　　　　　 – clop.
PANTALONE Come to woo a lady fine
ARLECCHINO (*chants*) Clip –
ZANNI (*responds*)　　　　　 – clop.

42. This *Lazzo* is not given in Part II as it is specific to this play and is described within the text.

ARLECCHINO (*chants*) Clip –
ZANNI (*responds*)   – clop.
PANTALONE Will that heiress soon be mine?
ARLECCHINO (*chants*) Clip –
ZANNI (*responds*)   – clop.
ARLECCHINO (*sings*) We'll have to wait a very long time
    Ad libs.
ARLECCHINO (*chants*) Clip –
ZANNI (*responds*)   – clop.
ARLECCHINO (*chants*) Clip –
ZANNI (*responds*)   – clop.
PANTALONE Here rides a suitor in his prime
ARLECCHINO (*chants*) Clip –
ZANNI (*responds*)   – clop.
ARLECCHINO (*chants*) Clip –
ZANNI (*responds*)   – clop.
PANTALONE Of noble form in raiment fine
ARLECCHINO (*chants*) Clip –
ZANNI (*responds*)   – clop.
ARLECCHINO (*chants*) Clip –
ZANNI (*responds*)   – clop.
PANTALONE That wealthy widow will be mine
ARLECCHINO (*chants*) Clip –
ZANNI (*responds*)   – clop.
ARLECCHINO (*chants*) Clip –
ZANNI (*responds*)   – clop.
ARLECCHINO (*sings*) And she'll never guess you're ninety-nine

    Pantalone hits Arlecchino across the back of the head with the bunch of
    flowers. The 'horse' rears up, nearly unseating Pantalone, who then has some
    difficulty in bringing the animal under control. When he does, they start off
    again on the original rhythm:

ARLECCHINO (*chants*) Clip –
ZANNI (*responds*)   – clop.
ARLECCHINO (*chants*) Clip –
ZANNI (*responds*)   – clop.
ARLECCHINO (*chants*) Clip –
ZANNI (*responds*)   – clop.

TOGETHER Cliperty-cloperty.

Repeat – then the 'horse' stops with a jolt and refuses to go further.

PANTALONE Why stoppeth thou, thou good and trusty Bucephalus! (*Arlecchino neighs.*) Proceed thou, thou good and trusty Bucephalus!

ARLECCHINO No.

PANTALONE What?

ARLECCHINO No. (*The repeated 'What' and 'No' getting louder each time.*)

PANTALONE (*very loud*) What!!!

ARLECCHINO No.

PANTALONE Oh, we'll see about that! (*Pantalone hits Zanni's rear and the 'horse' runs round.*) Let me dismount. (*Pantalone gets off. Arlecchino separates, but Zanni remains stooped under the blanket. Pantalone now speaks to the audience, who are given the role of townspeople of Bergamo.*) Greetings, noble citizens of . . . (*To Arlecchino.*) Where are we?

ARLECCHINO My home town, Bergamo.

PANTALONE Bergamo? Are you sure?

ARLECCHINO Of course, look at them. Where else do you get that look of vacant stupidity, except from the people of Bergamo?

PANTALONE Arlecchino!!! (*Meaning 'be careful'.*)

ARLECCHINO I'm not saying they are stupid, far from it. Under those masks of inanity, we – for remember I'm from Bergamo – are a people with a great talent and skill in every kind of villainy and skulduggery.[43]

PANTALONE (*to Arlecchino*) Do you want to be murdered in the street? (*To audience.*) Good kind people, forgive my servant. He has journeyed far and is tired.

ARLECCHINO Tired and hungry. Hungry! (*Mimes 'Hunger'.*[44])

ZANNI (*still under the cloth*) Hungry.

---

43. Similar wording as in *Home from the Wars* (Scene 1, page 25) – a memorised passage typical of *Commedia*.

44. *Lazzi of 'Hunger'*, No. 30, page 240

Pantalone pulls a leek from his bag, takes a couple of bites from it and hands it on to Arlecchino, who gnaws it and then hands it under the blanket to Zanni. Noise of eating – then Zanni releases a pile of horse droppings. Pantalone takes a pan and brush from his bag, gathers up the droppings and puts them in his bag.[45]

PANTALONE (*to Arlecchino*) Introduce me. Tell them who I am.

ARLECCHINO (*to audience in declamatory style*) My master, Il Signor Pantalone di Bisognose.

Pantalone executes a dance movement and bows with a great flourish.

PANTALONE My servant Arlecchino di . . . Bergamo. (*Arlecchino does an acrobatic movement of great agility and a bow to the audience.*) Wasn't there someone else? I don't think so . . . Oh dear, yes. (*Zanni is revealed.*) Zanni Padella da Roma!

Zanni bows, then all go into a short, high energy level dance routine.[46]

ZANNI Now, good people, we would have you know that our esteemed master, Il Messeur Pantalone di Bisognose, having made the long journey from Venice; the majestic, serene, and – (*As he speaks he folds the blanket neatly and carries it over one shoulder.*)

ARLECCHINO – wet.

ZANNI – city state, and –

ARLECCHINO – and what a state it's in – (*Holding nose.*)

ZANNI – and travelling via Vicenza, Verona, Parma, Palermo . . .

ARLECCHINO Palermo?

ZANNI All right, we lost our way a bit. We have at last arrived in the noble town of . . . Where are we?

ARLECCHINO Bergamo.

ZANNI In search of . . .

ARLECCHINO Beef Bergamos.

ZANNI In search of a c . . .

ARLECCHINO . . . a candle-lit supper, with beef Bergamos.

45. This short *Lazzo* is not given in Part II as it is specific to this play and is easiest described here.
46. *Lazzi of 'The Dance of Glee'*, No. 10, page 220

ZANNI A consort. (*Arlecchino mimes a violin.*) Not that sort of concert –
consort. A bride – a companion for his declining years; to soothe
his brow.

ARLECCHINO And stroke his . . .

PANTALONE Don't you dare. (*Appealing to the audience.*) Do any of you
know the whereabouts of La Donna Lucia . . . or any other such
wealthy woman? I care not if she be tall –

ZANNI *and* ARLECCHINO – and rich –

PANTALONE – or short –

ZANNI *and* ARLECCHINO – and rich.

PANTALONE Dark –

ZANNI *and* ARLECCHINO – and rich –

PANTALONE – or fair –

ZANNI *and* ARLECCHINO – and rich.

PANTALONE But she should be kind –

ZANNI *and* ARLECCHINO – kind of rich –

PANTALONE – and trusting.

ZANNI *and* ARLECCHINO – Enough to be gulled by an old swindler like
your good self.

PANTALONE Exactly. Er, what? Go thou among the people of the town
and garner what you can.

*Arlecchino and Zanni go among the audience to make further enquiries,
while Pantalone makes overtures to women in the front rows, asking after
their financial status and willingness to be his bride. The servants return to
the stage, Zanni brandishing a piece of paper which purports to give
directions for finding La Donna Lucia, who lives on the other side of town.*

Scene 3

Arlecchino, Pantalone, Zanni.

ZANNI Master, master, see I have it here. Yonder townsman – (*Pointing
into the audience.*) a cabinet-maker, I understand, has worked for La

Donna Lucia. (*To the supposed cabinet-maker.*) Is that not so? He speaks highly of her beauty and wealth, and has kindly writ down directions that we may find her. Her dwelling is some distance through the town.

PANTALONE Thank you, Sir, and all you good people of . . . Where are we? Ah, yes, Bergamo.

They huddle together and study the piece of paper, each one snatching it from one another, and interpreting it in different ways.[47] Pantalone is for starting to the left and Arlecchino to the right. Zanni's will prevails and he reads from the paper as they perform the Lazzo,[48] the exact form of which is tailored to suit the following text (which is of course open to elaboration or amendment).

ZANNI (*reading*) Follow the Via Marita, till you come to the end of the streeta. (*Walk.*) Turn left into the narrow Cammino Camarrio (*Walk.*) and out into the Strada Bellisimo. (*Walk.*) Keep straight on . . . and on and on . . . past Il Duomo (*Walk looking up at the great Basilica.*) and through the flower market (*React to flowers.*) and the vegetable market (*React to vegetables.*) and the meat market and turn sharp right at the little church of the Fasting Friar, and sharp left at the tavern of the Merry Monk. (*They stop here for a drink but they have only enough for one between them.*) And on past un orinatolo vecchio. (*They go into the urinal and turn their backs, then come out and continue their walk.*) You are now in the Via Capuleto.

PANTALONE Wait a minute – this isn't the Via Capuleto. Look, it's the Via Montegue –

ZANNI A street by any other name . . . Arlecchino, I thought you said you were born here!

ARLECCHINO I was. In the lower town – I've never been up here before. Oh dear, we'll have to go back.

They reverse their action back to where they left the inn, starting by walking backwards, and reversing into the urinal at all speed.[49]

Cross the piazza and in the west corner – (*Business of working out*

---

47. *Lazzi of 'Muttering and Mumbling'*, No. 44, page 253
48. *Lazzi of 'The Passeggiata'*, No. 49, page 256
49. *Lazzo of 'Going Backwards'*, No. 25, page 236

which is the west from the sun.) you will find the pleasant street, of which the third house is that of the wealthy Donna Lucia. (*The street should now run upstage/downstage, the house of Donna Lucia being to their right.*)

Scene 4

Arlecchino, Pantalone, Zanni, La Donna Lucia.

As they arrive in the street, La Donna Lucia appears from off right (by bringing on and mounting her stool, unless there is practical scenery). She mimes opening the shutters of her bedroom 'window', puts her head out and sings sweetly, welcoming the morn, which attracts the men's attention. They approach but she turns away, shutting the shutters behind her. Each in turn tries knocking at her door.[50] *They then try shouting her name through an imagined 'letterbox'. At last she flings open the window and puts her head out.*

PANTALONE We seek La Donna Lucia. Are you she?

DONNA Go away. Can't you read? (*She points to a notice, which can be imaginary.*)

PANTALONE (*reading the notice*) 'La Donna Lucia.'

DONNA Not that, underneath.

Pantalone tries to read some further writing, but as he can't find his spectacles, he enlists help – first from Arlecchino, who can't read anyway, and then Zanni. The three men are in a line, parallel to the 'footlights' and facing La Donna Lucia at her window stool (Zanni, Arlecchino, Pantalone).

ZANNI (*reading*) 'No door-to-door salesmen, pedlars, tramps, gypsies, vagabonds or rogues.' Dear lady, do I look like a vagabond? (*He bows and smiles.*)

DONNA Well, no, not you.

ARLECCHINO Do I look a rogue?

DONNA Er . . . No . . . But that old devil behind you does! (*Indicating Pantalone.*)

---

50. *Lazzo of 'Knocking'*, No. 32, page 242

ZANNI We, madam, are neither rogues nor –

ARLECCHINO – vagabonds.

ZANNI Pedlars nor –

ARLECCHINO – piddlers!

ZANNI But servants –

ARLECCHINO (*the following insertions by Arlecchino are made sotto voce*) Slaves!

ZANNI – to a most –

ARLECCHINO Disgusting!

ZANNI – illustrious lord –

ARLECCHINO Old bugger!

ZANNI – who seeks –

ARLECCHINO To swindle!

ZANNI – who seeks audience with –

ARLECCHINO Any bit of skirt with a few lire.

ZANNI – that renowned beauty of Bergamo, La Donna Lucia. Will you grant his request? How say you, fair one?

DONNA Gurn!

PANTALONE (*asking Arlecchino*) How says the fair one?

ARLECCHINO (*asking Zanni*) How says the fair one?

ZANNI (*to Arlecchino*) The fair one says: 'Gurn'!'

ARLECCHINO (*to Pantalone*) The fair one says: 'Gurn'!'

PANTALONE (*to his servants*) Stand aside. I shall make my address. And note how it's done; you may learn something. First, the approach. (*They cheer him on.*) They can't resist it. (*Ridiculous macho walk, hips thrust right forward, advancing on La Donna Lucia.*) Now for the soft talk. (*To La Donna Lucia.*) Hide not your fair face in your hands, sweet one. Be not ashamed of your maiden blushes. (*To his servants.*) They always blush. It's the thighs that seem to get them. (*To La Donna*

Lucia.) Respond with but a word and I am thine. (*To his servants.*) See, she is quite overcome. Your modesty inflames my passion. Will you be mine? How says my love? (*To his servants.*) She retires, so as not to seem too eager; she will return! (*She reappears.*) Didn't I tell you? (*To La Donna Lucia.*) Have you an answer for me, my love?

DONNA I have it right here. (*Produces a chamber pot and empties it over the hapless Pantalone.*)

PANTALONE I have never been so . . . (*Trying to shake off the contents of the pot.*)

ZANNI *and* ARLECCHINO Oh, yes you have – in Venice, Verona, Vicenza, Cremona and Milano.

PANTALONE That's true. I can't go on. Why should I suffer such humiliation? I resign – I shall return to Venice.

ZANNI You can't, we have not enough money left. Your only chance is to find a rich wife – we are destitute.

PANTALONE You're right. In youth I was much celebrated as a Romeo, but thou art more guileful and more nimble of wit than I at wooing such flibbertigibbets as yon. Zanni, pray intercede on my behalf.

ZANNI (*to La Donna Lucia*) My master of the noble line of Pantalioni, hearing of your great beauty, your fair face, your large –

ARLECCHINO Bank account! (*Sotto voce again.*)

ZANNI No . . . large . . . (*Arlecchino mimes bosom.*) No . . . largess, your full –

ARLECCHINO Coffers!

ZANNI Your soft –

ARLECCHINO Mattress!

ZANNI Your soft voice, your endless –

DONNA What ever else may be endless, it's not my patience.

ARLECCHINO My master has journeyed far to ask for your hand.

DONNA (*to Arlecchino*) What is your name? No, not him, *your* name?

ARLECCHINO I am nobody. Just a serving . . .

DONNA Signor Nobody . . . I'm coming down. Don't go away, Signor
Nobody.

*They huddle, congratulating Pantalone and waiting for her. When she has
come down to them, she only shows interest in Arlecchino.*

Now why do they call you Nobody? I think you're really somebody!

ARLECCHINO Yes, yes, but you will marry my master?

DONNA Marry him? Certainly not! But I will marry you.

ARLECCHINO But I have nothing.

DONNA I have enough for us both.

ARLECCHINO I am but a slave.

DONNA Yes – mine!

ARLECCHINO But what will become of my master?

DONNA Ex-master.

ARLECCHINO And my dear friend Zanni? (*Crying and embracing him.*)

DONNA We will keep them both on – as our servants.

ARLECCHINO If they are my servants, then I'm a master. (*He prances
about mimicking aristocratic movement.*) Il seignior Arlecchino di
Bergamo e Venezia. Zanni! Pantalone! Bow before your master.
Lower, lower – that will do. We will be married in Venice. Then
I can invite all my friends. Let us not delay. Pantalone! Zanni!

*Arlecchino gives the horse blanket to Zanni who puts it on Pantalone, who is
obliged to assume the back of the horse. Zanni takes the front. Arlecchino
helps the Donna onto the horse, hands her the flowers, and leads them off.*

They circle the stage with the 'Clip-Clop' Lazzo as before.

ALL Clip-clop, Clip-clop, etc. (*They exit.*)

Finis.

THE PATH
OF TRUE LOVE

A two-act play in the 'Golden Age'
style of the seventeenth century

Cast
Zanni – narrator and servant to Pantalone
Pantalone – aristocratic merchant and miser
Isabella – his daughter
Lelio – lover of Isabella
Franceschina – Servetta to Isabella
Captain Spavento – a Spaniard

Source
Based on several late-seventeenth-century scenarios,
and inspired by the *Lazzi* of the 'Golden Age' of *Commedia dell'Arte*

Playing time
60 minutes

Stage requirements
Approx. 5 x 4 metres stage space with wings on either side

Costumes
Traditional *Commedia dell'Arte* masks and costumes
for the 'comic' characters. The *Innamorati* in the fashion
of the late seventeenth century

Props
A chair, swords for Captain and Lelio. Optional: central screen, etc.

Music
Baroque style and instruments, preferably provided by the Zanni,
who is also the narrator

Introduction

The convention of having one of the servants address the audience, to advance the plot and delineate the characteristics of their masters, is extended here to make Zanni the virtual narrator. It is ideal if he is also a musician, playing pipe and tabor, or other portable instrument.[51] Its sources are from scenarios of around 1680, after which date those without an Arlecchino would have been the exception. In this play Zanni fulfils some of Arlecchino's functions, including his role as Pantalone's servant, though Arlecchino would never have been content to remain on the periphery of the performance.

In most respects the play follows a typical seventeenth-century scenario, as performed by one of the larger companies, though both the cast and the playing time are severely curtailed.[52] By the middle of the century the big companies were playing in purpose-built theatres, or temporary constructions in aristocratic ballrooms. Sets were often elaborate, and there would have been several scene changes. It is unlikely that any present-day company would have the resources to duplicate the extravagances enjoyed by Louis XIV in France or the Duke of Mantua in Italy, so the production here is thought of as being simply staged. The minimum requirements are an acting area of 5 by 4 metres, wings (or screens) at each side, and a central screen. The central screen can be painted to represent the trunk of a tree or other open-air feature, which can be turned by the Zanni to reveal the inside of a window for Act II. For performance, the atmosphere and the lighting should be light, bright and clean throughout. Tabs for the background would be satisfactory, although black should be avoided if at all possible.

Costumes can accurately copy the *Commedia dell'Arte* of the period. Lelio and Isabella are in the height of fashion. (Though Pantalone is a miser, he seems to make an exception when it comes to dressing his daughter, or is it that the actress playing her wouldn't be seen in anything less!) Pantalone's costume is important, as it is the main one to

---

51. If this is not possible, music can come from an offstage source, even mechanical.

52. The cast would have numbered between twelve and fifteen, and the playing time around two hours.

identify that it is a *Commedia* performance. He may wear pantaloons, or breeches, in dark red, with the red jacket under the long black cloak. His mask is brown with the aquiline nose, his hair and beard grey. He has a small stiletto and a purse at his waist. By this period the phallus/codpiece, would rarely have been seen. The Captain is clad as a military man, in the flamboyant Spanish mode. Like many another fraudster, he puts on a show of wealth in every way he can – well turned out but with just a few too many feathers and furbelows. Franceschina is an upper servant, only clearly distinguishable from her mistress dress-wise by her apron and cap.

In playing, it is important, in spite of the farcical element, not to play the characters so that they inspire ridicule. Here, Pantalone is perhaps the least sufferable, but his change of heart at the end must be made acceptable by his gravitas in all except the opening scene, when his amorous nature gets the better of him.

The pace is fast – and pickups must be instantaneous.

The Captain proposes to the wrong woman

Scenario

Act One

Scene 1

Zanni,[53] *Isabella, Lelio, Franceschina, Pantalone.*

Zanni enters and introduces himself to the audience. He announces the play *The Path of True Love* and identifies the cast as they enact a dumb-show in which Isabella and Lelio are playing a game of hide and seek, and Pantalone amorously chases the maidservant Franceschina. Then (in dialogue) Isabella warns Lelio that there will be trouble if her father catches them together. They exit in opposite directions.

Scene 2

Zanni, Captain Spavento, Isabella, Lelio, Franceschina, Pantalone.

Zanni is less sure of the identity of Captain Spavento, who now enters. He tells us that there have been reports of a military gentleman putting up at the local inn. Isabella runs on and almost collides with the Captain, whose gallantry she greets with haughty disdain. She exits and Franceschina is next on. Still fleeing from Pantalone, she bumps into the Captain who bows to her with equal grace before she too exits. Finally, the Captain is almost knocked over by Pantalone, who then exits after exchanging a few frosty words.

Scene 3

Zanni, Captain Spavento.

The Captain calls upon Zanni to identify the man he has just met. He is told that it is no other than Zanni's master, Pantalone, and so bribes the servant for information about the old man's financial status. He is told that though he lives frugally, he is believed to be a miser with hidden wealth.

---

53. As narrator, Zanni is onstage throughout the play.

Scene 4

Zanni, Isabella, Lelio, Franceschina, Pantalone.

Pantalone, now looking for Isabella, enters and not finding her, exits. Franceschina comes looking for Isabella to warn her that her father is on the warpath. She exits and in comes Lelio, also in search of Isabella. In an impassioned speech he pours forth an account of his misfortunes for the benefit of Zanni, the audience and the immortal gods.

Zanni – in a speech of some length, but taken at great speed – enlightens Lelio about a relationship that existed between Pantalone and Lelio's father: how he was cheated out of his fortune by Pantalone in a manner not only underhand but also criminal. Isabella enters, hears the last part of the story and begs Lelio not to destroy her father by bringing out the truth. Lelio agrees on condition that she promises to be his wife. Isabella says her father would never permit it. Pantalone, who has entered unobserved, seconds this. He orders Isabella to the house. Lelio says that he will marry Isabella and no one will stop him. Lelio exits. Pantalone, left onstage, tells the audience of Lelio's unsuitability and lack of means.

Scene 5

Pantalone, Captain Spavento.

Pantalone remains onstage. He chuckles unpleasantly about how he ruined Lelio's family. Captain Spavento enters, and tries to get into Pantalone's good books by various pleasantries. He meets with little success but launches into an oblique inquiry about the availability of Isabella's hand. The analogies and metaphors are so obscure that Pantalone imagines that the Captain knows something of his hidden hoard, and is panic stricken until the Captain comes out with it and asks for Isabella's hand in marriage. Pantalone is so relieved that, after a few questions concerning the Captain's own assets, he agrees. He advises the Captain to woo Isabella with fine words, and tells him to call upon her within the hour. The Captain leaves to prepare his proposal.

Scene 6

Pantalone, Franceschina.

Pantalone, alone onstage, is happy about the prospects of an advantageous marriage, until he realises that he will have difficulty in persuading his

daughter. He calls for Franceschina, and gives her instructions to notify
Isabella of his wishes. They exit in opposite directions. After a moment,
Franceschina returns with Isabella and relays Pantalone's message.
Isabella's response is 'Never!'

Act Two

Scene 1

Zanni, Isabella, Franceschina, Pantalone.

Zanni changes the scene by placing a chair centre stage right[54] (and
turning the screen if there is one[55]) and announcing that this is Isabella's
boudoir. Isabella and Franceschina enter stage left. They keep to an area
occupying about a third of the left side of the stage, now designated the
anteroom and separated from the boudoir by a mimed 'door'.[56] Isabella
thinks she has lost the key, but finds it and opens the 'door'. They enter
and she locks it behind her. She repeats her determination not to give in
to her father. He has entered left, tries the 'door' and finding it locked,
demands admission. Franceschina advises Isabella to pretend to acquiesce.
Not getting immediate admission he charges the 'door' just as Franceschina opens it, and he goes flying across the room. Isabella pretends concern for her father, which puts him off his stride a bit, and he is further
confused by her apparent submission. He exits.

Isabella, alone with Franceschina, again conveys her abhorrence of
Spavento, and performs a *grand 'Tirade'*[57] as required of the Innamorata.
After the expected applause, Franceschina tells Isabella that they must
change roles in order to discomfort Captain Spavento. They make a par-
tial change of costume and assume the voice and manner expected by
their change of status.

54. See Appendix 2, 'Onstage Locations', page 270
55. See introduction
56. *Lazzi of 'The Emperor's Props'*, No. 16, page 226
57. *Lazzi of 'Perquisites of the Role'*, No. 50, page 257

Scene 2

Pantalone, Captain Spavento, Isabella, Franceschina.

Pantalone and Captain Spavento enter the anteroom.[58] Pantalone knocks[59] at the 'door', tells Isabella that the Captain awaits her, and leaves Spavento, who rehearses his proposal while he waits to be summoned. When this doesn't seem to be forthcoming, he knocks at the 'door'. Isabella (now the maid) answers and uses every device to delay his admission. At last, he rudely pushes her aside, and advances on the supposed mistress seated with her back to him. He embarks on a grandiloquent proposal.

Between them, Isabella and Franceschina in their new roles put him through every possible indignity, including asking him to extemporise in verse, and perform a Galliard. Franceschina pulls faces at him and leads him a dance, but anxious to gain the imagined heiress, he at last gets out a proposal to Franceschina! All but Zanni freeze[60] – the Captain kneeling before Franceschina.

Scene 3

Zanni, Pantalone, Lelio, Isabella, Franceschina, Captain Spavento.

Zanni draws our attention to Pantalone and Lelio coming through the audience. Lelio has proof that Captain Spavento is a fraud and, once convinced, Pantalone is anxious to get to Isabella's room to stop the proposal. They arrive and burst through the 'door' to find Spavento on his knees before the maidservant Franceschina, who at that moment accepts the proposal. The Captain, discovering his error, instantly repeats his proposal to the true Isabella. Lelio draws his sword and fights with the Captain. Whilst still in contest, Lelio proposes to Isabella, is accepted, and disarms the Captain. He is about to deliver the *coup de grace* when he is stopped by Pantalone, who pardons the Captain on the understanding that he honours his proposal to Franceschina and enters the Pantalone household as manservant. Pantalone accepts Lelio as his son-in-law. Zanni speaks the final lines and all ends happily with the promise of a double wedding.

Finis.

---

58. The area outside the boudoir created by the mimed 'door'.

59. *Lazzo of 'Knocking'*, No. 32, page 242

60. *Lazzi of 'Asides and Freezes'*, No. 1, page 211

The Path of True Love

Act One

Scene 1

Zanni,[61] *Isabella, Lelio, Franceschina, Pantalone.*

Zanni enters playing.[62] *He stops centre and announces the company and the play:*

ZANNI The Felice[63] Company presents a *Commedia dell'Arte* romp entitled: *The Path of True Love.*

He moves left front and plays again in accompaniment to the following mime of hide and seek: Isabella runs rapidly across the stage, pauses briefly centre and continues, then doubles back and hides behind the central screen. Lelio follows, reaches the centre, hesitates, and runs off stage right.

Well, here's a how-d'you-do! I don't mean how-d'you-do, how-do-you-do? I'm not asking you – though I trust you be in the best of health – I'm telling you, 'here's a how-d'you-do' – A pretty kettle of fish! You all know me, Zanni, servant to . . . well, you know all that, and if you don't, you'll soon find out. No, the how-d'you-do I referred to is – Love – and as the saying goes: 'The Path of True Love never did run smooth'.

Isabella reappears from behind the central screen. Looks about her laughing, and runs off left.

That was La Donna Isabella de Bisognosi, and if I'm not much mistaken, she's the one in for the bumpy ride. She's playing hide and seek, bless her, with her Innamorato – (*Noises of the rather heavy-footed Lelio.*) Here he comes . . . (*Zanni again provides music.*)

---

61. As narrator, Zanni is onstage throughout the play.
62. Baroque style and instruments where possible.
63. 'Felice' standing in for your company name.

Lelio comes running on from his fruitless search, sees Isabella in the distant left and decides to hide. He goes behind the screen. Isabella re-enters, hesitates centre. Aware of Lelio's proximity, she creeps round to the back of the screen. Lelio comes out from the other side, circling round to avoid her. He catches up with her, and, grabbing her by the hand, pulls her behind the screen. Zanni stops the music and indicates: 'Shush! Listen!'

ISABELLA (*from behind the screen, getting louder in protest*) Lelio, Lelio, Lelio! (*She backs out from the screen.*) Lelio!!

LELIO (*backing out the opposite side*) Isabella.

ISABELLA Lel – i – o!

LELIO Is – a – bell – a! (*They draw towards each other till hidden by the screen.*)

ZANNI A certain elderly gentleman, namely my master Signor Pantalone, and in fact, father of the Lady Isabella, whom we have just met, has a little game of his own going.

Pantalone runs on from stage right. He is out of breath, and pauses centre, looks about him in great excitement and exits from where he came. Franceschina runs on from stage left, pauses.

And the name of the game is Franceschina, Isabella's maid.

Franceschina catches sight of Pantalone returning, gives a frivolous little scream and runs off left. Isabella and Lelio look out from behind the screen to see if all is clear, and come out of hiding.

ISABELLA Lelio, that was my father. If he catches us together he'll ban you from seeing me altogether. You better go. Quick, hurry – and I love you!

Lelio runs off right, blowing kisses as he goes. Isabella follows him to the wings, returning his kisses.

Scene 2

Zanni, Captain Spavento, Isabella, Lelio, Franceschina, Pantalone.

Captain Spavento saunters in from stage left. Isabella turns and almost bumps into the stranger. She tries to pass but he bars her way. He bows fulsomely.

SPAVENTO Charming, charming, most charming.

He lets her pass, and with a haughty toss of her head, she exits left. The Captain perambulates round the stage with an air of military arrogance.

ZANNI Now this is . . . well, I'm not sure who he is – some military gent, who has arrived recently in town. He has put up at the inn, and some say that he is very wealthy from prizes and plunder, and others say no such thing. Doubtless his name and his true colours will be made clear ere the comedy ends.

Franceschina comes running on from stage right and bumps into the Captain. She tries to pass but he bars her way. He bows to her with an equal flourish.

SPAVENTO Charming, charming, very charming.

He lets her pass, and with a little laugh and a bobbed curtsey, she exits left. The Captain next collides with Pantalone who enters at a trot and very out of breath, from stage right. He collapses into the Captain's arms.

PANTALONE I'll thank you to unhand me, Sir.

SPAVENTO But Sir, can you stand?

PANTALONE Sir, I have been standing for sixty years, and I expect to stand for a great many more, and without your help, Sir. Good day to you, Sir. (*He exits left.*)

Scene 3

Zanni, Captain Spavento.

The Captain comes downstage right opposite to Zanni downstage left (his position as narrator).

SPAVENTO (*to Zanni*) My good man, I say . . .

ZANNI Me, Sir?

SPAVENTO Of course you, who else? Come here.

ZANNI Come there, Sir? I come for no man but my master. (*The Captain holds up a large gold coin. Zanni quickly comes to his side.*) The Captain is very clever; he knows that any man with such a coin is my master. (*He holds out his hand but somehow the Captain manages to change the coin to a small copper one.*) The Captain is also very good at sleight of hand!

SPAVENTO Now you are, if my observation be correct, serving man to a certain elderly gentleman whom I have just met. Tell me is not that so?

ZANNI That is so. So?

SPAVENTO I need to know the name of that elderly gentleman whom I just now encountered.

ZANNI There I can oblige. The elderly gentleman in question is Il Signor Pantalone di Bisognose and none other than my master, so I know him well – sometimes too well. (*Rubs his backside.*)

SPAVENTO Pantalone di Bi . . . ?

ZANNI Bisognose, the very one. Will that be all, Sir?

SPAVENTO Would you say this Pantalone di Bisognose was a gentleman of wealth?

ZANNI I might if . . . (*Holds out his hand. Captain gives him another small coin.*) Well, it's like this, Sir. No one knows for certain, for he is a 'miser' (*Whispers the word.*) . . . of the worst kind, but he is reputed to have vast hidden wealth (*Aside.*) which so far I haven't located. (*He returns to his corner.*)

SPAVENTO Thank you – I shall not forget you. (*He exits.*)

Scene 4

Zanni, Isabella, Lelio, Franceschina, Pantalone.

The stage, apart from Zanni, is empty for a moment. Then Pantalone comes running on and stops centre.

PANTALONE Where is that darn girl? Zanni, have you seen her?

ZANNI Franceschina? – Yes, she went . . .

PANTALONE Not her, you fool, my daughter, Isabella. She's nowhere in the house.

ZANNI Oh no – (*To audience.*) No, we haven't seen her, have we?

Pantalone exits and Franceschina comes on.

FRANCESCHINA Have you seen Isabella?

ZANNI (*to audience*) No, we haven't seen her, have we? (*He prompts the audience to say: 'No, we haven't seen her.'*)

FRANCESCHINA She's going to get into trouble if her father catches her with that Lelio. (*She exits.*)

LELIO (*running on*) Has anyone seen Isabella?

ZANNI (*encourages the audience to shout out*) 'No, we haven't seen her.'

LELIO (*in soliloquy style*) But a moment ago she ran from me in a game, now she seems to run from me in earnest. I seek but no longer do I find. Why is she doing this to me? And why does she not stand up to her father? And why should he reject me anyway? Am not I of good birth? My family as noble as the house of Bisognosi? The supposed greater wealth of Pantalone is hidden, while that of my father, though now much reduced, is still apparent in a fine house, well and comfortably furnished, with good fare that all may see, and many share. Whereas the Casa Pantalone, though once a palace, is empty and in decay. I am plagued by an excess of whys; not wise of wisdom, but question marks as numerous as the stars. I ask the immortal gods, why, why, why? (*Beats his chest dramatically and strikes an heroic pose.*[64])

ZANNI (*applauds, after an appreciative pause*) Bravo! Bravo! (*To audience.*) That was his 'piece'. He does one in every show – it's in his contract. Bravo!

(*To Lelio, who is still holding his heroic pose.*) No reply? It would appear that the immortal gods are all otherwise engaged. But, Sir, if you would care for the answer from a mere mortal and none but a lowly serving man at that, I can tell you why Pantalone rejects you.

LELIO You can?

ZANNI In one word.

---

64. *Lazzi of 'Perquisites of the Role'*, No. 50, page 257

LELIO In one word?

ZANNI Well, one word – Money![65] (*The following is taken at great speed and with only a few exaggerated intakes of breath*.) Pantalone and your father were once business partners, and there was a deal over the provisioning of a merchant ship. Both put in large sums of the said commodity – that is – Money. (*Each time Zanni uses the word 'Money', Lelio says it with him in unison.*[66]) And the ship sailed forth from Venice in the expectation of substantial increase on the investment, giving them both more – Money. Whether to the Indies, to Java, Russe or Cathay, I know not. (*Isabella has entered and seeing Lelio in deep conversation with Zanni, holds back, and they are not aware of her presence.*) However, after some months it was given out that the ship had foundered in rough seas, with all hands and all cargo – that was – Money – lost. Years later, it was discovered that the ship had not sunk at all, but completed its journey and returned, loaded with spices, rich cloths, and cunning artefacts, which were diverted via the port of Genoa without your father's knowledge, and all the profits seized by Pantalone, and still later it had transpired that he had insured the ship against loss with bankers in Lombardy, and falsely taken the compensation. (*He does a drum roll or flourish on his instrument and strikes a pose expectant of applause.*)

LELIO Bravo! Bravo! (*To audience.*) That was Zanni's party piece. He tries to get one in – but it's not in his contract. (*Getting back into character.*) That means that Pantalone is not only the miser, skinflint and objectionable old rogue we know, but a criminal who deserves to hang.

Isabella lets out a cry, and starts to faint. Lelio, seeing her, catches her just in time and she falls into his arms.[67]

ISABELLA (*as she faints*) Oh, oh my poor father!

LELIO Oh, why does my beloved have to be the daughter of such a man? I will see that he is brought to justice.

ZANNI But there is no proof. Your father accused him but he protested

65. *Lazzi of 'Money'*, No. 42, page 251
66. *Lazzi of 'Interjections'*, No. 31, page 241
67. *Lazzi of 'Fainting'*, No 19, page 231

his innocence. That is perhaps why he dare not show his wealth and lives as if in penury. Since then, they have not spoken, and so his son is an unwelcome suitor for his daughter.

ISABELLA (*coming round*) Oh, Lelio, if you ever loved me, do not ruin my father. I know him to be miserly, even cruel, but he is my . . . (*Dissolves in tears.*)

LELIO I will do as you wish, if you consent to be my wife.

Pantalone has entered and finding Isabella in Lelio's arms, stands behind them towering with rage.

ISABELLA But my father would never permit it.

PANTALONE You are quite right; I would never permit it! (*Isabella rises.*)

ISABELLA What did I tell you? (*Faints again this time into Pantalone's arms.*[68])

LELIO Signor Pantalone of the grand house of Bisognose, I, Lelio del Flavia, of the truly noble family of Graziano, intend to marry your daughter, the fair Isabella, and you will not be able to stop me! (*Isabella revives.*)

PANTALONE We will see about that!

LELIO No, I shall see about it. (*He exits.*)

PANTALONE To your room, Miss. (*Isabella exits crying.*) Worthless young whippersnapper. Oh, noble pedigree and all that, but not worth a brass farthing! I should know, I had the pleasure of ruining his father.

Scene 5

Pantalone, Captain Spavento.

Pantalone starts to chuckle villainously and is just about to exit, when he once more bumps (physically) into the Captain who enters from stage left.

SPAVENTO Glad to find you in such good humour.

PANTALONE I am in my usual humour, Sir.

---

68. *Lazzi of 'Fainting'*, No. 19, page 231

SPAVENTO I am glad to hear that your usual humour is so merry. May I ask what you were laughing about?

PANTALONE You may not. What I choose to laugh at is my own affair, I hope.

SPAVENTO I beg your pardon. But here is a funny thing.

PANTALONE What's a funny thing?

SPAVENTO I was hoping to bump into you. And I did!

PANTALONE Well, now having had the pleasure of bumping into me for the second time today, I trust you will consider that is enough social contact for now, and permit me to say a good day to you.

SPAVENTO No, no, please do not go; there is something I wish to discuss with you. Now, you have something of which I'm sure you are very fond.[69]

PANTALONE (*aside*) He must mean my money!

SPAVENTO (*aside*) I mean, of course, his daughter. (*To Pantalone.*) As it were, a treasure . . .

PANTALONE (*aside*) How can he know?

SPAVENTO . . . which has so far remained hidden from me . . .

PANTALONE (*aside*) He has learnt of my secret hoard. One of the servants has betrayed me.

SPAVENTO . . . and so I hear, a shining beauty – refined – pure . . .

PANTALONE (*aside*) Gold. My gold!

SPAVENTO What did you say?

PANTALONE I said: 'My! Isn't it cold?'

SPAVENTO As I was saying, pure in thought and deed – virgo intacto.

PANTALONE (*puzzled*) Well, it has been through a few hands.

SPAVENTO But a time must come when the bird must fly the nest, and you must part with your treasure, and I am the one prepared to take

69. The following scene duplicates that in *The Duchess Mislaid* (Act II Scene 3, page 182), an example of the 'appropriation' typical of *Commedia*.

it off your hands. (*Pantalone nearly faints.*) Eh? What do you say to that? May I therefore formally ask for the hand of your daughter?

PANTALONE (*aside*) Pure? Refined? My treasure? He means my daughter. He doesn't know of my . . . Goodness!

SPAVENTO Now I am retiring from the wars, I must find myself a nice . . . (*Aside.*) rich (*To Pantalone.*) . . . little wife and settle down.

PANTALONE (*aside*) Just what I wanted – I hear he's very rich!

(*To Captain.*) I suppose you've taken a lot of booty in your time?

SPAVENTO Oh indeed, many a fine castle and fair town have I sacked in my time and put the treasures in my sack, and many a time have I wrung the secret hoarding place of a victim's gold, before I dispatched him to his Maker. To say nothing of the gifts showered on me by grateful kings, emperors, and potentates.

BOTH Kings, emperors . . . and potentates . . . (*The words sung and repeated ad lib, with appropriate dance movements.*[70])

PANTALONE I'm sure my daughter would be delighted to receive a proposal from such a handsome, cultured, courageous . . . (*Aside.*) and rich (*To Captain.*) . . . man, as your good self. May I soon be calling you son?

SPAVENTO Father! (*Embracing.*[71])

PANTALONE I will go and tell the dear girl. She will be thrilled. (*Aside.*) She'd better be! (*To Captain.*) However, if I may advise, I suggest you – how shall I put it? – persuade her with – er – well, fine words. I fear she has been educated.

SPAVENTO Educated? Oh, dear, yes I see.

PANTALONE Yes, educated beyond the strict social requirements of a lady of fashion, and has unfortunately acquired an unseemly penchant for the arts.

SPAVENTO Ah, the arts, oh dear.

PANTALONE And literature.

70. *Lazzi of 'The Dance of Glee'*, No. 10, page 220
71. *Lazzi of 'Embracing'*, No. 15, page 225

SPAVENTO (*worried*) Literature?

PANTALONE And poetry.

SPAVENTO (*worried*) Not poetry?

PANTALONE Yes, I fear so. She is in fact something of a bluestocking.

SPAVENTO (*very worried*) A bluestocking?

PANTALONE But . . . on a very shapely leg! (*'Nudge-nudge' Lazzo.*[72] *They laugh together; the Captain much relieved.*) I suggest that when you approach her, you win her with some well-chosen phrases, perhaps the odd Latin or Greek quotation. Or something up to the moment – Dante, or Petrark. Captain, pray call upon her within the hour.

SPAVENTO I go to prepare a fitting proposal. Within the hour – Father! (*Exits.*)

PANTALONE Within the hour – son! That will put paid to Master Lelio. (*Happy.*) There's going to be a wedding. (*Worried.*) Oh dear, oh dear!

Scene 6

Zanni, Pantalone, Franceschina, Isabella.

ZANNI (*to audience*) Pantalone knows that it won't be easy to tell Isabella. So what does he do? He calls for Franceschina . . .

PANTALONE (*calling*) Franceschina! (*Franceschina enters.*)

ZANNI . . . and tells her that she must prepare Isabella for the Captain's proposal.

Pantalone beckons Franceschina close to him, and talks into her ear. We can hear the sound but not understand a word of what he is saying. He gesticulates wildly, with actions that seem to indicate everything from gentle cajoling to downright fury.[73] *She responds with the odd word such as:*

FRANCESCHINA What? Who? Not him! Oh, she won't like that! – I'll see what I can do.

They part; Pantalone exiting right and Franceschina moving left where she meets with Isabella. She beckons her to come close and we get a similar scene

72. *Lazzo of 'Nudge-nudge, wink-wink'*, No. 47, page 255
73. *Lazzi of 'Muttering and Mumbling'*, No. 44, page 253

*to the one just played but with Franceschina whispering and gesticulating
and Isabella making interjections.*[74]

ISABELLA What? Who? Not him! Never! Oh, we'll see about that!

They exit.

End of Act One.

Act Two

Scene 1

Zanni, Isabella, Franceschina, Pantalone.

ZANNI To see what happens next, we must change the scene to
Isabella's boudoir – (*He places a solitary chair downstage right facing the
wings and turns the central screen, if there is one, to represent an interior.*)
Isabella's boudoir! Here she comes!

*Isabella, distressed and rebellious, sweeps in from off left, followed by
Franceschina.*

ISABELLA I will not marry that odious creature. Never, never, never!

*They keep to an area occupying about a third of the left side of the stage, now
designated the anteroom and separated from the boudoir by a mimed
'door'*[75]. *Isabella tries the handle of the 'door' but finds it locked.*

Have you got the key?

FRANCESCHINA What key?

ISABELLA The key to my boudoir.

FRANCESCHINA No, you locked the door. (*Isabella finds the 'key' about
her, and they enter. Isabella locks the 'door' after them.*) It's no good, my
pet, he'll have his way, you know what he's like.

ISABELLA Not this time – you know what I'm like – (*She sits on the chair
facing an imaginary dressing mirror.*)

74. *Lazzi of 'Muttering and Mumbling'*, No. 44, page 253
75. *Lazzi of 'The Emperor's Props'*, No. 16, page 226

FRANCESCHINA (*to audience, coming downstage*) What's it they say? When an irresistible force meets an immovable object – something like that. Anyway, that's them two. (*Pantalone comes on stage left, tries to open the 'door' but finds it locked.*) Here comes the force! (*He knocks angrily.*[76]) See what I mean?

PANTALONE This is your father.

ISABELLA And I thought it was the Angel Gabriel.

PANTALONE Are you going to open this door?

ISABELLA No!

FRANCESCHINA Immovable object.

PANTALONE No? Open it at once. Do I have to break it down?

FRANCESCHINA More force. (*Conciliatory to Pantalone.*) Yes, Signor Pantalone. Do you want something?

PANTALONE Open this accurséd door.

FRANCESCHINA Oh, is it locked? Just a moment, Mistress Isabella is just finishing dressing.

PANTALONE I'll give her thirty seconds, then I'll break the door down. I'm counting now – one, two . . . (*Etc. He paces up and down, counting threateningly.*)

FRANCESCHINA (*quietly to Isabella*) You'll have to give in to him.

ISABELLA Never.

FRANCESCHINA Listen to me.

ISABELLA I will not listen, it's no good – I can be as adamant as he is.

FRANCESCHINA Just pretend.

ISABELLA Pretend?

FRANCESCHINA Pretend – trust me. I'll have to open it. (*Isabella gives her the key.*)

PANTALONE (*getting louder on the last counts*) Twenty-eight, twenty-nine, thirty! Right, time's up!

76. *Lazzo of 'Knocking'*, No. 32, page 242

He prepares himself and with one shoulder forward makes a mighty charge for the door, just as Franceschina unlocks it. Of course he comes flying in, skids right across the stage, falls and ends up with only his feet visible from the opposite wing. With a cry of assumed alarm, Isabella rushes off to assist her father.

ISABELLA Oh, dear Father, I pray you are not hurt. (*From off right.*) Here let me help you.

PANTALONE (*half off*) Leave me alone – don't fuss.

They come back onto the stage. Pantalone, nursing his bruises, but trying to make as little of it as possible; Isabella all filial solicitations.

Now, daughter, there is something of import of which I need to inform you.

ISABELLA Yes, Father, but are you sure you are not hurt?

PANTALONE I am quite unharmed. Now, sit down and listen to what I have to say and don't interrupt.

ISABELLA (*sitting*) Yes, Father.

PANTALONE Now you know that I have always had your best interest at heart?

ISABELLA Yes, Father.

PANTALONE And what I say is best?

ISABELLA Oh yes, Father.

PANTALONE Well, it's time you were married, my girl.

ISABELLA Oh no, Father.

PANTALONE Oh, yes, daughter.

ISABELLA (*Franceschina gives her nudge*) Yes, Father.

Pantalone is somewhat suspicious of her apparent submission, but continues.

PANTALONE Well, there is a fine military gentleman, of good address, whom I have chosen to be your husband. His name is Captain Spavento dell Val Inferno. (*Unseen by Pantalone, Isabella mimes her disgust to Franceschina.*) He will call within the hour, propose to you and you will of course accept him.

ISABELLA Never!

PANTALONE What did you say?

ISABELLA (*Franceschina kicks Isabella covertly*) I said: 'I'd never do anything but obey my father in his every wish.'

PANTALONE What? You'll do as I say?

ISABELLA Of course, Father.

PANTALONE (*aside*) Strange. (*To Isabella.*) You're all right? Not ill or something? Well, that's settled; I am relieved. So, make yourself look your best. This is a great . . . well . . . Franceschina, see she doesn't take too long and . . . Well, I'll leave it to you two women to . . . (*He almost dances with joy and adds aside.*) Splendid, splendid . . . but odd! (*Goes through 'door' and offstage.*)

ISABELLA I will not look my best. I will not marry that odious creature. Never, never, never!

She flings herself onto the chair, buries her head in her hands, and won't respond to any of Franceschina's approaches. Franceschina comes downstage and talks to the audience in intimate terms.

FRANCESCHINA Ooh, she is difficult. No, you've seen nothing yet. No, just you wait; any second now. Watch!

Isabella straightens up in her chair, clenches her fists, and starts to stamp her feet in a glorious tantrum.

ISABELLA (*rising*) Captain Spavento. I, marry Captain Spavento! (*She follows this with tears of rage and paces the stage expressing her anger.*) Captain Spavento! (*She goes into tears of despair and takes up highly theatrical postures of anguish.*) Captain Spavento! (*Roars with contemptuous laughter, as from a Jacobean mad scene and then uses his name to spark off each of a full gamut of emotions, expressed in sound and gesture. A truly operatic display.*[77])

If the audience don't spontaneously applaud, Franceschina, after a momentary pause, encourages them. Isabella bows gracefully.

---

77. *Lazzo of 'Perquisites of the Role'*, No. 50, page 257

Isabella and Franceschina conspire

FRANCESCHINA Do you have an encore?

ISABELLA (*thinks a moment and then declaims in tragic vein*)
Rather would I the cloister seek,
And never more with mankind speak,
Or cast myself to the raging foam,
Or in desert far make my home,
Or with cruel knife, my own life take,
Than marry him, for my father's sake. (*Acknowledges more applause.*)

FRANCESCHINA So you won't change your mind?

ISABELLA Never!

FRANCESCHINA Not ever?

ISABELLA Never ever, whatever!

FRANCESCHINA (*slowly – planting every word*) Well, as *you* won't change
your mind, and *Pantalone* won't change his mind, what we'll have to
do is make the *Captain* change his mind!

ISABELLA What?

Isabella and Franceschina freeze.[78]

ZANNI Now in the *Commedia dell'Arte*, as often in life, servants are, shall we say – more worldly wise – better at coming up with practical solutions than their betters, so it is Franceschina who has a plan to save Isabella from the unwanted marriage. What could that be? Why, an old favourite, perhaps you've guessed it; Franceschina and Isabella will change places.

Largely mimed scene, worked between Isabella and Franceschina, in which they change headgear etc.[79]

Are you ready?

Isabella and her maid complete the transformation, advise Zanni that they are ready, and take up their positions; Franceschina – as the Mistress – sits at her mirror, Isabella – now the maid – is helping her complete her toilet. Zanni plays a drum roll.

Scene 2

Pantalone, Captain Spavento, Isabella, Franceschina.

PANTALONE (*voice offstage left*) After you, honoured Sir, you are my guest.

SPAVENTO (*voice offstage left*) No, indeed no, we are in your house, unknown territory for me, as it were – pray lead the way.

Pantalone enters with Captain Spavento close on his heels. Pantalone ushers his guest forward into the anteroom – that is the area separated from Isabella by the boudoir 'door'.

PANTALONE (*knocks on the 'door'*[80]) Isabella, my dear, there is someone here to see you.

FRANCESCHINA (*as herself*) She won't be long.

PANTALONE Well, Captain, my good fellow, give her a moment or two,

78. *Lazzi of 'Asides and Freezes'*, No. 1, page 211
79. *Lazzi of 'Exchanging Clothes'*, No. 17, page 227
80. *Lazzo of 'Knocking'*, No. 32, page 242

THE PATH OF TRUE LOVE

then it's all up to you. I shall leave you to your conquest. (*Pantalone exits.*)

After bowing to Pantalone, the Captain paces nervously to and fro, silently rehearsing his proposal. He forgets his words, stops and consults a scrap of paper on which he has them written. Somewhat timidly, he knocks on the 'door'. No answer. He tries again and this time Isabella answers it, in the character of the maid.

SPAVENTO I wish to pay my respects to La Donna Isabella de Bisognosi.

ISABELLA Yes, Sir, I'll see if she's at home.

She almost closes the 'door' on the Captain, so he can hear, but not see, what is going on inside. She 'minces' back to Franceschina. Note: each time she crosses between the Captain and Franceschina, she takes very small mincing steps, twice as many as required as an additional delaying tactic.

Madam, there's a gent here what says he wants to pay his respects. Is you at home?

FRANCESCHINA (*sotto voce*) I don't talk like that! (*Aloud.*) Ask him his name.

ISABELLA (*'minces' back to the Captain*) My lady wishes to be informed as to who it is what wants to pay to her his respects.

SPAVENTO I am Captain Spavento dell Val Inferno.

ISABELLA (*back with Franceschina*) He's at your service and his name is Captain . . . (*Returns to Captain.*) Who did you say?

SPAVENTO (*getting angry*) I am Captain Spavento dell Val Inferno.

ISABELLA (*crosses again to Franceschina*) Captain Spavento and he's making an infernal nuisance of himself.

FRANCESCHINA Ask him if he has an appointment.

ISABELLA (*back with Captain*) My lady says have you an . . .

The Captain pushes rudely past Isabella – the supposed servant – sending her flying, and launches into a flamboyant proposal to the figure seated with her back to him, who pulls a face at him from behind her fan.

SPAVENTO Though I am a soldier, Madam, used to the canons roar . . .
and fearless of the Saracen's blade . . . I tremble before your beauty.

Franceschina turns to him, lowers her fan, and pulls a 'Gurney'.[81] *The
Captain is taken aback and put off his stride.*

(*Aside.*) Courage, Spavento, think of the money. (*To Franceschina.*)
Where was I?

ISABELLA You was trembling.

SPAVENTO Ah, yes. Although I tremble before your beauty . . . my
ardour gives me courage to press my suit.

FRANCESCHINA Your suit, Sir? Pray, Sir, what is the purport of your
impassioned address? Pray continue; I am all of a flutter. Is that not
so, Franceschina?

ISABELLA Quite so. I've never seen her in quite such a flutter. In fact
she is not a regular flutterer.

FRANCESCHINA Thank you, Franceschina; that will do. I'm on
tenterhooks as to what the Captain is about to say.

ISABELLA Tenterhooks, Madam? What does that mean?

FRANCESCHINA You know – Spargee voces in vulgum ambiugas.

ISABELLA Oh, I see.

FRANCESCHINA You were going to say, Captain? (*The Captain has been
put off his stride and forgotten what he was going to say. He hesitates.*) Take
your time, Captain, we don't mind waiting. Do we, Franceschina?

ISABELLA No, we don't mind.

*They assume attitudes of enforced patience; sing under their breath, suppress
yawns while the Captain tries to recover himself.*[82] *He makes several attempts
to start, then turns away and consults the scrap of paper from his pocket.*

SPAVENTO (*starting up with a squeak*) Although . . . (*Starts again.*)
Although you are most tender in years, and I an old warhorse of
some thirty summers, I trust the disparity . . .

81. A particularly hideous facial distortion, the word 'Gurney' is courtesy of Harpo
Marx.

82. *Lazzi of 'Tedium'*, No. 60, page 263

FRANCESCHINA I beg your pardon; how many summers?

SPAVENTO Some . . . er . . . thirty . . . er five?

ISABELLA Ooooh! He must have been through some bad winters.

SPAVENTO (*again fast, parrot-fashion*) Although you are most tender in
years, and I an old warhorse of some forty – (*They glare at him.*)
Forty-five? (*They continue to glare.*) Fifty – summers, I trust the
disparity will not impede a union, so much to be desired by your
noble father and my humble self.

FRANCESCHINA Franceschina, would you say that the gentleman is
making me a proposal of marriage?

ISABELLA Oh, I wouldn't know, Madam. I'm only an ignorant . . .

FRANCESCHINA That will do, Franceschina.

ISABELLA Yes, but I think he'll have to do better than that.

FRANCESCHINA That's just what I was thinking. Very well, Captain,
pray continue. Both myself, and my maid, attend your every word.
Do we not, Franceschina?

SPAVENTO (*angry, in a series of theatrical poses*) I am Captain Spavento
dell Val Inferno, the Chastiser of the Infidel, the Turk Terrifier, the
Hero of Salamanca. From me the hoards of Asia flee. The cities of
the plain tremble and the walls of Jericho fall again. Am I to be
insulted by a mere wench and her skivvy!

There is a slight pause before Franceschina and Isabella burst into applause.

FRANCESCHINA Bravo, Captain – that is more like it. You are beginning
to interest me.

SPAVENTO I come not to banter pretty words but to storm the bastion,
to mount the tower and lay claim to the castle of your heart! (*More
applause from the girls.*) Your lips . . . (*Franceschina coquettishly pouts her
lips in a kiss.*) Your eyes. (*She flutters her eyes.*) Your nose. (*She pats her
nose.*) Your hair! (*She strokes her hair. The Captain hesitates and
Franceschina thrusts out her bosom, meaning 'Don't forget that'.*) Your
bosom fair, your dainty foot beyond compare. Your ankle fine. Say
but yes and I'll be thine.

Many a battle have I enjoined and many the feats of arms.
Never was I, before defeated, till I surrendered – to your charms.

FRANCESCHINA Oh, bravo, Captain – you're a poet. What other
talents, have you hidden? Tell me, Captain, do you paint?
Compose? Sculpt in stone?
Sing bass? Tenor? Baritone?
I think I have it, tell me, is it true? You love to cut a caper,
Come, Captain, here's your chance
Show me, just how well you dance?

SPAVENTO Dance, Ma'am? You expect me to dance? I fear . . .

FRANCESCHINA You fear, Sir? You tremble again? Where is this famous
courage you boast?

SPAVENTO Courage, Ma'am, I do not lack, but dancing – dancing is
not my forte.

FRANCESCHINA In that case, good day to you, Sir – I would not dream
of giving my hand to one who refused to dance for me. Is that not
so, Franceschina?

ISABELLA Oh, very so. Madam puts great store on dancing. Come
Captain, show us your Gay Galliard.

SPAVENTO But . . . but . . . there is no music.

ISABELLA Oh, I'm sure Zanni would oblige.

*Zanni plays. The Captain dances. To avoid the obvious, it is rather better if
he surprises everyone by dancing well; something in military mode (within
the capacity of the actor). Isabella and Franceschina applaud. The Captain
takes a bow, and indicates Zanni, who also takes applause.*

FRANCESCHINA Tell me, Captain, when your foe flees your wrath, do
you let them go? Or do you pursue them?

SPAVENTO To the ends of the earth, till I have them in my grasp!

FRANCESCHINA (*seductively*) And one more thing: are you a gambling
man?

SPAVENTO Like many a soldier who has diced with death, I am
prepared to chance a wager.

FRANCESCHINA Then, Captain, I wager you can't catch me.

She stands close to the Captain, holding her skirts, bouncing up and down and ready for flight. The Captain starts to roar.

SPAVENTO Cavalry, at the gallop – chaaaarge!!! [83]

He chases her around the stage. She employs every trick of evasion and mockery, including climbing over the chair, hiding behind Isabella, and changing direction so swiftly, the less agile Spavento goes careering off in all directions.[84] (Note: The mimed 'door' and anteroom remain.) At last he captures her and holds her in a powerful embrace. Zanni who has been giving a musical accompaniment to the chase brings it to a climax as they embrace. All except Zanni freeze![85]

Scene 3

Zanni, Pantalone, Lelio, Isabella, Franceschina, Captain Spavento.

ZANNI Meanwhile – not far off –

He points out Pantalone and Lelio, coming through the audience. Lelio is attempting to importune an initially reluctant Pantalone and will not stop until he has made him listen. Both mime and gesticulate, but we only hear Pantalone's voice.

PANTALONE What? What are you saying?

ZANNI Lelio has discovered the truth about Spavento, who is nothing more than a penniless adventurer. At first Pantalone will not believe it –

PANTALONE I don't believe it!

ZANNI – but is soon persuaded –

PANTALONE I am persuaded!

ZANNI – and they both rush to Isabella's boudoir.

SPAVENTO (*unfreezing and going on his knees before Franceschina*) I lack for fine words to express my longing, so like a plain soldier, I ask in plain words for your hand in marriage.

83. *Lazzi of 'Charging'*, No. 5, page 215
84. *Lazzi of 'Chasing'*, No. 6, page 216
85. *Lazzi of 'Asides and Freezes'*, No. 1, page 211

FRANCESCHINA Oh very well, if you really want little me – it's yes!

PANTALONE (*bursting in through mime 'door'*) What is going on? Captain, what are you doing with my maidservant?

SPAVENTO Maidservant?

PANTALONE Certainly – this is my daughter Isabella.

The Captain, who is between Franceschina and Isabella turns from one knee to the other so that he faces the true Isabella and repeats his proposal to her.[86]

SPAVENTO I lack for fine words to express my longing, so like a plain soldier, I ask in plain words for your hand in marriage.

PANTALONE No, that will not do. You can't have two wives. You scoundrel.

LELIO (*brandishing his sword*) I'll kill him.

The Captain flees for his life but as he can't escape, he draws his sword and they fight. [87] *Isabella, anxious that Lelio should not get hurt, tries to hold him back, her arms round his waist. Franceschina, from less clear motives, has her arms round the Captain, likewise trying to pull them apart.*

LELIO (*to Isabella, firmly but not unkindly*) Desist, woman, leave me be. This is man's work. (*She releases her hold.*)

SPAVENTO (*to Franceschina*) Desist, wench, this is indeed man's work.

She lets go. They continue to fight. Soon Lelio's superior swordsmanship shows and he does an 'Errol Flynn' parrying and reposting without looking, as he speaks to Isabella.

LELIO Fair Isabella. I will stand the torment no longer; I beg, I entreat, I demand, that you become my wife.

ISABELLA If that's a proposal, Lelio my sweet, shouldn't you be on your knees?

LELIO (*going onto one knee before Isabella, but still duelling with the Captain without looking at him, he repeats*) Fair Isabella, I will stand the torment no longer; I beg, I entreat, I demand that you become my wife.

86. See *Lazzi of 'Proposing'*, No. 54, page 259
87. See 'Stage Fighting', Appendix 1, page 270

ISABELLA Of course I will, my darling – *Yes, yes, yes!*

Lelio suddenly turns and disarms the Captain and is about to give the coup de grace, when Pantalone stops him.

PANTALONE Stop there! Stop I say! I'm not having my maid's husband killed!

ALL Franceschina's husband?

PANTALONE Certainly. He proposed to her, didn't he?

FRANCESCHINA He did!

PANTALONE And you said 'yes'. I heard you.

FRANCESCHINA I suppose I did. (*Beginning to like the idea.*)

PANTALONE Well, there you are. He's quite presentable, speaks well. I'm sure he'll make quite a good butler for my household. Servants of good address are so hard to get these days; that is unless you would like him in your household, Lelio, when you marry my daughter, Isabella.

ISABELLA Did I hear you rightly, Father?

PANTALONE Certainly. He proposed to you, didn't he?

ISABELLA Yes, he did, Father.

PANTALONE And you said 'yes', didn't you, girl? Three times if I recall.

ISABELLA Yes, Father, but . . .

PANTALONE No buts about it; I order you to marry him. Couldn't find a better fellow. I insist on it. And you will obey me; do you hear?

ISABELLA Yes, Father, of course, Father. Anything you say.

ZANNI And so, as in all comedies, there is a happy ending and we bring it to a close with a dance to celebrate the double wedding of Franceschina and Spavento, and of Isabella and her Lelio.

Zanni strikes up the music and they dance, bow and all exit, still dancing.

Finis.

FOOL'S GOLD

*One-act play with early Mask types,
and extensive use of 'Illusory Mime'*

Cast
Zan Padella – the 'Crafty' Zanni
Zan Mortadella – the 'Stupid' Zanni
Pantalone – their old master

Source
Written for three of the earliest characters, and on a storyline
from the Roman playwright, Plautus. It is not intended as
an accurate period reconstruction as it betrays later stylistic
influences

Playing time
30 minutes

Stage requirements
Approx. 4 x 5 metres
Wings or screens either side are needed for offstage business

Costumes
All three Masks are dressed traditionally, but using a muted palette

Props
Treasure map, spade, small treasure chest and contents
Key, etc.

Music
Optional

Introduction

Although *Fool's Gold* takes its characters from the earliest period of the *Commedia dell'Arte* – historically, Pantalone is the first *Commedia dell'Arte* character to be mentioned by name, and his two servants Zan Padella and Zan Mortadella are very early examples of the Zanni pair – it contains elements that would not have been part of a typical performance from that time, and so belongs to experimental *Commedia* rather than period reconstruction. It takes the concept of 'reality' suggested by the 'pretend' facet of the genre, and extends it to consider the nature of actual and theatrical 'reality'. However, it is true to the nature of the three traditional Masks concerned, and as a workshop or performance piece it gives the actors a chance to explore them in some depth. There is also the opportunity to practice advanced skills: audience involvement, performing partnerships and especially the *Commedia* version of '*illusory mime*'.[88]

This last needs great precision and considerable rehearsal time. Avoid any of the 'artistic' embellishments we sometimes associate with the French style of mime, but be open to comic possibilities of the relationship between the three Masks. In the 'treasure chest' sequence, Pantalone 'creates' the objects with flourish and flair, to fool his servants. Padella already has his own universe – he has persuaded Mortadella and the audience of the presence of the 'bush' and 'tree', and wants to show his superiority to the slow-witted and blundering Mortadella, in supporting his master.

Mortadella is full of misgivings and confusions; when he has faith, he can lean against the 'tree' and be stung by the 'nettles'. But he is full of doubt, and not totally mesmerised by either Padella or Pantalone. Neither is he confident enough in himself to voice his convictions, like the little boy in *The Emperor's New Clothes*.[89]

Although the period of the play is set in the last years of the sixteenth century, the essential need for wings – the 'onstage' and 'offstage', expressing two different realities – precludes the use of a trestle stage. It needs a space with a minimum acting area of 4 by 5 metres, with wings – or screens to take their place.

88. See *Lazzi of 'The Emperor's Props'*, No. 16, page 226
89. Ibid.

Pantalone's costume can be based on the traditional one, but is perhaps best if the image is not too clearly defined; the colours less vivid, the materials worn, crumpled, distressed.

The two serving men are both called Zanni, being a name and also an occupation; this can be shortened to Zan when included with an identifying appendage, such as Mortadella (Sausage) or Padella (Frying Pan). They are dressed alike in the early basic Zanni costume made from old sacks or rough hessian.[90] As these are hardly distinguishable, the face-masks must clarify the marked difference in their characters: Mortadella is rounded, open-eyed, snub-nosed, stupid, lovable; Padella is sharp-featured, narrow-eyed, crafty. In build, he tends to be lean and hungry-looking, though his movement is quick and muscular. Mortadella, more rounded, flabby, slow in wit and movement. He too is hungry, but not lean. As Zanni brothers, Padella is the forerunner of Brighella and Mortadella of Arlecchino.

The production (and lighting if there is such) should have a certain mellow quality; the season is the end of summer; the time, the early evening of a hot day.

The Zanni watch as Pantalone follows the treasure trail

90. It has worked equally well in modern dress; the old man in blazer and slacks, the servants in torn jeans. In the production illustration, Padella is dressed in dark clothes and Mortadella, light.

Scenario

Scene 1

Padella, Mortadella.

The first Zanni, Zan Padella enters (downstage right) and in a stage whisper talks to the audience and asks them all to keep as quiet as possible. During this, Zan Mortadella keeps running on and off (from downstage right), appearing and disappearing, fooling about. Padella ticks him off for making a noise which will give their presence away and tells him to hide himself behind a totally imaginary 'bush' (stage centre right). Mortadella is eventually persuaded of its existence and hides behind it, while Padella hides behind an equally invisible 'tree' (stage centre left), as in the *'Emperor's Props' Lazzi*.

Scene 2

Pantalone, Padella, Mortadella.

Pantalone, their old master and the object of their snooping, now enters (downstage left) muttering to himself – turns tail, and exits – then returns reading aloud from an old treasure map. He follows the instructions and counts the paces out loud. He can see the 'bush' and the 'tree', established by Padella, but not the Zanni hiding behind them. When he circles the tree, Zan Padella moves round so as to avoid him. Following the instructions of the treasure map takes him offstage, counting as he goes (upstage right). He returns still counting, crossing the stage towards the opposite wing (upstage left). He pauses just short of making an exit and says: 'X marks the spot – well, it must be just there', indicating a point just offstage. He exits.

Scene 3

Pantalone, Padella, Mortadella.

The Zanni come out from hiding and move closer to the wing (upstage left) to see what Pantalone is up to. He returns suddenly, just failing to catch the Zanni who retreat behind the 'tree'. But he has rumbled their presence – and calls out their names. Failing to get any response, he exits calling for them, pretending that he hasn't guessed where they are. They come out from hiding and he catches them by again returning suddenly. He tells them that he needs their help in digging up a treasure and they follow him off (upstage right).

Scene 4

Pantalone, Padella, Mortadella.

Noise of digging off (from upstage right). Mortadella returns immediately. The Zanni perform a *'Relay & Relate' Lazzo*.[91] Pantalone who is offstage makes sounds of 'digging'. Padella keeps coming on and off to *'Relate'* to Mortadella, what's going on. Mortadella then *'Relays'* it to the audience. Mortadella is alone onstage when Pantalone and Padella enter lugging an imaginary treasure chest. Mortadella is asked to help, but as he can't see the 'chest', he just gets in the way and makes difficulties. The 'chest' is brought downstage centre and all three do a *'Looking' Lazzo*[92] to make sure they are unobserved. Next, with an invisible key, Pantalone unlocks the invisible 'chest', raises the lid, and leads them in a mime of admiring and playing with the treasure. Mortadella has difficulty in perceiving the items.

Scene 5

Pantalone, Padella, Mortadella.

Pantalone says that he must make arrangements with his banker to find a safe place, and commands the Zanni to guard the 'chest'. He exits (upstage right). Left alone, at first they take their responsibility seriously, but Padella senses an opportunity and suggests that they steal the treasure. Mortadella is unwilling but is persuaded when it is explained to

91. *Lazzi of 'Relay & Relate'*, No. 55, page 260
92. *Lazzi of 'Looking'*, No. 36, page 246

him that it is really for their young master Lelio, Pantalone's nephew, whom Mortadella loves and to whom it rightfully belongs. They open the 'chest' and load themselves up with treasure. Pantalone is heard approaching, so they rapidly replace all the items back in the 'chest', with a mime in exact reversal of the one just completed.

Pantalone enters – he has 'forgotten to lock the treasure chest'. He takes a single (imaginary) 'gold coin' from the 'chest' and gives it to Padella to share with Mortadella, and makes a great play of locking up the treasure. Padella persuades Mortadella to steal the key. Mortadella picks Pantalone's pocket, and draws out a *real* key, which he hides about him, as Pantalone exits. Once alone, they try the real key in the imaginary lock of the 'chest' – it won't fit, so Padella goes off with the 'gold coin' to drown his sorrows.

Scene 6

Mortadella.

Alone, Mortadella laments his lack of a coin; he confesses to the audience that he would like a sausage. Perhaps there was something – just one little coin perhaps, left in the mud where they were digging. It would be worth a try. He goes off to the site of the digging and soon returns to tell us that his spade has struck something. A little more digging and he comes back lugging a *real* chest. He opens it with the *real* key and finds coin and treasure, which seem palpable to him, but perhaps he is mistaken and they are an illusion? He will keep a few coins for himself – the rest he will take to his young master, Lelio, who will probably give him a beating for making up such stories – still, it's worth a try. He exits.

Scene 7

Pantalone, Padella.

Padella returns and complains that no one will accept his 'gold coin' and he has been beaten black and blue for his impudence. He stops moaning for a moment to listen to the sound of digging again. Pantalone enters in a fury, and demands to know where the treasure has gone. Padella indicates the 'chest'. 'Not that one – the real one, I left in the ground,' says Pantalone. All Padella's protestations are in vain, as Pantalone chases the unfortunate Zanni.

Finis.

Padella and
Mortadella

Fool's Gold

Scene 1

Padella, Mortadella.

The first Zanni (Zan Padella) enters furtively (downstage right). He is followed by the second Zanni (Zan Mortadella) who is immediately 'shushed' off by Zan Padella, who then comes downstage centre, and addresses the audience in a stage whisper:

PADELLA Good! Excellent! Keep it up. Remember not a sound, please – you know the old saying: 'see all, say nowt.' The merest noise from one of you and it would ruin everything. (*Mortadella creeps back on.*) What was that? (*Mortadella runs off. Padella suppresses any laughter from the audience.*) As I was saying. (*Mortadella creeps on and comes downstage.*) If he – (*Mimes Pantalone.*) should suspect for an instant that he is being watched, the whole plan will be scuppered.[93] (*Suddenly turning on Mortadella.*) . . . And that goes for you too, not a sound from either end. (*Lazzo.*[94]) Now go and hide behind that thorn bush over there.[95]

MORTADELLA Thorn bush?

PADELLA Yes, that one there.

MORTADELLA I can't see no bush. (*To audience.*) Can you see a thorn bu . . .

PADELLA (*angry*) That one – that one – that one!

He pushes Mortadella centre stage right, who mimes hitting into a bush and shows Padella that he's got a thorn in his finger. Padella drives Mortadella round to the back of the 'bush', who this time comes out claiming that he has been stung by nettles.

MORTADELLA There are nettles behind that bush – I'm not sitting on those nettles.

PADELLA You go behind that bush and I'll hide behind this tree.

MORTADELLA I can't see any tree.

PADELLA This tree – this tree – this tree! (*Padella mimes leaning against a 'tree' upstage left. Mortadella comes close, trying to find the 'tree'. He duplicates Padella's lean, but in the wrong place, and falls.*) No, this tree, here. (*Mortadella tries again, closer to Padella and manages to lean against it.*) Now hide behind the bush and keep quiet.

Mortadella goes behind the 'bush'. Pause. He comes out looking for Padella, who mimes coming from behind the 'tree' and waving. They return to their positions. Pause. Then Mortadella comes out again.

MORTADELLA Padella, come here a minute. (*Padella joins Mortadella downstage centre.*) Who are we hiding from?

PADELLA (*angry*) I told you – Pan-tal-o-ne.

---

93. *Lazzi of 'Mimicking'*, No. 40, page 249
94. *Lazzo of 'Either End'*, No. 14, page 224
95. *Lazzi of 'The Emperor's Props'*, No. 16, page 226

MORTADELLA Oh. (*Starts to walk back then thinks of another question.*) Padella, why are we hiding from Pantalone?

PADELLA I told you – I told you – (*In a stage whisper.*) He's found a map, and he's searching for . . . (*The rest of the sentence goes into Mortadella's ear.*)

MORTADELLA (*loud*) Hidden what? (*Padella whispers again.*) Treasure? (*Padella barely lets him get the word out, setting about him brutally.*)

PADELLA Idiot, fool, nitwit, numbskull, nincompoop, lout, loon, dolt, dunderhead!

Padella gives Mortadella a blow or kick on each word.

MORTADELLA Padella?

PADELLA What?

MORTADELLA You've forgotten 'clodhopper'. You always call me a clodhopper. I like it when you call me a clodhopper.

PADELLA Shut up. Get behind the bush, and keep quiet. He's coming.

Scene 2

Pantalone, Padella, Mortadella.

Pantalone enters (from downstage left) with a determined walk – stops – he has forgotten something – exits. The heads of both Zanni come out from their hiding places. Pantalone returns with a map in his hands. The Zanni hide.

PANTALONE (*muttering*) Nor-nor-nor – east? By 20 degrees . . . That's no use. Got to have a starting point. Ah, here we are. (*Reads.*) Place your back 'gainst the old oak tree . . . facing where the setting sun shall be . . . (*Lazzo of ignoring the 'hidden' Zanni. He goes round the tree to find the west.*) Paces six, and five and one . . . Why the devil doesn't it say twelve? Then six. (*Ends up facing the 'thorn bush'.*) Then four more. Can't go four paces; this bush must have grown since my grandfather's day. I'll have to go round it. (*The terrified Mortadella goes round further to avoid him.*) Turn sharp right and paces two . . . Left again and full five score. (*Exits counting, centre stage right.*)

MORTADELLA (*coming out of hiding*) Shall we follow him?

PADELLA Yes . . . No – he's coming back.

PANTALONE (*he re-enters counting*) Eighty-nine, ninety, ninety-one . . .
(*Etc.*)

*He crosses and exits upstage left. Returns, rubs his hands and chuckles
gleefully, indicating that he has found the spot – just offstage. Exits again.*

Scene 3

Pantalone, Padella, Mortadella.

*Padella watches from the upstage left wing, mimes Pantalone's actions to
Mortadella, who re-mimes them downstage for the audience.*[96]

MORTADELLA (*mimes digging and tells the audience*) He's digging a hole.
(*He runs upstage, Padella mimes digging. Mortadella repeats the action for
the audience.*) He's still digging.

*On the third mime the Zanni bash into each other, Mortadella letting out a
great scream. Pantalone is heard from off. The Zanni hurry to hide behind
the 'bush'. Pantalone enters.*

PANTALONE What was that? (*Pause.*) Nothing eh? Only the rustle of a
bird . . . or perhaps two birds, fluttering in the thorn bush – that's
all. (*Aside.*) It would seem that I am observed. Ah, but old Pantalone
wasn't born yesterday – I shall outwit them. (*Loud.*) Padella, Mortadella,
my good faithful servants, where are you? (*The Zanni, in doubt, still
hide.*) I need you both. (*Exits calling for them. Mortadella moves nervously
upstage left after him. Padella follows just behind. Pantalone suddenly
re-enters, confronting Mortadella.*) Ah, just the person I want to see.

MORTADELLA Why me?

PADELLA To give you a good hiding. (*They change places.*[97])

PANTALONE Ah, the other person I want . . .

PADELLA Want me?

MORTADELLA Yes, for a good hiding. (*They change places again.*)

96. *Lazzi of 'Relay & Relate'*, No. 55, page 260
97. *Lazzi of 'Changing Places'*, No. 4, page 214

PANTALONE Come on, both of you. I'm on the point of digging up a great treasure. A chest of gold, hidden by my good grandfather, Il Magnifico Messer Pantaleone de Bisognosi.

PADELLA (*getting it right with difficulty*) Il Magnifico, Messer Pantaleone de Bisognosi.

MORTADELLA Heel Nifico – Messer Pant or on loan to Big Conk Nosey.

PANTALONE God rest his soul. Well, I'm not quite so strong as I used to be and will need your help to get the chest from where it lies buried. Come along.

Scene 4

Pantalone, Padella, Mortadella.

All three exit, but Mortadella returns almost immediately and tells us what's happening:[98]

MORTADELLA We're digging a hole. (*Goes off again briefly and comes back.*) We're digging a . . . Oh yes, I told you. It's quite a big hole. We haven't found anything yet . . .

PANTALONE (*off*) Keep digging, Zan Padella, that's it, keep digging.

Mortadella goes off and shouts. He re-enters, miming that he's had a shovel-full of earth in the face.

That's it, now heave. Clear a little more earth away. (*Etc.*)

Pantalone and Padella enter, lugging a totally imaginary 'chest'.

Come on, Mortadella, lend a hand.

Mortadella makes it clear that he is having difficulty in seeing the 'chest', in the same way that he couldn't see the 'tree', and is at a loss how he should help.

PADELLA Not there, you'll send us all flying . . . Now you're shoving me. (*They swivel round and Pantalone is knocked over by the 'chest'.*) Now you've knocked the master over.

98. *Lazzi of 'Relay & Relate'*, No. 55, page 260

MORTADELLA He wasn't pushed – he fell. (*They bring the 'chest' centre-stage.*)

PANTALONE Now see if anyone is looking – we don't want any Nosey Parkers.

'Looking' Lazzo.[99] *Then Pantalone gets an invisible 'key' from his pocket, unlocks the 'chest', and slowly opens the lid.*

Ahh! Behold, what treasure!!

PADELLA What treasure!

MORTADELLA What treasure??

PANTALONE What gold!

PADELLA What gold!

MORTADELLA What gold??

Pantalone leads them in a mime sequence, of admiring and playing with the imagined contents: counting and juggling with coins, holding goblets and statuettes, trying on bangles and necklaces, crowns and coronets. Pantalone with great conviction, Padella with less so, Mortadella with doubt and confusion, though he does try to hold objects passed to him and is told off for nearly dropping them.[100]

Scene 5

Pantalone, Padella, Mortadella.

PANTALONE Well, I have to make arrangements with my banker . . . to . . . to put it in his vaults. Will you guard it for me? With your life if needs be. (*Shuts 'chest'.*) With your lives! (*Aside to audience, as he exits upstage right.*) Fools!

The Zanni start by acting out their new responsibility, playing sentries and keeping a lookout, but soon get bored and end up sitting on the 'chest'.[101]

---

99. *Lazzi of 'Looking'*, No. 36, page 246
100. *'Illusory Mime'*, see *Lazzi of 'The Emperor's Props'*, No. 16, page 226
101. Ibid.

PADELLA Well?

MORTADELLA Well?

PADELLA Well.

MORTADELLA What?

PADELLA We'll have to steal it.

MORTADELLA Stealing's wicked.

PADELLA Now don't start that again, I've explained it to you. We are just 'appropriating' it for young master Lelio – to whom it really belongs – so that he can run away and marry the beautiful Isabella.

MORTADELLA (*dancing a jig*) Appropriate an appropriate sum, for the most appropriate one . . .

They open the 'chest', fill their pockets and anywhere else they can stuff the supposed treasure. Noises off of Pantalone returning. They reverse the routine exactly, replacing things in the 'chest' and closing the lid just in time.

PANTALONE (*entering upstage right*) I forgot to lock the chest; silly old fellow that I am. (*He mimes taking a single 'coin' from it and closes the lid.*) As you've been such trustworthy fellows, I'll give you a gold piece – you'll have to share it, but it will buy you lots of good things.

PADELLA Good things to eat?

MORTADELLA Sausages. (*Lazzo of 'Listing' foods.*[102])

Pantalone hands the 'coin' to Padella and locks the 'chest'.

PADELLA (*whispers to Mortadella*) Get the key from him.

PANTALONE Well, my faithful Zan Mortadella, and you too, my trustworthy Zan Padella . . . My good servants – nay – my dear friends, whom I can trust . . . (*Aside.*) to be up to every possible villainy.

During this speech, Mortadella is trying to pick Pantalone's pocket. He succeeds in the end in drawing a real key from Pantalone's belt. He is puzzled by the reality of the key.

---

102. *Lazzi of 'Listing'*, No. 35, page 246

PANTALONE (*indicating the 'chest'*) Guard it with your life. (*He exits upstage right.*)

PADELLA He's gone – open it up. (*Mortadella tries the real key.*) You fool, you've got the wrong key – it doesn't fit. Now what are we going to do? We can't carry it far; it's too heavy. It's hopeless . . . (*By turns, he gets angry, tearful, apathetic and then angry again as he tries to force open the 'chest'.*) It's hopeless – I'd go and drown my sorrows if I only had a few sous. (*He remembers the 'coin'.*) I shall eat and drink and eat and drink some more and you're not having any of it – you're too stupid.

He exits (upstage right) taunting Mortadella.

Scene 6

Mortadella.

Left alone, Mortadella tries to sit on the 'chest'. He falls, cries, mopes, sits still – finally thinks!

MORTADELLA (*to audience*) Do you suppose one little coin might have gone astray? Been left in the mud? If I dig round out there, there might be. Don't suppose so, no – but I would like a sausage. It's worth a try. (*He exits to where the digging took place, but keeps returning.*) (*Off.*) The earth's nice and loose. I'm digging a bit to the side. (*On.*) I said I'm digging a bit to the other side. Oh, you heard me. (*Off.*) There's something here. My spade hit it. (*On.*) I said my spade hit something. (*Off.*) Wait a moment.

He enters dragging a real chest. He tries the real key and finds that the chest opens and he goes through some of the moves of the previous mime displaying the objects for real.

(*To audience.*) Pardon me, are there any among you ladies and gentlemen who think they see a gold coin here? (*Holding it up.*) Or a bag here? (*Holding coin bag up.*) Or some pearls here? (*Holding them up.*) Or a chest here? (*Kicks it, and hurts his toe.*) Ow! I hope not – for then you would be as stupid as I am – and that would be unthinkable, as everyone knows I am the most stupid creature ever born. (*Pause.*) Still, sometimes it's good (*Playing with gold.*) to see the world a little different than other people. What will I do? Why, I'll put one – no, one, two, three, four – no, three is all I'll need. Three pieces of my imaginary gold in my own pocket, and the rest I shall take to my young and much-loved master Lelio – though I expect he will soon prove its non-existence by a good hiding. Your servant, ladies and gents. (*He exits with the chest on his shoulder downstage right.*)

Scene 7

Pantalone, Padella.

PADELLA (*returning from upstage right*) What's the matter with the world? First the butcher: 'What kind of trick is this?', he says. Won't change my coin and chases me out of the shop. Then the baker, and the little woman who runs the sweet stall. Then I went to the money-changer and though I explained how I was given it by Signor Pantalone himself, they brought in a constable who gave me a very rough time – I'm black and blue.

Noise of digging off left; Pantalone is searching for the real treasure chest. Padella listens.

PANTALONE (*running on*) Help! Thief ! Someone has stolen my gold!

PADELLA But master, it's here, where you left it. (*Indicates the imaginary 'chest'.*)

PANTALONE No – you fool – the real gold – that I left in the ground. It's you, you rascal – you've made off with it.

Noisy chase about the stage, preserving the fiction and the location of the imaginary 'chest'; going round it, Padella jumping over it, and Pantalone tripping over it.

Padella exits in full flight from the furious Pantalone.

Finis.

HARLEQUIN MARRIED

Mime sketch
by William Grantham Parker

Cast

Harlequin – pantomist and dancer, at present out of work
Columbine – his wife, a dancer, also unemployed
Collette – their daughter (*child performer*)
Pierrot – a lodger
Joey – the Landlord
Little Joe – Joey's horrid child (*child performer*)

Source
Typical of the Art Deco *Commedia dell'Arte* of the 1930s,
the plot having derived from Victorian Melodrama
and with an echo of the 1930s Depression

Playing Time
20 minutes

Stage requirements
Any interior space, box set or curtains with
offstage entrance to indicate the 'front door'

Costumes
Art Deco *Commedia dell'Arte*

Props
Table, cupboard, 4 plates, 4 stools, guitar, prop clock,
money tin and rent book, policeman's hat, tin drum,
judge's wig, hamper of food and wine, etc.

Music
More or less throughout. Early ragtime and novelty pieces
and children's music from the early twentieth century

Introduction

This is a short and entirely mimed one-act play conforming to, what is perhaps even today, the popular misconception that the historical *Commedia dell'Arte* was silent. It was written by my father, probably in the late 1930s, to which style it clearly belongs. As a boy of eight or nine I played the part of Little Joe on several occasions, during the 1940s. It should be worthy of revival as an exercise in Art Deco *Commedia dell'Arte,* and as such it could be quite stylish.

It has much in common with an earlier style from the 1840s and still to be seen at the Peacock Theatre of the Tivoli Gardens in Copenhagen, where balletic dancing ability is demanded from most of the cast. It also inherits the stereotypical two-dimensional nature of the Victorian Harlequinade. The mime requires skill, but little in the way of characterisation. The costumes are important and must evoke the Art Deco style of the paintings of Barbier,[103] or the bronze statuettes of the period. Harlequin should wear the all-over leotard of tri-coloured diamonds, or perhaps – as he is 'at home' – tri-coloured tights with white shirt and black bow, like Bakst's design for the ballet *Carnaval*.[104] He is the only one with a mask and this should be a very minimal black domino. It can be painted on the face, as is the usual practice in the ballet.

103. George Barbier (1882-1932), Parisian art deco illustrator specialising in fashion and ballet.

104. Leon Bakst (1866-1922), designer for many of the ballets given by Diaghilev's Ballet Russe, which included Fokine's *Carnaval* (1910) with Nijinsky as Harlequin and Kasarvina as Colombine.

Columbine here is the balletic version of the heroine, in a decorated romantic length tutu, over which she wears the apron of domesticity. Collette exactly duplicates Columbine's costume in every detail, in a smaller size. Pierrot presents the familiar image of baggy white trousers and a smock, with pompoms down the front, overlong sleeves and his face 'en farine'.[105] His head is covered with a black skullcap or bandana.

Joey (his name taken from Joseph Grimaldi) wears the costume of the famous clown with the addition of a stovepipe top hat. He smokes an oversize cigar. Little Joe duplicates his father – minus hat and cigar. He carries some sort of bag from which he draws various items, like the judge's wig and the policeman's helmet.

The set is simple and clean, like a drawing from a 1930s children's book. It represents a very poor kitchen: a bare table centre stage, on which are four empty tin plates. There are four stools, an empty cupboard, and a mantelpiece or shelf, on which stands a rather large prop clock, with hands that can be moved (from the front). There is also a tin for the rent money and a rent book.

105. 'Floured': The origin of the mime's white face is said to have originated with the Bakers Guild's contribution to the mystery plays.

Harlequin Married

DISCOVERED ON

Harlequin *sitting on a stool. He is reading the one o'clock racing edition. He mimes terrific concentration, his head travelling from side to side, reading. He turns the paper over, repeats. His finger travels down a list of horses. Stops. Excitement as he finds a sure winner. Despondency when he turns the paper over and finds it isn't running. Repeat all, ad lib. Cross and uncross legs in excitement. (Emphasise the dancer's habits; toes always pointed and feet turned out.)*

Columbine *is sweeping up. (Don't forget she is a dancer – exaggerate dancing positions as she works.) She mimes terrific annoyance with her husband, by peeping over his shoulder, reading, and making derisive movements. She deliberately knocks into him as she works, first from one side, then from the other. She sweeps the floor all round him, making him raise his feet. As soon as he goes to another stool to escape her, she follows and repeats her actions there. She changes her broom for a duster, and finds every opportunity to disturb* Harlequin *with this, including shaking it under his nose to make him sneeze.*

REPEAT ALL, AD LIB

Collette *is sitting at the table doing her homework on a slate. She is doing a sum, adding 2 + 2 + 2. She can't get an answer. She counts on her fingers, shakes her head, and tries again. Repeat ad lib. Asks her mother to help.* Columbine *tries, but she can't get an answer either.*

She asks Harlequin *– he waves her away.* Columbine *tries to do it again, and again asks* Harlequin. *They keep harassing him but he will not help, so* Columbine *snatches the newspaper from him, tears it, and throws it to the ground.*

Harlequin *rises, stamps his foot in annoyance.* Columbine *rises, she stamps.* Harlequin *stamps both his feet furiously.* Columbine *responds till both are dancing a flamenco. When he outdoes her with his 'zapateado', she crosses the stage, defiant, her nose in the air, and bends to dust.* Harlequin *takes his slapstick and slaps her on the behind.* Columbine *turns and slaps his face.* Harlequin *sits and weeps.* Collette *stands and weeps.* Columbine *sits sulking.*

103

PIERROT'S ENTRANCE

Pierrot *enters carrying his guitar – he has been busking.* Harlequin, Columbine, *and* Collette *jump up miming: 'Have you brought money?'* Pierrot: *'No, no'. He turns out his empty pockets.*[106] *No money, no hope, no nothing. In a spasm of melancholy he goes to smash his guitar. He is stopped by* Columbine *who takes it and hangs it on the wall.*

Pierrot, *very melancholy, rubs his stomach; he is very hungry.*[107] *He turns over the empty plates. Goes to the empty cupboard. They all mime very, very hungry. They sit on their stools, disconsolate.*

Collette *gets an idea! 'Thinks' Lazzo.*[108] *She dances merrily before them. They ignore her.*

Collette *shakes each by the shoulder: 'Watch me'. She does a merry dance, then starts a 'mime game' coming in from the door with a huge basket. It is very heavy. She takes the contents from the basket – an imaginary chicken, a flask of wine, a long loaf of bread. They all pretend with her, sitting at the table; very pleasant table manners, eating and enjoying the imaginary food. Laughter and fun.*

THERE IS A LOUD KNOCK AT THE DOOR

They all freeze with fear. The knock is repeated. Columbine *points to* Harlequin: *'You answer it.' He shakes his head: 'No, you answer it'. She shakes her head: 'No'. They both point at* Pierrot. *Another violent knock. Terrified he shakes his head violently: 'No' and points at* Collette. *Showing no fear whatsoever, she gets up and goes to the door.*

ENTRANCE OF THE LANDLORD, JOEY

Joey *strides in, followed by his son* Little Joe *carrying a large bag.* Harlequin's *family and their lodger,* Pierrot, *rise apprehensively.* Joey *demands to see the rent book.* Columbine *runs to the mantelpiece and takes it to* Joey. *He examines it: 'You have not paid for three months.' He questions (mime of course): 'So? Two and two and two are?' She suggests: 'Three?' He looks at*

106. *Lazzi of 'Money'*, No. 42, page 251
107. *Lazzi of 'Hunger'*, No. 30, page 240
108. *Lazzi of 'Thinking'* , No. 61, page 264

The landlord demands the rent

Collette *who tries: 'Five?'.* Joey *indicates: 'Six, Six, Six . . . Well, where is it?'* Columbine *goes to the tin on the mantelpiece and shows* Joey *that it is empty.*

He turns on Harlequin *who shows an empty purse, and then* Pierrot, *who turns his pockets inside out as before. Fear from the family – anger from* Joey: *'The furniture, the house, the guitar (Twangs Pierrot's guitar), all mine or give me my rent.' He swaggers about and hits things with his stick, etc. Then attempts to embrace* Columbine. Harlequin *intercedes.* Joey *sneers, demands: 'My money then.'*

During which time Little Joe *(having put down his bag) is dancing round* Collette, *pulling her hair and pinching her. While his father's attention is elsewhere,* Little Joe *steals the moneybag from his father's belt and hides it in the cupboard. He grins, grins, grins.*

Joey *misses moneybag, roars and stamps: 'My moneybag! Gone, gone, gone!' They all search furiously –* Harlequin, Columbine, Collette, Pierrot, *very frightened.* Joey *very angry and threatening.* Little Joe *grins, grins, grins.*

Joey *finds moneybag in the cupboard, and accuses them: 'You thieves, thieves, thieves!'* Harlequin, Columbine, Collette, Pierrot: *'No, no, no, no!'*

Little Joe *throws cartwheel in great glee. He draws a judge's wig from his bag and hands it to* Joey, *who makes a big play of removing his top hat and putting on the wig.* 'Kneel' *he demands. They kneel.* Joey *accuses:* 'You, and you, and you, and you, stole my money.' Harlequin, Columbine, Colette. Pierrot: 'No, no, no.' 'Yes, yes, yes, yes.' 'No, no, no, no.'

Joey: 'Hang, hang, hang, hang!' *Rises, thumps the table.* Harlequin, Columbine, Collette, Pierrot *sink down.*

Little Joe *throws a cartwheel in great glee – draws a policeman's hat from his bag and gives it to* Joey. Joey *puts it on.*

He puts Harlequin, Pierrot, Columbine *and* Collette *in a row behind each other. Then puts* Collette's *hand on* Columbine's *shoulder,* Columbine's *hand on* Pierrot's, Pierrot's *on* Harlequin's, *until they are linked like convicts, setting himself at their head.* Little Joe *takes a tin drum from his bag, and bangs out a march, taking up the rear.*

They tramp round the stage. After a single circle, Collette *drops off the end and goes to the front of the stage and indicates that she has an idea. She finds* Harlequin's *slapstick and gives it to* Columbine *who is at first reluctant to take it. She passes it on to* Harlequin, *who is at first also reluctant. When he does get the idea, he taps it on the floor, first behind and then to each side and front of* Joey, *who stops, and freezes in different attitudes at each slap of the slapstick.* Harlequin *throws the slapstick to* Pierrot *who immobilises* Little Joe.

Harlequin *takes the moneybag from* Joey's *belt, and starts to stuff the coins in his own purse.* Columbine *stops him with an admonishing finger. She opens and examines the rent book. She is puzzled and repeats the 'calculation' mime. She still can't get an answer.* Collette *comes to her aid and mimes:* '2 + 2 + 2 = 6.'

Columbine *takes six coins from the bag and puts them in the tin on the mantelshelf. She replaces the rest in the moneybag. When she turns away,* Harlequin *is seen by the audience to filch one more coin and put it in his purse.* Columbine *puts the moneybag back on* Joey's *belt. Taking the slapstick again,* Harlequin *does a series of taps and slaps which implement* Joey's, *and* Little Joe's *progress to and through the 'door'.*

Joey and Little Joe march round the room

HARLEQUIN PUTS BACK THE CLOCK

Harlequin *goes to the clock, taps it with his slapstick, moves the hands of the clock back half an hour, taps it again. They take up their positions and repeat exactly the moves of the mimed dinner. There is a knock at the door and as before,* Collette *opens the door and* Joey *bursts in demanding the rent.* Columbine *produces the rent book. Mimes: 'Six coins, is that right?' Takes the money from the tin, and hands it to the* Joey. *He is puzzled but accepts the money and signs the rent book.* Little Joe *sulks, because the family can't be taken off to jail.* Joey *and* Little Joe *exit.*

The family resumes its domestic activities. Columbine *continues the housework,* Pierrot *plays his guitar,* Collette *dances, and* Harlequin *studies the Sporting Times. He finds a sure winner, and shows the audience his coin.* Columbine *notices this, and with the usual admonishing finger, takes the coin from him. She puts on a headscarf and taking a large empty shopping basket, exits.* Harlequin, Pierrot *and* Collette *go to the table and sit and wait.*

They stare at the empty plates, stylised mimes of hunger,[109] and impatience for Columbine's return.

A HAPPY ENDING

Harlequin *gets a thought. He taps the clock with his slapstick and moves the hands forward half an hour. Immediately there is a gentle knock at the door.* Collette *opens the door and* Columbine *enters with the full basket. She sets the fare on the table and they repeat for a third time the eating routine, but now, with real items of food including a bottle of wine and four glasses.* Harlequin *pours out the wine.*

They freeze as they raise their glasses.

Finis.

---

109. *Lazzi of 'Hunger'*, No. 30, page 240

THE HAUNTING OF PANTALOON
A Harlequinade

*One-act play
based on the early Victorian
'spoken' Harlequinades*

Cast

Clown
Player 1 – Later, Pantaloon
Player 2 – Later Columbine, Pantaloon's daughter
Old Actor – Later, Harlequin

Source
Based on early Victorian 'spoken' Harlequinades,
and a popular theme inspired by Dickens

Playing time
30 minutes

Stage requirements
Approx. 4 x 5 metres

Costumes
Based on traditional illustrations
'Penny Plain and Twopence Coloured' prints

Props
Chair, mop, plate, nightshirt, coat hanger.
Satchel for Clown, pen, paper, inkpot, slapstick, etc.

Music
Early Victorian, sentimental and comic tunes,
live or recorded as available

Introduction

In the seventeenth century when the *Commedia dell'Arte* eventually succeeded in getting a foothold in England, two traditions were soon established, depending on which actor played the leading role. Performers like John Rich (known as 'Lun'), whose talent was for mime rather than speech, presented a silent Harlequin, but others, like Garrick himself, spoke a scripted version. The source material from this date (complete plays not just scenarios) is plentiful, but piteously infantile. How the mighty Masks of the *Commedia dell'Arte* have fallen! Pantalone has become Pantaloon – a two-dimensional character with hardly a saving grace, inflexible in mind but so weak in body that he must rely on his henchman, Clown, to carry out his tyrannical demands. He is very old, too old one would have thought to have fathered a Columbine, very much younger than her predecessor Colombina, and a creature as simpering as the most feeble of Dickens' heroines. Worst of all, the earthy Arlecchino has become the tiptoeing Harlequin, with the intelligence of a three-year-old. This may be blamed on the fourth character, Clown; or, one should say, on Joseph Grimaldi, creator of the role. In the early years of the nineteenth century Grimaldi presented a character of such comic genius, that it stole from Arlecchino the comic lead, and diminished him to the status of dancing partner and characterless lover.

That being said, I hope you will still find the following play, which may owe some small debt to that popular Mr Dickens, entertaining and playable. It always receives whoops of delight, cries of 'He's behind you', boos for the tyrannical Pantaloon, and gales of childish laughter, which makes it great fun to perform – even if there is little to offer in the way of character development.

From an artistic point of view, the potential merits are largely visual. The only thing to be commended about Pantaloon is his superb costume – that of a Regency dandy, which its once modish owner still wears in his declining years. Clown's costume is equally striking, having a distant relationship with that of Pierrot. Grimaldi considered the white face and white gown rather too bland for the audience of Regency London, and added coloured trimmings to the gown and paint to his face in a large number of variations. Columbine – who has still not outgrown the shortened crinoline and pantaloons in which upper-class Victorians dressed their daughters – has all the light and prettiness, of the early years of Victoria's reign. The spangled, tri-coloured, all-over leotard in red, yellow and blue set the popular image of Harlequin from this time on. Gone was the powerful simian mask of the *Commedia dell'Arte*, exchanged for a simple black Domino, whereas the floppy cap of his low origins blossomed into a glorious Regency bicorne.[110] All the costumes play well before any background – but if there are the resources, there is the possibility of adding the naivety of a tuppence-coloured setting.[111]

Scenario

Prologue

Clown, Old Actor, Player 1, Player 2.

Five minutes before the advertised time of performance, Clown appears in his full costume and displays a placard announcing *A Harlequinade*. Players 1 and 2, not yet in their roles of Pantaloon and Columbine, support him, and entertain with dancing, juggling, magic or other skills.

Harlequin, disguised as the Old Actor in an all-covering cloak and over-mask, enters and recites a dismal classic ode. The others gang up on him, and tell him that the audience are expecting a Harlequinade. They ridicule him when he offers to play Harlequin. He pulls off the cloak and over-mask to reveal his costume of many colours, and chases them, hitting them with his slapstick. Players 1 and 2 exit.

Scene 1

Harlequin, Clown, Columbine, Pantaloon.

Harlequin and Clown stop centre stage to catch their breath. They greet each other as fellow players, but then realise that they need a Columbine to perform in the Harlequinade. They are considering where they might find one when Player 2, now costumed as Columbine, appears next to

110. It is usual to remove the bicorne revealing the skullcap underneath after the early scenes.

111. 'Penny Plain and Twopence Coloured' prints for Juvenile Theatres, still to be had from 'Pollocks', No. 1 Scala Street, London W1.

them. She points out that they need four actors for the Harlequinade. Harlequin and Clown go through a *'Counting' Lazzo*[112] to show that there are four of them but Columbine persuades them that they are but three, and still need a Pantaloon. Clown suggests that they do without a Pantaloon for once, as he spoils their fun. They all dance at the thought, but are soon stopped by the entrance of Player 1, in the character of Pantaloon. He demonstrates his unpleasant nature by forbidding any more dancing, expressing his dislike of children – especially boys, ordering Columbine to her room, and forbidding Harlequin to see his daughter. As a parting shot he calls Harlequin a 'dancing Jackanapes'.

Scene 2

Harlequin, Clown.

Clown laughs at Harlequin for being called a Jackanapes. Although Harlequin has no idea what a Jackanapes is, he doesn't like being called one. Clown teases him, and Harlequin chases him with his slapstick. Clown stops running and asks why he is being hit. Harlequin says his name is 'Harlequin', and he doesn't like to be called other things. They perform several *'Name' Lazzi*[113] including one involving the audience, before leaving the matter and discussing what Harlequin is going to do about his love for Columbine. Clown suggests that he write her a letter, which he, Clown, will deliver. Clown provides paper, pen and ink, and his back as a writing board. They part in opposite directions, Clown promising to put the letter into Columbine's hands.

Scene 3

Clown, Pantaloon, Columbine.

Columbine and Pantaloon enter; she in tears, he lecturing her on obedience. They pace to and fro. Clown, trying not to be noticed by Pantaloon, makes several covert attempts to hand the letter to Columbine. Pantaloon becomes suspicious and they keep passing the letter between them, performing a *'Letter' Lazzo*.[114] Pantaloon gets the letter and reads it aloud

112. *Lazzo of 'Counting'*, No. 7, page 218
113. *Lazzi of 'Names'*, No. 45, page 254
114. *Lazzi of 'The Letter'*, No. 34, page 244

in mocking tones. Pantaloon takes Columbine by the arm and pulls her offstage. In the tussle, Columbine drops her shawl as they exit, followed by Clown.

Scene 4

Harlequin, Clown, Columbine.

Harlequin returns and dances longingly with Columbine's shawl. Then a very agitated Clown enters – so agitated that he can't get a word out. So he plays a mime and guessing game with Harlequin, and eventually makes Harlequin understand that Columbine has been locked in her room. Harlequin is at a loss what to do. Columbine, having escaped, joins them, and the three perform a *'Thinking' Lazzo* to formulate a plan.[115]

Scene 5

Harlequin, Clown, Columbine, Pantaloon.

As they pace back and forth, Pantaloon enters from the wings and joins them. He is sleepwalking and follows their moves. They get a fright, but he doesn't see them and goes to his chair, still fast asleep. Harlequin comes up with an idea and asks to be brought a mop, an old nightshirt, a coat hanger, a plate and a crayon. Columbine and Clown quickly bring in the items from which Harlequin makes the 'ghost'. He puts the nightshirt on the hanger, paints a face on the plate, and attaches both to the mop.[116] Columbine and Clown hide out of sight.

Scene 6

Pantaloon, Harlequin.

Harlequin wakes Pantaloon, manipulates the 'ghost' puppet and, speaking in sepulchral tones, tells Pantaloon that he is dead, and must forever haunt the night, in punishment for the misdeeds and miserliness of his life on earth. Pantaloon promises to reform, if only he were given another chance. The 'ghost' extracts a promise from him to bless the union of his daughter, Columbine to Harlequin.

---

115. *Lazzi of 'Thinking'*, No. 61, page 264
116. *Lazzi of 'Making do with'*, No. 38, page 248

Scene 7

Harlequin, Columbine, Pantaloon, Clown.

The 'ghost' disappears; Pantaloon, woken by Columbine, is at first in his usual ill humour, but recalling his 'dream', changes his manner, asks for Harlequin and greets him warmly as a suitor for his daughter's hand. He jokes that he had always hoped for such a union, but would not force Columbine, if she were set against it. Columbine agrees to marry Harlequin 'just to please her father'!

The Harlequinade concludes with a dance and the traditional rhymed couplets.

Finis.

'I'll rub my eyes and it will go away . . .'

The Haunting of Pantaloon

The Preamble

Clown, Player 1, Player 2.

Shortly before the advertised time of the performance, Clown, in the full Grimaldi get-up, goes around the venue with a placard, telling all and sundry where and when the Harlequinade is to be given. At the same time Player 1 (who will later become Pantaloon) and Player 2 (who is to be Columbine), accompanying Clown or separately, go round creating interest in the show. The goal is to involve the public and generate an expectation of the excitement ahead. Players 1 and 2 should not be seen in their role costumes; what they do wear will depend on any additional entertaining skills they can offer, and also they will probably need to be at least partially underdressed. The exact form of this preamble will depend on the venue, and whether the performance is to be given in a theatre or other setting. In either case, it should lead seamlessly into the prologue.

The Prologue

Clown, Old Actor, Player 1, Player 2.

Clown comes onto the performing area and places a stand with a placard announcing that the Harlequinade will take place 'Soon'. Clown goes, and returns a few minutes later and hangs an addition to the placard – 'In 5 Minutes'. He leaves again, and then returns and replaces the previous notice with 'Right Now'. Music starts. Players 1 and 2 enter. Clown removes the stand and the notices. Each of the artistes comes forward in turn with a short display of their own speciality – juggling, acrobatics, magic or dance.

The Old Actor, masked and in a great all-enveloping cloak, makes an entrance, brushing all aside. The other performers draw back a little in amazement!

OLD ACTOR Theodorous Tonk – actor! At your service. Noble lords and ladies and infant prodigies, I shall commence with an epic poem entitled *The Fall of Troy*:
'On Ilium's stone-clad towers,
The sinking sun sheds a dying light,
And soon the city and surrounding plain,
Are encased in the black mantle of night . . .

The other three, behind the Old Actor, are creeping in on him threateningly.

But still the sound of distant battle is heard,
By the Queen, awaiting word, of how the day has fared.
A knock is heard at the massy door.
O Woe! O Woe! . . . '

OTHERS Whoa ! . . . (*Indicating the audience.*) They don't want any more of this. They want to see a Harlequinade.

OLD ACTOR Speak up . . . a what?

CLOWN A Harlequinade.

OLD ACTOR A lemonade?

PLAYER 1 No, no, no – a Harlequinade.

OLD ACTOR A marmalade?

PLAYER 2 No, no, no – a Harlequinade.

OLD ACTOR Ah, a hearing aid?

OTHERS (*loud*) Harlequinade.

OLD ACTOR No need to shout – a Harlequinade. They don't want a Harlequinade; they want to hear my poem . . . (*They drown him out.*) Well, all right, a Harlequinade – as long as I can be in it.

OTHERS (*ridiculing him*) And who would you play?

OLD ACTOR Harlequin of course!

They turn away laughing, during which time the Old Actor removes his cloak and over-mask to reveal the Harlequin beneath. He sets about Players 1 and 2 with his slapstick, who exit to avoid further blows.

Scene 1

Harlequin, Clown, Columbine, Pantaloon.

Clown laughs[117] until Harlequin turns on him. Clown runs, Harlequin chases. Centre stage they both stop to get their breath. Harlequin does a 'Double Take'[118] at Clown.

HARLEQUIN Wait a minute – you're Clown, aren't you?

CLOWN Yes, and you're Harlequin.

HARLEQUIN It's nice to see you, Clown – it's been a long time.

CLOWN Yes it has. But it's nice to see you.

HARLEQUIN Sorry about the beating, old chap.

CLOWN That's all right. Just like old times.

HARLEQUIN Are we going to do a Harlequinade for the boys and girls here?

CLOWN Yes, that would be fun.

HARLEQUIN Well, that's two of us – Harlequin and . . .

CLOWN . . . and Clown!

HARLEQUIN But we can't do a Harlequinade without a Columbine.

CLOWN Where can we get a Columbine? That's what I'd like to know.

Player 2, now fully transformed into a Victorian Columbine, enters from upstage and stands between them.

HARLEQUIN (*to Columbine*) I don't suppose you know anyone who could play . . . (*Realising.*) Columbine! That's good, we are all here. A Harlequinade always has . . . a Harlequin!!

COLUMBINE A Columbine . . .

CLOWN A Clown . . .

COLUMBINE And a Pantaloon.

117. *Lazzo of 'Grimaldi's Laugh'*, No. 26, page 236
118. *Lazzi of 'Clocking and Double Takes'*, No. 8, page 218

HARLEQUIN Yes – that's the four of us . . .

COLUMBINE But we are only three.

HARLEQUIN No, four. (*He now starts the Lazzo*[119] *by first counting himself.*) One . . . (*He then walks behind Columbine and counts her.*) Two . . . (*Then behind Clown counting him.*) Three . . . (*He finds himself at the other end of the line and counts himself again.*) Four!

COLUMBINE That's not right. (*She stays in her position between them, pointing to each in turn.*) One, two, three.

HARLEQUIN (*starts from the other end with the same results*) One, two, three, four.

CLOWN I'll settle this. (*He goes to the front facing the other two with his back to the audience. He points to Harlequin, and then to Columbine.*) One, two. Oh, dear, now there are only two of us.

COLUMBINE (*after enlisting the help of the audience*) There you are, there are three of us – and we haven't got a Pantaloon . . .

CLOWN Goody-goody – he always spoils the fun.

HARLEQUIN Yes, and he always stops us dancing.

The three of them dance. After a few bars, Player 1, now Pantaloon, enters.

PANTALOON Now stop all this prancing at once.

CLOWN It's not prancing, it's dancing.

PANTALOON Well, whatever it is – stop it!

COLUMBINE But Father, we're dancing for all the children.

PANTALOON Children? Bah, are there children here? I hate children. Are there any boys here? Nasty things, boys – they've all got sticky pockets. And the girls are as bad, they're all flibbertigibbets . . . (*Columbine comes to the defence of the girls in the audience. Ad Lib.*) Now you, Miss, stop all this and get back to your housework – and as for you . . . (*Turning on Harlequin.*) Don't let me catch you hanging round my daughter again, you good-for-nothing, dancing Jackanapes. (*Exits with Columbine.*)

---

119. *Lazzo of 'Counting'*, No. 7, page 218, is included in Part II, but also given here as it forms part of the dialogue.

Scene 2

Harlequin, Clown.

Clown stays onstage, pointing the finger and laughing at Harlequin for being called 'Jackanapes'.

HARLEQUIN (*to audience*) Fancy calling me a Jackanapes. Jackanapes. Fancy calling me a Jackanapes! I don't know what a Jackanapes is, but I don't think I like it.
I know Jack Sprat, Jack Straw, Jack and Jill,
Jack the Giant Killer, Jack-of-all-trades, Jack-in-a-Box,
Jack Rabbit, Jack Knife, Jack Tar, Jack Daw,
Jack Ass, Jack Pot, Little Jack Horner, and the Union Jack,
But Jackanapes no one knows,
If they call me that, it'll come to blows.

CLOWN Jackanapes! Ha, ha, ha! (*Harlequin chases Clown, hitting him with the slapstick.*[120]) My turn. (*Harlequin hands slapstick to Clown, who now chases Harlequin.*) Thank you! Your turn again. (*Harlequin chases and keeps hitting Clown with the slapstick. Clown stops running.*) Wait a minute, why do you keep hitting me?

HARLEQUIN I don't know, I can't remember. I must have had a good reason.

CLOWN Well, I hope it was a good reason. I don't like being hit for nothing, Jack.

HARLEQUIN What did you say?

CLOWN I said: 'I don't like being hit for nothing.'

HARLEQUIN And then?

CLOWN That's all, that's all I said, Jack.

HARLEQUIN That's it! You called me Jack.

---

120. Clown's mocking laugh (*Lazzo of 'Grimaldi's Laugh'*, No. 26, page 236) initiates the *Lazzi of 'Chasing'*, No. 6, page 216

CLOWN Well, what's the matter with that, Jack?

HARLEQUIN It's not my name.

CLOWN It's a very nice name.

They play a 'Names' Lazzo with the audience.[121]

HARLEQUIN Well, it's not my name; my name is Harlequin. What's your name?

CLOWN Clown.

HARLEQUIN No, not what's your job – I mean what's your real name?

CLOWN Joe.

HARLEQUIN Joe what?

CLOWN That's right.

HARLEQUIN What's your second name?

CLOWN Yes, Watt's my second name.

HARLEQUIN How should I know?

CLOWN I just told you, Watt's my second name . . . Oh, just call me Joe, Harlequin.

HARLEQUIN Joe Harlequin? Then you must be a relation of mine!

CLOWN No, I'm not, I'm Joe. This is . . . (*Recalling child's name from the audience.*) And that's . . . (*Another name.*) And you're Harlequin – and you're in love with Columbine.

HARLEQUIN How did you know?

CLOWN Everyone knows that.

HARLEQUIN Do they?

CLOWN So what are you going to do about it?

HARLEQUIN I don't know. (*Starts to cry.*) That nasty old Pantaloon won't let me see her. I don't know what to do . . .

CLOWN Well, why don't you write her a letter?

121. *Lazzi of 'Names'*, No. 45, page 254

HARLEQUIN I could write her a letter!

CLOWN What a good idea. I'd never have thought of that.

HARLEQUIN If only I had a bit of . . . (*Clown hands Harlequin a sheet of paper which he takes from his bag.*) Paper! But it's no use I haven't got a . . . (*Clown gives him a pen.*) Pen! Or any . . . (*Ink.*) Ink! Now I've nowhere to write! (*Clown turns his back to Harlequin and leans forward.*) No, I can't play piggyback now. I might spill the ink.

CLOWN No. My back's for you to write on.

HARLEQUIN I wouldn't like to write on your back – it would spoil your shirt.

CLOWN No, no, you write on the paper, which you put on my back.

HARLEQUIN What a good idea. What shall I say?

CLOWN Dear Columbine . . .

HARLEQUIN That's a good idea. (*Writing on Clown's back.*) 'Dear Columbine'. Anything else?

CLOWN Tell her you love her.

HARLEQUIN 'I love you . . . '

CLOWN For ever and ever.

HARLEQUIN '. . . for ever and ever.'

CLOWN So, I'll say ta-ta for now.

HARLEQUIN 'I'll say ta-ta for now.'

CLOWN Hoping that this finds you in the pink.

HARLEQUIN 'Hoping that this finds you in the pink.'

CLOWN Yours faithfully, Clown.

HARLEQUIN 'Yours faithfully, Clo . . . No! Harlequin!' There we are – sealed with a kiss. (*He kisses letter.*) Will you see she gets it?

Harlequin exits right.

Scene 3

Clown, Pantaloon, Columbine.

Clown is about to leave when Pantaloon and Columbine enter, walking close together. She is in tears, and Pantaloon, though we can't hear most of what he is saying, is lecturing her on obedience. They pace to and fro. Clown makes several covert attempts to hand the letter to Columbine. Pantaloon becomes suspicious and they keep passing the letter between them in a 'Letter' Lazzo.[122] *Pantaloon gets the letter, and reads it aloud, in mocking tones.*

PANTALOON (*reading*) 'Dear Columbine, I love you for ever and ever. So, I'll say ta-ta for now. Hoping that this finds you in the pink. Yours faithfully, Harlequin!' That settles it. I'll lock you in your room, Miss.

Pantaloon grabs Columbine by the arm and pulls her offstage. In the tussle Columbine drops her shawl as they exit. Clown follows them off.

Scene 4

Harlequin, Clown, Columbine.

Harlequin returns and dances longingly with Columbine's shawl. Then a very agitated Clown enters – so agitated that he can't get a word out. So he plays a mime guessing game with Harlequin.[123]

HARLEQUIN (*Clown points, with other hand on hip*) You're a teapot? (*Clown shakes his head and mimes being tall.*) You're a coffee pot? (*Clown crouches low.*) You're a little potty? (*Clown mimes beard.*) You've been eating spaghetti and you choked yourself; that's why you can't speak! (*Clown points again, with his other hand on hip.*) A teapot? (*Clown mimes old man.*) . . . with a walking stick? (*Clown mimes putting on pants.*) You're putting on a pair of trousers? (*Clown shakes head.*) You're not putting on any trousers? Fancy coming in here without any trousers! (*Clown comes close to Harlequin and pants.*) Not trousers? You're out of breath? You're out of breath because someone has run

---

122. *Lazzi of 'The Letter'*, No. 34, page 244

123. This *Lazzi* is not included in Part II. It is very similar to those of Chico and Harpo Marx in several of their films (*A Day at the Races*, 1937; *At the Circus*, 1939).

off with your trousers. (*Short gasps from Clown.*) Not trousers – only short pants! You're a dog? Little pants?

Clown puts his hand over Harlequin's mouth to shorten what he's saying.

Pantsss Pants Pant!!! (*As modern game of charades.*) Pant . . . Small word 'The'? Panther . . . There's a panther loose? Help! Help! Not a panther? Another little word 'A' Panta? Panta an idiot? Third syllable. (*Clown mimes 'moon in the sky'.*) Sun? Moon? Rhymes with? Boon, soon, goon, June, loon. Loon? Pant – a – loon – ah Pantaloon! What about him? (*Clown mimes locking a door.*) He's locked up? He's locked someone up? (*Clown mimes girl.*) He's locked up a jellyfish?

CLOWN (*finds his voice*) Not a jellyfish – a girl! He's locked up Columbine.

HARLEQUIN This is terrible. I'll break the door down. I'll call him a Jackanapes with knobs on. I'll squash him between two bits of bread and say: 'How's that for a bacon butty?' I'll cut off his beard! And tickle his tummy with it. I'll . . . I'll . . . I'll . . . [124] What shall I do, Joe? What can I do? (*Columbine enters and stands next to Harlequin. To Columbine:*) Do you know that wicked Pantaloon has locked up my dear Columbine in that dark damp attic . . . ? Columbine!!!

CLOWN Columbine! How did you get out?

COLUMBINE My name is Columbine, that means a dove;
I flew out of the window on the wings of love. (*Shows key to Clown.*)

HARLEQUIN Sweet Columbine, will you be mine,
And let our hearts in marriage entwine?

COLUMBINE To wedding vows, I gladly agree,
But till Father relents, it cannot be.

CLOWN Yes, it's no good unless he agrees to it.

HARLEQUIN Oh dear, we'll have to think of something.

They perform a 'Thinking' Lazzo.[125]

124. *Lazzi of 'Listing'*, No. 35, page 246
125. *Lazzi of 'Thinking'*, No. 61, page 264

Scene 5

Harlequin, Clown, Columbine, Pantaloon.

The 'pacing about' of the Lazzo widens to come close to the wings, and on the last turn, Pantaloon tags on to the end of the line. Harlequin, Columbine and Clown are alarmed at first, but he is sleepwalking and doesn't see them. He goes to his chair and sits there, still fast asleep. They take a few more 'thinking' steps, and then Harlequin has an idea.

HARLEQUIN I've got it! Bring me a mop – an old nightshirt – a clothes-hanger – a plate – and a crayon.

They bring the props and Harlequin makes the 'ghost'. He puts the nightdress on the hanger, draws a face on the plate, and attaches both to the mop.[126]

Scene 6

Pantaloon, Harlequin.

Clown and Columbine hide. Harlequin holds the 'ghost' prop by the mop handle and manipulates it like a rod puppet.

PANTALOON (*waking*) What was that? I thought I saw . . . a ghost. I'll rub my eyes and it'll go away. (*'Ghost' hides.*) That's better. (*It reappears.*) No, there it is again. (*To audience.*) Can't you see it? What is it? I wonder if it speaks? I will address it. Oh, ghostly spectre, I conjure you to tell me, what are you?

HARLEQUIN (*as 'ghost', in sepulchral tones*) I am not a what – I am a what was.

PANTALOON A what was? Well, what was you?

HARLEQUIN A miserable wretch; my name was Pantalooooon.

PANTALOON But, I'm Pantaloon.

HARLEQUIN No, Pantaloon is dead.

PANTALOON Dead? I'm not dead.

126. *Lazzi of 'Making do with'*, No. 38, page 248

HARLEQUIN Yes, dead and gone, gone for good – jolly good – and now I am doomed to walk the earth . . .

PANTALOON Wait a minute, Mr Ghost. If I am Pantaloon, and now I'm dead, why can't I be the ghost?

HARLEQUIN Err . . . (*Thinks.*) You were too mean and miserly to pay your dues to the Amalgamated Union of Ghosts and Spectres, and so I have to haunt for you till the crimes you committed in your days of living are all . . .

PANTALOON But I didn't do any crimes.

HARLEQUIN You gave nothing to Children in Need – you even stole 20p from a blind man, and you never smiled, or sang, or danced.

PANTALOON Shall I dance now?

HARLEQUIN Too late, too late.

PANTALOON Oh no, I don't want to be dead. How long do I have to be dead for?

HARLEQUIN For ever and ever.

PANTALOON Oh no, not for ever and ever! I don't mind being dead for half an hour, but I don't want to be dead for ever. Is there no hope for me?

HARLEQUIN You could try smiling. (*Pantaloon smiles grimly.*) Is that a smile? It's not very good. Try laughing. (*Pantaloon tries. To audience.*) That's not very good either, but at least he's trying.

PANTALOON Bring me back to life, please, Mr Ghost. I'll be ever so kind and generous and full of love and laughter.

HARLEQUIN Will you give to Children in Need? (*Pantaloon nods wildly.*) You won't steal from a blind man again? (*Pantaloon shakes his head.*) Do you promise to give your blessing to the marriage of your daughter, to Harlequin? (*Pantaloon shakes his head: 'No'. Harlequin makes the 'ghost' rear up angrily.*)

PANTALOON Must I? Oh very well, they have my blessings, and a bag of gold as a wedding present. Ha, ha, I feel better already. I can sing, I can dance.

He dances wildly, finishing by collapsing into his chair. He breathes heavily and soon falls asleep, snoring loudly.

Scene 7

Harlequin, Columbine, Pantaloon, Clown.

Clown and Columbine reveal themselves. Harlequin stays out of sight.

CLOWN He's gone to sleep again – good. All we need to know now is, if he's still the same old skinflint he always was.

COLUMBINE Shall I wake him? Father dear, Father . . .

PANTALOON (*waking in a bad temper*) What is it? What do you want? Can't you . . . (*Remembering.*) I seem to have been dreaming. (*Changes to his reformed self.*) Ah, my dear Columbine, all by yourself? Where's that good fellow Harlequin? Yes, fine young fellow. (*Harlequin makes himself seen.*) Ah, there he is, just the sort of chap to make a good husband for you, Columbine. Always thought so. Can't see why you don't care for him. Still, I won't force you to marry him – but it would have made me so happy.

COLUMBINE Well, Father, I will marry him – just to make you happy of course.

Music strikes up, and Columbine and Harlequin start to dance.

PANTALOON Stop that. (*Pause.*) Don't you know – the first dance is with her father!

To his surprise, Pantaloon is taken in a ballroom hold by Harlequin and they whirl round together in a polka. Columbine and Clown laugh and clap their hands. After a spell, Columbine taps her father on the shoulder.

COLUMBINE May I cut in?

Harlequin and Pantaloon bow to each other. Harlequin takes Columbine in his arms, the music changes to a waltz, and they dance together. Pantaloon and Clown join in, and all change to a line, facing the audience, to bring the dance to an end.

They come forward for the final tag.

HARLEQUIN And so the old tale's been told once more,

ALL Much-of-a-muchness, as before,

COLUMBINE And Papa's repentant –

HARLEQUIN – Till next time.

HARLEQUIN *and* COLUMBINE The Lovers –

PANTALOON Pantaloon –

CLOWN – and Clown –

ALL Once more come, to play – the town.

Music and they dance off in a farandole.[127]

Finis.

'That settles it, to your room, Miss'

127. Simple walking and skipping dance, in which the dancers join hands and follow a leader in weaving and circular patterns.

THE DUCHESS MISLAID

Large-scale two-act play,
featuring most of the well-known
Masks of the seventeenth century

Cast

The House of Bisognose
Pantalone – an elderly merchant
Isabella – his daughter
Brighella – their manservant
Pedrolino – a mute Zanni
Colombina – maid to Isabella

The Inn
Burattino – the innkeeper
Franceschina – his wife
Padella – their manservant
Spinetta – their maidservant

Guests at the Inn
Captain Spavento – a Spaniard
Tropolino – his batman
Torolino – his other servant
Tartaglia – a Papal Nuncio
Fuomo and Fuoco – two rival captains

The House of Graziano
Doctor Graziano
Lelio – his son
Arlecchino – Lelio's man
Fritellino – the house Zanni

The Convent
Fiorinetta – the Abbess
Sister Lupina – a Little Sister of Mercy
Sister Rosa – a Little Sister of Mercy

Characters in The Night Scene
The Penitent
Three Bravos
The Decoy
The Courtier (The Body)

Source
Based on scenarios to be found in Flaminio Scala's
published Scenarios of 1611[128]

Playing time
95 Minutes, plus interval
Act I – 50 Minutes   Act II – 45 Minutes

Stage requirements
Large space, preferably flexible theatre,
for near in-the-round production

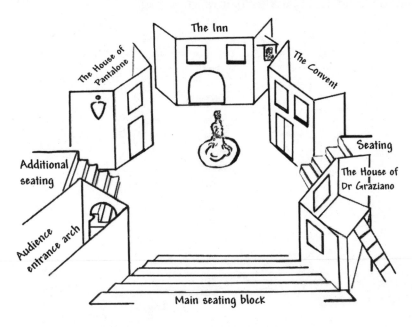

Suggested setting for near in-the-round performance

128. See *Scenarios of the Commedia dell'Arte: Flaminio Scala's 'Il Teatro Delle Davole Rappresentative'*, trans. Henry F. Salerno, New York University Press, 1967

Note on costumes and props

This play breaks the early (and valuable) convention we have enjoyed in the previous plays, of keeping props to a minimum and limiting the complexity of the staging.

However, there should be no great difficulty in simplifying the production: the Renaissance fountain could be replaced with a village pump; the incident with the blunderbus can be omitted for example; and full hobbyhorses could be replaced with cut-out horses' heads on broom handles – or mimed. They are given here as examples of the type of elaboration that gradually developed towards the end of the seventeenth century and into the eighteenth.

Among the large number of props needed for a full production there would be a long trestle table and four stools, trays and drinking vessels, hunting horns, six hobby horses, dogs (in the original production: cut-outs on 'rigid' leads), a wheelbarrow, etc.

Introduction

LE TAVERNIER.

The Duchess Mislaid is the longest of the plays in this book, demands the largest cast, the greatest rehearsal time, and is the most demanding in terms of set, props and costumes.

It was first presented at the Oval House Theatre, a community and educational centre in London, which in addition to its popular *Commedia* group of professional and student performers, was also able to provide set and costume designers and makers from among the students and teachers in other disciplines. If it is to be produced it will require similar facilities and aims, unless the company is large and well subsidised. The cast is intentionally large, to provide a variety of roles, requiring different levels of skill and ability.

Apart from the possibility of providing a useful performance vehicle for school or community theatre, individual scenes can be selected as workshop projects, either from the scenario or from the scripted version. Several important Masks not included in the other plays – the Doctor, Brighella, Burattino, etc., can be studied here, as well as introducing a further selection of traditional *Lazzi*.

As will be seen, it is envisaged as being produced in a flexible space (partially in the round), and so does not strictly belong to any of the traditional forms of presentation such as the trestle, apron or proscenium stage. It also makes use of modern lighting and sound effects. However, it is very true to the nature of the *Commedia* Masks and the plot is an amalgam of several themes from Flaminio Scala's published scenarios of 1611. Surprisingly – or perhaps because – it was a theatre featuring actresses in the female parts, there are few roles for whores or courtesans in the *Commedia dell'Arte*, and they are even referred to less frequently than one would have supposed. Characters such as the two whores and their madam do appear in written Italian drama, and the somewhat blasphemous assumption of the name 'convent' is typical of seventeenth-century literature.

The stage directions are more detailed than would be usual, so as to stress the importance of the visual element. They are there as a guide for the director, who is of course free to adapt them as he or she thinks fit.

Pantalone and Dr Graziano fulfil their ascribed positions in the *Commedia dell'Arte*. They are dressed, move and speak according to the 'conventions', modified by the personality, skill and temperament of their portrayers. Pantalone's costume and character are described in the introductions to previous plays. The Doctor dresses in an academic gown, very similar to those in use today; he has a distinctive black quarter-mask, only covering his forehead and nose, and a black hat with a very wide brim. More details of his dress and manners are described in *Playing Commedia*.[129]

Burattino is another Mask we meet for the first time in this play.[130] Like Pulcinella, he is a Mask that takes on various trades and vocations, but always retains his basic persona of the solid bourgeois; the employer rather than the employee, subservient to his betters and harsh to his underlings. He has an extraordinary costume – the base being the standard loose Zanni suit, in coarse, off-white material, but spattered with little bows of tags in different colours. It may share an origin with the coloured patches worn by the early Arlecchino. The few known pictures of Burattino don't give us much indication of how his facemask would have appeared. As he is apparently fond of his food and wine, he might well have features reflecting his habits: full cheeks and a russet complexion. For some reason in the original production his mask was pale blue and it seemed to work.[131]

Arlecchino himself can appear in his costume with the irregular patches from the earliest period, or one in the style of the Biancolelli triangles, being careful to avoid the spangled look of the Victorian Harlequin. His 'Mysterious Lady' disguise represents a widow and so

129. Pages 163–70.

130. Burattino became the generic name for a glove puppet in Italy – though unlike Punch, nothing of the *Commedia* character seems to have survived.

131. It is a good idea to make the masks as different from each other as possible, both in colour and feature.

should be black; though supposed to be the Italian Duchess of Ferrara, the costume would not be unlike that of Goya's Spanish Duchess of Alba.

There are numerous engraving of Brighella; he wears a type of livery – the standard Zanni costume with the addition of green frogging down the front of the jacket, the sleeves, and at the sides of the trousers. He has an olive green mask with sloe-shaped eyes, plenty of black hair and a beard of which he is very proud. Padella and Fritellino are 'conventional' Zanni types, but differentiations can be made in the shade of their suits (off-white to any shade of earthy browns, reds and greens). Their hats and the character of their facemasks can also be varied. Pedrolino, being the ancestor of Pierrot, should be in near-white, with his sleeves too long – the costume a hand-me-down from a much larger Zanni. There is the choice of his wearing no mask and, like Pierrot, appearing 'en farine', or wearing a white half-mask with a small snub nose.

The Innamorati ('The Lovers'), the three captains and the military servants do not have 'fixed' costumes, but are dressed in what was then contemporary costume, and so conform to the period in which the production is set. In the present case, that gives us all the richness of mid-seventeenth-century attire. Spavento is a Spaniard, so if one wants to be very precise this can be borne in mind. His appearance should be grand, if shabby. Fuomo and Fuoco are to be dressed alike, inspired by a locality considered exotic at the time – Hungary, Russia or Turkey.

Tartaglia[132] wears clerical dress, with a large sash and medallion proclaiming his status. He wears one of the most interesting of traditional *Commedia* masks; flesh-coloured with a pair of green-framed spectacles balanced on the end of his nose.

Of the women (no facemasks of course), Isabella, as we have said appears in the fashion of the day (Italian or French). The maids, Colombina and Spinetta, in simple long dresses, aprons and caps.[133] Franceschina would be similar, in perhaps darker colours. With the inmates of the 'convent' we have a challenge. One might start with the undergarments worn by Venetian courtesans and cover, or partially cover them with the headdress and gown of the nun – which, dating from the fourteenth century, has only recently (and sadly) been abandoned. Whether

---

132. In this play, Tartaglia the Stutterer takes on his 'lawyer' guise (see *Playing Commedia*).

133. The time when Colombina can only be distinguished from her mistress by a flimsy apron is a little later (circa 1690) as for *Path of True Love* (page 54).

all three should wear the high Venetian pattens (see illustration) would be a decision to be made at the time. It would be imposing for the Abbess, and humorous for Sister Rosa, who could be caught in the 'padded knickers' when she is admonished.

Any play, written or improvised, will have a life of its own, not entirely obeying the intentions of its author. The fictional characters will obey their own evolution – the survival of the fittest. The author may set out with the idea that one character is the main protagonist, but another may usurp the position. Characters that the author might wish to predominate, fade, and others come into focus. So here, the Captain has slipped beyond his original brief into a many-faceted character, leaving others less well rounded. The performer may alter all this and a small part, like that of Pedrolino, may come to dominate every scene he or she appears in.

A Venetian courtesan

The Area [134]

The audience are handed masks and carnival novelties as they pass through an arched 'Entrance Gate', which brings them to the piazza of a small Italian town. In the very centre is a Renaissance fountain surmounted by a statue. Around the perimeter are the five 'houses' of the play: practical constructions of two storeys, with a doorway and at least one practical upper window.

Directly facing us is the inn, 'The Load of Bull', hosted by Burattino and his wife, Franceschina. Rooms are to be taken here by the captains and the Papal Nuncio.

134. See diagram, page 131

To stage left of the inn are the shuttered windows of a bordello known as the 'Convent of the Little Sisters of Mercy', which is run by the elegant Donna Fiorinetta, known as the Abbess, with her two 'nuns': Sister Lupina and Sister Rosa.

To stage right of the inn is the House of Pantalone di Bisognose, displaying his coat of arms; here he lives with his daughter Isabella and his servants, Brighella, Colombina and Pedrolino.

On the extreme left is the House of Dr Graziano, graduate of Bologna University, his son Lelio and their servants, Arlecchino and Fritellino.

The main block of seating is between the 'Entrance Gate' (downstage right) and Dr Graziano's – but other seating banks are situated by each of the houses.

Scenario

Prologue – Night Scene[135]

Three cloaked figures, The Drunk, The Client, The Decoy, Three Bravos, Sister Rosa, Sister Lupina.

Light streams from the 'convent' window. There are sounds of revelry from the 'convent', inappropriate for such an establishment; then an angry female voice and the sounds of a rapid descent of stairs. The door opens and a female's leg kicks out a half-dressed 'penitent'. Sister Rosa throws his trousers from the upper window. Next a well-dressed man follows a woman decoy across the piazza, but is intercepted by three bravos who attack, rob and strip him, leaving him dead by Pantalone's door. A cock crows. Dawn breaks.

---

135. Due to the greater length of the play, the original titles assigned to each scene have been retained to help identification during rehearsal and workshop sessions.

Act One

Scene 1 – The Awakening

Burattino, Arlecchino, Brighella, Sister Rosa, Franceschina, Pedrolino.

Burattino is seen at the inn window, blowing a hunting horn. He disappears – like the cuckoo in a clock. Brighella then appears at Pantalone's door sounding a horn. Arlecchino, putting his head out of the Doctor's window, asks what's happening. It's the morning of the hunt. Arlecchino blows his horn. Sister Rosa of the 'convent' complains that her sleep is being disturbed. Franceschina shakes bedding from the inn window.

Scene 2 – Waking Pantalone

Pedrolino, Brighella, Pantalone.

A sleepy Pedrolino comes from out of Pantalone's house, stepping over the body on the doorstep. He washes perfunctorily at the fountain, and then sits on the step next to the body, picking his feet, including one belonging to the body. Then he finds an extra hand – *'Extra Limbs' Lazzo*.[136] He takes fright, but can't get back into the house, so bangs on the door. This brings out Brighella, who examines the body, but finding nothing of value, calls up to the window to wake Pantalone. When Pantalone eventually appears, Brighella reminds him that he is due to go hunting with Dr Graziano, and asks what he should do with the body. Pantalone tells him to put it on the Doctor's doorstep.

Scene 3 – The Doctor Tripping

Arlecchino, Dr Graziano, Burattino, Padella, Spinetta.

Dr Graziano, on entering with his servant Arlecchino, trips full length over the body. When he has ascertained that the man really is dead, he calls for an undertaker. Burattino, the innkeeper, whose many additional trades include that of undertaker, offers various expensive funeral packages, but is told that it will be a pauper's internment at the City Father's expense. Burattino calls for Padella and Spinetta, who bring in a wheelbarrow and remove the body in a mock funeral cortege.

---

136. *Lazzi of 'Extra Limbs'*, No. 18, page 230

Scene 4 – Lover's Meeting

Pantalone, Lelio, Dr Graziano, Isabella, Arlecchino, Colombina.

As he goes into his house, Dr Graziano calls for his son, Lelio, who puts his head out of the upstairs window. Pantalone comes from his house and calls for his daughter, Isabella, and then exits again in search of her, just missing her as she appears at the window above him. The two lovers face each other across the piazza. Lelio tries to make conversation, but she is haughty and scornful. He calls out for Arlecchino, who comes out of the door below him. 'Who is the haughty female at the window opposite?' asks Lelio. Isabella has called for Colombina who replaces her at the window. Arlecchino says that she is Isabella's maidservant whom he fancies. The face at the window changes, so that Lelio and Arlecchino see a different woman each time they look. At last all are properly named and identified, but the lovers are left with some antagonism for each other.

Arlecchino sounds the hunting horn

Scene 5 – Questions

Dr Graziano, Arlecchino, Pantalone, Brighella.

Dr Graziano enters with Arlecchino and quizzes him for information on his neighbour Pantalone, whom he is about to meet for the first time. He is interested to know if Isabella would make a good match for his son. They exit,

139

and are replaced by Pantalone and Brighella. Pantalone is eager to learn what he can about the Doctor, and especially about his financial status.

Scene 6 – Departure for the Hunt

Dr Graziano, Pantalone, Lelio, Isabella, Brighella, Arlecchino.

Dr Graziano and Pantalone greet each other. Unsure of each other's names, they work a *'Fragmented Sentences' Lazzo.*[137] They then call for their offspring, who are formally introduced to each other. The young people greet each other with disdain. Burattino comes on to announce the departure for the hunt. Arlecchino and Brighella appear as we hear noises of horses, dogs and hunting horns. The Zanni run to and fro. Pantalone, the Doctor, Isabella, Lelio, Burattino and now Franceschina appear with hobbyhorses; Colombina and Pedrolino with dogs.[138] They depart amid much noise and clatter.

Scene 7 – Arrivals

Brighella, Padella, Arlecchino, Spinetta, Tartaglia, Tropolino, Torolino, Sister Lupina.

Left alone, the remaining Zanni enumerate the tasks to be done, but opt for a little nap by the fountain. They perform a *'Bee' Lazzo*[139] and other business settling down. The Papal Nuncio, Tartaglia, arrives seeking accommodation. He knocks at the inn door but gets no response. The Zanni at the fountain, disturbed by the knocking, gag and bind the Nuncio to the inn door, so they can go back to sleep.

Singing off. Tropolino, batman to Captain Spavento, arrives looking for a billet for his master. He releases Tartaglia and makes Padella open the inn. Spinetta, who has been asleep behind the fountain throughout the scene, is woken to show them to their rooms. Torolino, Spavento's second servant comes on carrying a large chest. Brighella, Arlecchino and Padella are curious about its contents. Torolino hints at what it might be, but won't be drawn. He points out how heavy it is, and that he has the key on his belt. He takes the chest into the inn. Brighella in a whisper tells Padella to try and get the key, and they exit. Tropolino

137. *Lazzi of 'Fragmented Sentences'*, No. 21, page 233

138. See *notes on costumes and props*, page 132

139. *Lazzi of 'The Bee, the Fly and the Flea'*, No. 3, page 214

waits for Torolino at the door. Sister Rosa from the 'convent' comes out with milk for her cat. She is pleased to see that the military has arrived in town. Torolino, having deposited the chest, tells Tropolino that the key has already been stolen. They are not worried, as they know that it is not the one to open the chest. They leave to fetch their captain.

Scene 8 – Brighella Confides

Brighella, Padella.

Left alone, Brighella recapitulates the plot so far for the audience, and tells them about his plans to enrich himself; either by discovering Pantalone's hidden hoard, or making off with the contents of the Captain's chest, which he believes to be full of booty from Spavento's campaigns. Padella enters and tells Brighella that he has managed to steal the key.

Scene 9 – Return from the Hunt

Brighella, Arlecchino, Padella, Fritellino, Colombina, Pedrolino, Dr Graziano, Lelio, Pantalone, Isabella, Burattino, Franceschina.

Fritellino, Colombina and Pedrolino enter and explain that the hunt has been aborted. Dr Graziano and Pantalone have quarrelled. The Doctor and Pantalone ride in threatening each other. The lovers, who have been forbidden to communicate with each other, follow them. Surprisingly Isabella blows a kiss to Lelio as they disappear into their houses. Franceschina and Burattino come on and comment on other matrimonial possibilities facing the lovers.

Scene 10 – The Arrival of Spavento

Pedrolino, Captain Spavento, Tropolino, Abbess and the full company (so far seen).

Sounds of bugle and drums arouse the locals who come to see what's happening, and we get a first glimpse of the Abbess at the window of the 'convent'. Pedrolino watches the approach of Spavento and his men, still some way off, and mimics them for the benefit of the crowd. Tropolino and Torolino enter with drum and bugle, followed by Captain Spavento, who harangues the onlookers, telling them of his intention to settle in the quiet town. All exit.

Scene 11 – A Love Letter

Fritellino, Dr Graziano, Pedrolino, Pantalone, Colombina, Arlecchino, Isabella.

Fritellino brings out a table and chair for Dr Graziano, who sits outside his house studying a Latin text. Pedrolino brings a table and chair for Pantalone who sits, going over his accounts. They studiously ignore each other. The Doctor returns to his house to consult a reference. Pantalone goes indoors to check a receipt. As he goes he almost bumps into Colombina, who is carrying two large jugs to get some milk. On her return she bumps into Arlecchino and sexual banter takes place between them, ending with Arlecchino showing her a letter from Lelio to Isabella. Both try to read the name of the addressee on the cover, without much success. Isabella appears and claims the letter. She just manages to avoid Pantalone as he returns to his chair.

Scene 12 – The Sussing

Burattino, Tartaglia, Arlecchino and the full company (so far seen).

A complex scene in which various plot developments are made simultaneously. As they come out of the inn, Tartaglia is admonishing Burattino for leaving the establishment in such unworthy hands. He looks up the appropriate penalty in a pocket-book and fines Burattino on the spot. With the money, Tartaglia orders wine for the two of them. Dr Graziano at his table calls for wine and a glass for the innkeeper, which is brought by Spinetta. Spavento and Tropolino enter and walk about while they discuss the occupants of the various establishments. Spavento too calls for wine and an extra glass for Burattino who buzzes about, drinking at each table and answering questions from Tartaglia, Spavento, and lastly Pantalone who has joined in – without, however, supplying any wine. We learn from Tartaglia that he is on a mission to find the disgraced Duchess of Ferrara who, on the accession of a new Pope, is to be pardoned and reinstated. Other members of the cast enter and all draw close, to hear that there is a likelihood that the Duchess will arrive in the town incognito, if she is not already here. He admits that: 'The Duchess has been mislaid.' All onstage freeze in attitudes of astonishment, except Arlecchino who comes forward to announce to the audience that there will be an interval.

Act Two

Scene 1 – The Siesta

Arlecchino, Dr Graziano, Brighella, Isabella, Pantalone, Lelio, Colombina, Padella.

Arlecchino comes on and explains to the audience why none of the other characters are about; it's early afternoon and everyone is taking a siesta – no one would dream of being about at . . . Arlecchino stops talking and hides. Dr Graziano slips out of his door and gains admission to the 'convent'. Brighella steals on with a hammer and a jemmy; he goes to the inn and is let in by Padella. Lelio comes looking for Isabella and exits again. Isabella comes looking for Lelio. Pantalone comes out and looks at her suspiciously as she returns to the house. He turns suddenly and catches Lelio, who retreats rapidly. From the inn, Franceschina beckons to Pantalone. At first he is doubtful but soon takes up the invitation. Lelio enters and, observing that Pantalone is out of the way, goes to Pantalone's house and knocks. He plays a game of hiding and makes a grab for Isabella as she comes out to look. Arlecchino watches Colombina come from Pantalone's house and, to his surprise, enter the 'convent'. The Doctor comes out of the 'convent'. Isabella and Lelio separate and return to their houses. The Doctor, finding Arlecchino talking to the audience, tells him to get back to work and then exits. Arlecchino is about to exit when Colombina come out of the 'convent'. He is shocked and annoyed with her until she explains that it is part of the plan to help the lovers. She leads a perplexed and protesting Arlecchino into the 'convent'.

Scene 2 – The Lover's Knot

Isabella, Lelio, Brighella, Pantalone, Dr Graziano.

A love scene in which Isabella tries to break from Lelio and chides him for not being able to improvise in the romantic vein of his letter. When he does release his hold on her, she is reluctant to part and is about to submit to his embrace when they are each seized by their respective parents, dragged apart and sent to their rooms. The scene ends with Pantalone and Dr Graziano setting into each other in a comic brawl. The Doctor seems to get the worst of it and beats a hasty retreat.

Scene 3 – *A Father's Permission*

Burattino, Captain Spavento, Pantalone, Isabella, Colombina.

Captain Spavento and Burattino enter. They see Pantalone, and Burattino introduces Spavento and Pantalone to each other in high-flown classical mode, likening them to Mars and Jupiter. Left alone, the Captain raises the question of marriage to Isabella, in such obscure terms that Pantalone thinks the Captain has gained some information on his hidden savings. When the misunderstanding has been cleared up and Pantalone has been assured of the Captain's financial position, he agrees that the wedding should take place immediately, though he delays discussion of the dowry. Pantalone promises to send Isabella out shortly. The Captain leaves to consider his proposal. Brighella crosses from the inn to Pantalone's house unobserved. Isabella enters accompanied by Colombina. Pantalone informs Isabella of his decision. She is appalled at the thought of marrying Spavento and refuses. For his part, Pantalone refuses to listen to her objections and tells Colombina to bring the girl to her senses. He exits, and Colombina advises Isabella to pretend to acquiesce. She says that she has got together with the other servants and they have come up with a plan to prevent the unwanted marriage. They exit.

Scene 4 – *Spavento Proposes*

Captain Spavento, Tropolino, Sister Lupina.

Spavento and Tropolino enter from the inn. The Captain lets his batman know that he is about to propose to a woman he has never seen. Tropolino tells him that Isabella is a most acceptable choice. He then describes her as tallish, fairish and elegant (or in a manner appropriate to the actress in the part). Tropolino exits. The Captain is rehearsing his proposal when he hears Sister Lupina calling for her cat, 'Spiv'. 'Can she mean me?' he wonders. When he sees her, he is very doubtful that this is the tallish, fairish and elegant-ish Isabella, but none the less, launches into a passionate proposal, which so terrifies Lupina that she throws up the saucer of milk she was carrying and runs for her life in a *'Comic chase'* Lazzo.[140] Enter Tropolino who tells his Captain that he is trying to propose to the wrong woman!

140. *Lazzi of 'Chasing'*, No. 6, page 216

Scene 5 – *The Arrival of Fuomo and Fuoco*

Captain Spavento, Tropolino, Fuomo, Fuoco, Spinetta, Padella, Burattino.

Spavento and Tropolino become aware of approaching rivals and hide. Twin captains, Fuoco and Fuomo enter, and knock on the door of the inn. They speak in an outlandish language that none at the inn can understand. Tropolino comes out from hiding and translates in a *'Gibberish'* Lazzo.[141] They are here in search of heiresses or wealthy widows, and need a room. They go into the inn. The Captain mustn't delay. Tropolino again describes Isabella – tallish, fairish and elegantish – and exits.

Scene 6 – *Spavento Proposes Again*

Captain Spavento, Sister Rosa, Abbess.

Now Sister Rosa come from the 'convent' and orders a plate of cream buns. She sits at the inn table, eating them. Spavento, still doubtful, approaches her, but can make little of her answers as she speaks with a mouthful of buns. Her tone is however very friendly and she appears to accept his offer of marriage. But soon it becomes clear that she has only agreed to an assignation, and leads him towards the 'convent'. The Abbess appears at the upper window and admonishes Rosa for her gluttony. The Captain explains his error, saying that he seeks a special lady. Rosa exits, and the Abbess, promising to help, comes down to meet him.

Scene 7 – *Spavento meets his Match*

Captain Spavento, Abbess.

The Abbess suggests various fetishes that she thinks might suit Spavento. These he rejects and confesses to her that he is looking for a wife to recoup his depleted fortunes. A warm intimacy grows between them and they agree that it seems they are fellow fraudsters. They make a pact to keep each other's secrets. The Abbess retires.

141. *Lazzi of 'Gibberish'*, No. 24, page 235

Scene 8 – Spavento Doesn't Propose

Captain Spavento, Isabella.

At last the true Isabella comes from Pantalone's house; she is sullen and spoiling for a fight. She is taken aback when she finds Spavento gentle, kindly and with no intention of proposing, and only offers avuncular advice; she should not submit to her father but find someone of her own age. She kisses him affectionately and exits. Somewhat wearily, Spavento returns to the inn.

Scene 9 – The Arrival of the Mysterious Lady

Colombina, Arlecchino, Padella, Burattino, Tartaglia, Dr Graziano, Tropolino, Captain Spavento.

Colombina, in the male disguise of 'Roberto', page to the supposed Duchess, enters from the 'convent'. She tells the audience that she and the other Zanni, with the help of the 'Little Sisters of Mercy' have devised a plan. From the 'convent' comes a cloaked and masked female. Colombina goes to the inn and knocks on the door, while the 'Mysterious Lady' keeps out of sight. As the page, she asks for a room for 'my mistress, a lady travelling incognito'. She is told they have none, but when Burattino appears, thinking that this might be the Duchess of Ferrara, offers accommodation. Colombina and the Mysterious Lady go into the inn.

Tartaglia arrives from out of town and Burattino meets him with the news that the 'Duchess' is here. They both go into the inn. Tropolino tells Spavento of the opportunity afforded by the arrival of the Mysterious Lady. Spavento replies that he is no longer keen on the idea, as he has formed an attachment for the Abbess. However, duty calls and he will propose to the Mysterious Lady.

Scene 10 – The Mysterious Lady Interviews Spavento

Burattino, Arlecchino, Captain Spavento, Colombina.

The Mysterious Lady is ushered out of the inn by Burattino. The audience will by now have realised that it is Arlecchino in drag. Burattino asks him to take a glass of wine while a room is prepared. The Captain is already seated at the other end of the table. Burattino introduces him to the 'lady' and exits. The Captain soon launches into his proposal. The 'lady' says that she is quite impressed but that there are others to be seen. She calls for Roberto, her page, and ask him to put Spavento's name on the list. The Captain withdraws but remains onstage. The 'lady' calls for Burattino: 'Who's next?'

Scene 11 – *The Mysterious Lady Interviews Fuomo and Fuoco*

Arlecchino, Burattino, Fuomo, Fuoco, Colombina.

Fuomo is announced and proposes in *'Gibberish'*.[142] Enter Fuoco, who seeing Fuomo on his knees before the 'lady', draws his sword and they fight. Fuomo, getting the worst of it, is directed to the house of the Doctor. Fuoco's proposal is so violent that Arlecchino takes flight. There is a comic chase,[143] ending in Arlecchino, held tightly in Fuoco's grasp, calling for help. Spavento comes from hiding, fights and wounds Fuoco. Spavento's name is put on Roberto's list above Fuoco and Fuomo.

Scene 12 – *The Mysterious Lady Interviews Doctor Graziano*

Fuoco, Dr Graziano, Lelio, Arlecchino, Colombina.

Fuoco seeks Dr Graziano, who is just coming onstage with his son, and is told to go to the waiting room. The Doctor prompts Lelio to propose to the 'lady', but, on his son's suggestion, offers himself instead. Lelio watches from a little way off. During the course of the Doctor's proposal he proclaims that he knows who the mystery 'lady' is. Arlecchino is relieved to find it is just one more metaphor (likening him to Diana) and the Doctor is also put on the list by Roberto. The Doctor and Lelio exit.

Scene 13 – *The Mysterious Lady Interviews Pantalone*

Arlecchino, Burattino, Pantalone.

Burattino announces Pantalone. Arlecchino makes fun of his master, but when the old man collapses in his attempt to get on his knees for the proposal, Arlecchino finds two stools and they continue the rest of the interview seated side by side. Arlecchino extracts a promise from Pantalone that he will permit a marriage between Lelio and his daughter, and provide her with a suitable dowry. Arlecchino agrees to marry Pantalone.

142. *Lazzi of 'Gibberish'*, No. 24, page 235
143. *Lazzi of 'Chasing'*, No. 6, page 216

Scene 14 – The Dénouement

Full company.

There is a loud thudding noise emanating from the inn – the sound of a trunk being dragged down the stairs. Burattino goes to investigate. All the cast (apart from Tartaglia) gradually gather onstage as Burattino returns holding Brighella by the ear. Franceschina has Padella in similar fashion. They have been caught trying to steal the Captain's chest. The Captain is called for, but doesn't want the chest opened. They insist and the Captain's secret is revealed: he has no treasure – there is nothing in the chest but stones and some old rags. He confesses that he is a fraud and a liar. He says that the Abbess, now standing next to him, can tell them all about him. How he regrets that it were not full of treasure. Had it been, he would lay it at the feet of the Abbess, who, to him, was no whore but a most noble lady. Tartaglia enters and stands between Arlecchino and the Abbess. After an extended spell of stuttering he is able to identify the Abbess as the true Duchess of Ferrara. He accuses Arlecchino of being a false claimant to the title, and, as such, punishable by law. Arlecchino is seized, but the Duchess speaks in his defence: 'It is only that prankster Arlecchino, licensed to take on any role and grant us the gift of laughter.'

In rhymed couplets she reminds everyone that this is just a play of the *Commedia dell'Arte* and all the characters merely players. Though she insists she really *is* the Duchess mislaid.

Finis.

Burattino and Pantalone

The Duchess Mislaid

Act One

Prologue – Night Scene

The Penitent, The Decoy, The Courtier, Three Bravos, Sister Rosa, Sister Lupina.

The lights dim to near blackout, except for the light streaming from the 'convent' window. A clock chimes three o'clock. Noises of laughter and lovemaking from the 'convent's' upper window. Then we hear the 'sisters' getting angry with a 'penitent'. Shouting and noises of hurried flight down the stairs. The door opens and a female leg (that of Lupina) kicks out the 'penitent' – a grotesque figure without breeches. Rosa leans out of the window.

ROSA The gentleman seems to have forgotten something.

She throws his breeches at him and shutters the window. Lupina locks the door. As he tries to put on his breeches he becomes aware of the three bravos who enter severally and converge centre. The 'penitent' makes good his escape, still struggling to pull up his trousers. A masked courtesan (the Decoy) enters, pursued by a well-dressed courtier, who tries to follow but is intercepted by one of the bravos who drops a coin into the hand of the decoy who then vanishes. The courtier draws his sword, which is quickly knocked out of his hand. He tries to escape, but finds himself surrounded by the other Bravos. They stab, rob and strip him, leaving him dead on Pantalone's doorstep. Pause. They exit.

The 'penitent' re-enters still trying to get into his breeches. He is puzzled and frightened by the corpse. He counts the clock striking four. Then, almost immediately, five. He runs off, scared as it strikes six.

A cock crows. Dawn breaks.

Scene 1 – *The Awakening*

Burattino, Arlecchino, Brighella, Sister Rosa, Pedrolino, The Body.

The upper window of the inn opens. Burattino sticks his head out and gives a blast on a hunting horn and then disappears again, like the cuckoo in a Swiss clock. Brighella appears at the door of Pantalone's house with a hunting horn, which he blows. Arlecchino puts a sleepy head out of the Doctor's window.

ARLECCHINO Eh? What? Eh?

BRIGHELLA The hunt, Arlecchino. Get your master Dr Graziano ready for the hunt.

Arlecchino disappears. Brighella blasts his horn again. Burattino appears, blasts horn again. Arlecchino reappears and blows a great raspberry. Rosa opens the 'convent' window.

ROSA Can't a lady get her sleep?

BURATTINO Aren't you saying your matins yet, Sister Rosa?

BRIGHELLA She was up too long saying her vespers!

Burattino disappears, and is replaced by Franceschina shaking out the bedding. Rosa closes her window. Brighella goes back into his house.

The stage empty, a sleepy Pedrolino enters from Pantalone's door, stepping over the dead body without noticing it. He comes downstage centre and 'Gawps' at the audience.[144] At the fountain he washes with two drops. He sits on the body picking his feet. Lazzo of finding an extra arm and then a third leg.[145] Terror! He tries to get back in but the door has shut on him. He bangs on it in panic. Brighella appears and is shown the body. He expertly checks for anything of value – purse, rings – but finds nothing.

Scene 2 – *Waking Pantalone*

Pedrolino, Brighella, Pantalone.

BRIGHELLA (*calling up to Pantalone's shuttered window*) Signor Pantalone!

---

144. *Lazzo of 'Gawping'*, No. 22, page 234
145. *Lazzi of 'Extra limbs'*, No. 18, page 230

No response. He picks up a pebble and throws it at the window. Still no one. Pedrolino, trying to help, throws horse dung which hits Pantalone full in the face as he opens the shutters. Pantalone empties a chamber pot over Brighella, and goes.

BRIGHELLA Signore Pantalone! It's time to get up, your early morning call, Sir. Wake up, you silly old bastard.

Pantalone returns, this time hitting Pedrolino with a slipper. He disappears again and returns with a blunderbuss, and scatters the Zanni with wild shot. It knocks the head off the fountain statue. Brighella takes a shield and tries again.

But you threatened to beat the life out of me, if I didn't wake you early! You have a most important day today.

PANTALONE (*appearing*) Important you say? Why, what have I on today, Brighella?

BRIGHELLA Apart form your nightcap, you appear to be as naked as the day you were born – and considering how long ago that was, it ain't a pretty sight.

PANTALONE Rascal. I'm asking you about my appointments.

BRIGHELLA Ah, well Sir . . . without flattery, I think your appointments would do credit to many a younger man, but I'm not –

PANTALONE No, my schedule – my commitments – the things I have to do today.

BRIGHELLA That's what I'm trying to tell you. This morning you are going hunting with the Innkeeper Burattino and Dr Graziano.

PANTALONE Dr who?

BRIGHELLA Dr Graziano.

PANTALONE And who the devil is Dr Grazi . . . ?

BRIGHELLA . . . ziano. Surely you remember your new neighbour, the one with the son – Dr Graziano.

PANTALONE Oh, yes, oh yes . . . (*Not remembering.*)

BRIGHELLA And you're hoping to marry your daughter.

PANTALONE I can't marry my daughter; it's incestuous.

BRIGHELLA Marry *off* –

PANTALONE And the same to you . . .

BRIGHELLA I mean, marry *off* your daughter.

PANTALONE Oh, I see. Yes, it's all coming back to me. Hurry then. Are the dogs and horses ready? Give my compliments to Dr Grazi . . .

BRIGHELLA . . . ziano.

PANTALONE Yes, well give him my compliments. I have but to change the garb of Morpheus (*Taking off nightcap, and replacing it with a hunting hat.*) . . . for the livery of Diana.

BRIGHELLA Signor Pantalone?

PANTALONE Now what is it?

BRIGHELLA I forgot to mention, there's a body on the doorstep.

PANTALONE A body?

BRIGHELLA . . . a body.

PANTALONE Anyone we know?

BRIGHELLA No, a stranger; murdered I'd say. What shall I do with him?

PANTALONE Put him on Dr Graziano's doorstep.

Pantalone disappears from the window and Brighella and Pedrolino move the body to the Doctor's door.[146] *That done they go back into the house of Pantalone.*

Scene 3 – *The Doctor Tripping*

Arlecchino, Dr Graziano, Burattino, Padella, Spinetta, The Body.

The Doctor is heard from inside his house admonishing Arlecchino in high-flown language.

---

146. *Lazzi of 'Moving a Body'*, No. 43, page 253

DR GRAZIANO (*improvised ending*) . . . and as the ancient sages were wont to extol: 'Pride cometh before a . . . '

On entering he trips full length over the body.

ARLECCHINO . . . a fall!

DR GRAZIANO (*getting up*) The completion is correct, but inapt – for my descent from a position of vertical dignity to horizontal recumbency was not the result of the random vector, mood, mode, motive force or motion of falling.

ARLECCHINO It wasn't?

DR GRAZIANO Dear me, no. It was the result of a deliberate action on the part of another – gratuitous precipitatus florum causus[147] – or in the vernacular: 'tripped up'. A dastardly ploy by that rascal there – who is, I doubt not from his posture, this moment planning to spring a further attack upon my person!

They draw back from the supposed threat, Arlecchino cowering behind the Doctor. After a pause Arlecchino plucks up courage and advances towards the body.

ARLECCHINO He doesn't seem to have much spring in him. In fact . . .

DR GRAZIANO You may be right. There is a certain pallor . . . Let me see . . . (*Starts to examine the body, improvised words diagnosing the 'illness'.*)

ARLECCHINO But isn't he dead, Doctor?

DR GRAZIANO Dead? You're right. Dead right!! Well, he should have taken my medicine. Send for the undertaker.

They come downstage. Arlecchino prepares to charge off, but is caught by the tails by Burattino,[148] who has just appeared between him and the Doctor.

DR GRAZIANO Good morning, Burattino. Sorry I can't pause now – official business you know. I'm looking for an undertaker. (*Burattino holds a business card under the Doctor's nose. Reading.*) 'B. Burattino, Private Investigator – Divorces arranged. Co-respondents found . . .'

BURATTINO Oh, sorry. (*Takes another card from large selection.*)

147. An example of the Doctor's dog Latin.

148. *Lazzi of 'Getting Nowhere'*, No. 23, page 234

DR GRAZIANO (*reading*) 'B. Burattino, Purveyor of Cooked Meats. Pies our . . . '

BURATTINO No, this one.

DR GRAZIANO 'Bartolomao Burattino – Funeral Director . . . '

BURATTINO (*reading over the Doctor's shoulder*) ' . . . Undertaking's our Undertaking.'

DR GRAZIANO Ah, yes, the very person. I . . .

BURATTINO Yes, quite, a dear departed parent; your father perhaps? My condolences. Nothing too good for a father.

DR GRAZIANO It is not my father.

BURATTINO Ah, not your father, quite so – a brother, what a loss!

DR GRAZIANO Not my brother. Merely . . .

BURATTINO Your uncle . . . Well, you'll still want the best . . .

DR GRAZIANO Not an uncle, damn you.

BURATTINO An aunt?

ARLECCHINO It ain't an aunt.

BURATTINO Not an aunt? Quite so, a son. To die so young, dear me . . . Nothing but the best. May I suggest four black horses?

DR GRAZIANO No horses.

BURATTINO No horses? Ah, a daughter, still . . .

DR GRAZIANO It is not a member of my family. It's a nobody.

BURATTINO Quite so, a dear departed nobody.

ARLECCHINO The Body of a No-body.

DR GRAZIANO (*to audience*) Ah, interesting etymological example here: when is a body not a body?

ARLECCHINO (*music hall style*) When it's a Nobody![149]

---

149. *Lazzo of '. . . Two Bits'*, No. 64, page 266

BURATTINO How sad, how sad! May I suggest solid mahogany, silver handles, silk and velvet furnishings, six mourners . . . (*The Doctor is violently shaking his head.*) Teak? Yes, teak with brass handles, No? Oak with lead? You can't mean deal? (*The Doctor and Arlecchino still indicate 'no'.*) Plywood? How about a large cardboard box? (*Starting to understand.*) And does the bill go to you, Doctor?

DR GRAZIANO Certainly not – to the City Fathers.

BURATTINO Got it! One City Father's funeral, third class, coming up. (*Calling.*) Spinetta, Zan Padella! (*They put their heads out of the inn.*) One City Father's Funeral – pronto.

They disappear, re-appearing a moment later with skimpy and dilapidated funeral accoutrements.[150] *Padella brings a wheelbarrow into which the body is dumped.*[151] *Burattino, Padella and Spinetta go into OTT mock mourning. They parade off.*

DR GRAZIANO (*to Arlecchino*) Remind me to put my bill in for treatment and attendance. Now where is my son? (*Goes into his house calling.*) Lelio, Lelio. (*He is followed by Arlecchino.*)

Scene 4 – Lover's Meeting

Pantalone, Lelio, Dr Graziano, Isabella, Arlecchino, Colombina.

PANTALONE (*coming out of his house*) Isabella! Isabella! Where has the girl got to? Isabella!

He goes back into the house. Lelio appears at the upper window of the Doctor's house, Isabella at Pantalone's upper window.

ISABELLA *and* LELIO (*together*) Were you calling, Father? (*They look at each other; embarrassed laughs.*)

LELIO We appear to both have fathers.

ISABELLA Yes.

LELIO How remarkable.

150. Possible opportunity for suitable anachronisms; black armbands, draped tophats (see Introduction, page 2).

151. *Lazzi of 'Moving a Body'*, No. 43, page 253

ISABELLA What?

LELIO That we both have fathers.

ISABELLA Why?

LELIO Well . . . er, both to have two fathers . . .

ISABELLA Sir, I have only one, and one is quite adequate.

LELIO I meant one each.

ISABELLA I cannot share your enthusiasm. I would have thought fathers fairly frequent.

LELIO I beg your pardon?

ISABELLA Please, do not apologise.

LELIO I meant, that I did not hear you.

ISABELLA I said, that there is a positive plethora of paternal progenitors.

LELIO Oh yes. (*Calling.*) Arlecchino. (*Arlecchino instantly appears below.*)

ISABELLA (*calling back into the house*) Colombina, Colombina.

LELIO (*down to Arlecchino in a stage whisper*) Arlecchino, who is the haughty dame in the window opposite?

ARLECCHINO Eh?

LELIO I said, who is the fair but haughty dame in the window there?

While they talk, Columbina has taken Isabella's place in the window frame. Lelio, intent on Arlecchino, doesn't notice right away.[152]

ARLECCHINO I believe it's Colombina, a serving maid of Signor Pantalone. That I mean to find out for myself. I saw her first, so hands off, Master.

LELIO A serving maid? Never. (*He sees Colombina.*) No, not her. (*Isabella takes Colombina's place again.*) Her! (*When Arlecchino looks up they have changed places again.*)

---

152. This *Lazzi* is not included in Part II as it is specific to the scene and should be clear from the stage directions.

ARLECCHINO That's what I said, her . . . (*Now both women are at the window.*) Oh, her.

ISABELLA (*to Colombina*) Well, who is it?

COLOMBINA I think his name is Arlepino, or sino, or rino, or something. But he looks a right villain, whatever his name. (*She giggles; both Lelio and Arlecchino are gawping.*)

ISABELLA No, not that lout down there.

COLOMBINA Which lout then?

ISABELLA The other lout, upstairs, with his mouth open like a trout.

COLOMBINA Oh, that lout; that must be the new doctor's son, Lilio, or Lelico, or Lalico or some such.

ISABELLA Anyway, he's an idiot . . . a handsome idiot, but an idiot. (*Isabella withdraws.*)

COLOMBINA And the other one's an idiot, and he's an ugly idiot. (*She closes the shutters.*)

Scene 5 – <u>Questions</u>

Dr Graziano, Arlecchino, Pantalone, Brighella.

The Doctor joins Arlecchino.

DR GRAZIANO Is my son ready yet? – the great dandy.

ARLECCHINO He's just coming, Master.

DR GRAZIANO By the way, did you find out anything for me about this Panta . . .

ARLECCHINO . . . talone – yes, he's got a long nose, a short temper and a pretty maid.

DR GRAZIANO A pretty made what?

ARLECCHINO A pretty made, pretty maid.

DR GRAZIANO That to the pretty maid. (*Rude gesture.*)

ARLECCHINO That's what I intend, Master.

DR GRAZIANO What I want to know is – if he has a fair daughter and a large purse. Or failing that, a large daughter and a fair purse.

ARLECCHINO He has a fairly short daughter – and if I know you, Master, he will shortly have a lighter purse – that is, if it isn't already an empty one.

DR GRAZIANO You gather he is without . . . (*Mimes 'Money'.*[153])

Arlecchino Well, his servants are unpaid, his house bare, cold and comfortless.

DR GRAZIANO Then we are wasting our time on him.

ARLECCHINO On the other hand, it is rumoured that he is . . . (*'Hiding Money' mime.*[154])

DR GRAZIANO Ah, salting it away. Keep up the enquiries. I will see what I can discover during the hunt. (*They exit.*)

Enter Pantalone followed by Brighella.

BRIGHELLA She won't be long Master – she's lost her gloves.

PANTALONE As long as that's all she's lost, we should still be able to raise a good settlement on her. Do you think that this Grazi . . . ?

BRIGHELLA . . . ziano.

PANTALONE Graziano, would be suitable?

BRIGHELLA Lord, Master, he's as old as God, even as old as you are. You couldn't wish him on your daughter.

PANTALONE No, not him you fool, his idiot son. I mean, has this Graz-i-ano the wherewithal?

BRIGHELLA He boasts estates in Perugia, but I think his state is in – pecunia.

PANTALONE You mean he's in an impecunious state? Are his servants paid?

BRIGHELLA Tenfold – in promises.

---

153. *Lazzi of 'Money'*, No. 42, page 251
154. Ibid.

PANTALONE Not like me, eh?

BRIGHELLA No, you promise the same as you pay – nothing.

PANTALONE Right, that way I never get behind. Keep your eyes and ears open and I will discover what I can during the meet.

Brighella returns to the house. Isabella, now in hunting dress, joins her father.

Scene 6 – Departure for the Hunt

Dr Graziano, Pantalone, Lelio, Isabella, Brighella. Arlecchino, Franceschina, Fritellino.

The Doctor enters in hunting gear with Lelio in tow. He greets Pantalone.[155]

TOGETHER Ah . . .

PANTALONE Doctor Graz . . .

DR GRAZIANO Senior Pant . . .

TOGETHER . . . ee . . .

DR GRAZIANO . . . ziano . . .

PANTALONE . . . talone

TOGETHER A great . . .

DR GRAZIANO . . . pleasure.

TOGETHER What a fine . . .

DR GRAZIANO . . . morning.

PANTALONE . . . day.

TOGETHER Yes, what a fine . . .

DR GRAZIANO . . . day.

PANTALONE . . . morning.

TOGETHER Allow me to present . . . Where is that . . . ?

DR GRAZIANO . . . boy?

155. *Lazzi of 'Fragmented Sentences'*, No. 21, page 233

PANTALONE ... girl?

TOGETHER Ah, there you are. My ...

DR GRAZIANO ... son.

PANTALONE ... daughter.

DR GRAZIANO Lelio.

PANTALONE Ah, Lelio, this is Isabella.

DR GRAZIANO Ah, Isabella. Charmed. Isabella – Lelio.

PANTALONE Lelio – Isabella. (*They introduce the young people to each other, who give one another a frozen stare.*) Ah, here comes our host, Signor Burattino.

Burattino enters in hunting dress.

DR GRAZIANO Are the horses ready, Arlecchino?

Arlecchino enters and puts his hand to his ear. There are sounds of horses off.

PANTALONE Are the dogs assembled, Brighella?

Brighella puts his hand to his ear. Sound of dogs off.

BURATTINO To horse! Gentlemen, Ladies.

DOCTOR *and* PANTALONE To horse!

Burattino, the Doctor and Pantalone exit. More noise of dogs, horses and hunting horns. The Zanni run to and fro. Pantalone, the Doctor, Isabella, Lelio, Burattino and now Franceschina appear with hobbyhorses. Colombina, Pedrolino and Fritellino appear with dogs. All exit except Brighella, Padella, Arlecchino, and Spinetta who hides herself behind the fountain.

Scene 7 – Arrivals

Brighella, Padella, Arlecchino, Spinetta, Tartaglia, Tropolino, Torolino, Sister Lupina.

Brighella, Padella and Arlecchino stand and watch the departing hunting party.

BRIGHELLA They're off.

PADELLA They're off.

ARLECCHINO Yes, they're off. They've gone. Left us by ourselves.

ALL Leaving us to do the work.

BRIGHELLA Sweep the floors.

PADELLA Muck out the stables.

ARLECCHINO Clean the bog.

ALL Have a little nap.

They make themselves comfortable round the fountain. 'Bee' Lazzo by Brighella etc.,[156] *until all is quiet except for the snoring. The Papal Nuncio, Tartaglia, enters via the Entrance Gate. He locates the inn and knocks at the door. No reply, so he knocks again. The Zanni go on sleeping.*

ARLECCHINO (*only half awake*) Someone is knocking. Knock, knock, knock. (*Pause.*) Someone is knocking. Knock, knack, kneeek.

PADELLA (*kicking Arlecchino*) K-nobody is k-nocking. (*The knocking continues.*)

BRIGHELLA Yes, there is, and he's knock, knock, knocking at your door – not at mine.

ARLECCHINO Yes, and he's not knocknotting at my door. He's at your door, Padella.

PADELLA Go to sleep – you're dreaming someone's knocking.

BRIGHELLA There is someone knocking at the inn – go and see to him Zan Padella, so that I can get back to sleep.

Padella rises and like a sleepwalker approaches Tartaglia. He shakes his finger 'er-er', then takes off his own cap, cushions the knocker with it and returns to the fountain to sleep. Tartaglia then uses his cane on the door. Arlecchino gets up and breaks the cane across his knee, then goes back to the fountain. Tartaglia calls up to the window.

TARTAGLIA Hey, you within, I require a r-r-room.

BRIGHELLA He'll be requiring a c-c-coffin if he doesn't shut up.

TARTAGLIA As an inn you are r-r-required by law to open for the t-t-traveller.

156. *Lazzi of 'The Bee, the Fly and the Flea'*, No. 3, page 214

PADELLA He'll be t-t-travelling further than he expects in a minute.

TARTAGLIA I d-d-demand that . . .

Padella and Brighella go to him, gag him and truss him up to the door, and put a 'No Vacancies' sign round his neck. They go back to sleep.

TROPOLINO (*heard singing, off*) Down the road,
Comes a soldier with his load,
Pom-tiddle-om-pom, pom-tiddle-om-pom, pom pom pom.
Batman to a captain bold,
Down the road,
Comes a soldier with his load (*he enters*),
Pom-tiddle-om-pom, pom-tiddle-om-pom, pom pom pom.
In search of women, wine and gold,
Pom-tiddle-om-pom, pom . . .

This must be the place. What a dump – but beggars must . . . (*He looks round the square, reading the plaques and trade signs.*) 'Casa Pantalone'. 'Dr Graziano, M.D. D.D. Dr of Lit, Phil, and Zoo'. 'Holy Convent of the Little Sisters of Mercy'. ' The Load of Bull' – Ah, here I'll find rooms for the Captain and yours truly. (*Reading the card round Tartaglia's neck – Tartaglia is trying to speak.*) This must be a very rich town if they can afford to hang up a Papal Nuncio as a door ornament. (*'Double Take' Lazzo.*[157]) Papal Nuncio! (*He untrusses Tartaglia.*) Unless I am very much mistaken, I see from your uniform you are an emissary from the papal court of his Holiness Clement the Umpteenth.

TARTAGLIA I am indeed – and I have been b-b-barbarously assaulted in this heathen town. May I know the n-n-name of he who has brought me su-su-succour in my hour of need?

TROPOLINO Oh yes, I'm the s-s-sucker. Tropolino, late of the Dragoons, now batman, confidant and dog's body to that renowned Captain Spavento dell Val Inferno. And Sir, how came you to be in this fowl – and by that I do mean trussed up – condition?

TARTAGLIA I was trying to gain admittance to the inn when I was s-s-set upon by that gang of v-v-v-v-v – rogues, now slouching by the fountain.

157 *Lazzi of 'Clocking and Double Takes'*, No. 8, page 218

TROPOLINO (*he goes over to the fountain*) Good morning, good morning. (*Kicking Arlecchino.*) – I need a room.

ARLECCHINO Nothing to do with me.

PADELLA (*being kicked*) Nothing to do with me.

BRIGHELLA (*before kick*) Nothing to do with me. (*Tropolino forces them up.*)

TROPOLINO Well, it's one of you. (*To Brighella.*) Too villainous. (*To Arlecchino.*) Too stupid. (*To Padella.*) Beer stains, smells of cooking and horse dung. An ostler, if ever there was one. Right, Sir Ostler – your best room for my master, Captain Spavento, honoured soldier and . . .

PADELLA Oh we don't have rooms for soldiers. No, they drink the best wine –

ARLECCHINO – break the furniture –

BRIGHELLA – piss in the corridors –

ARLECCHINO – put the maids up the spout –

PADELLA – and don't pay.

TROPOLINO (*threateningly*) The very best room for the Captain; suitable accommodation for myself and my colleague Torolino – preferably near the maids or the kitchens. And the second best room for His Eminence; whom you have so recently and shamefully maltreated. Quick, jump to it!

A version of Tropolino's song is again heard off.

TOROLINO Down the road,
Comes a soldier with his load,
Pom-tiddle-om-pom, pom-tiddle-om-pom, pom pom pom.
With a trunk of a Captain bold,
(*He enters carrying a great chest on his shoulders.*)
Down the road,
Comes a soldier with his load,
Pom-tiddle-om-pom, pom-tiddle-om-pom, pom pom pom.

Torolino is a big man – a soldier – used to taking orders and not having to think too much. He breaks up his sentences in military fashion.

TOROLINO Trooper Torolino, reporting delivery of – one trunk, chest or coffer – property of Captain Spavento. Delivered herewith – as per orders of – himself, Captain Spavento into care of – Sergeant Tropolino.

TROPOLINO Where's the Captain?

TOROLINO Half-league hence – bivouacked, awaiting confirmation of acquisition of suitable billet.

TROPOLINO Oh, yes, this fellow (*Padella*) was just assuring me that they will be honoured to have the Captain as their guest. (*Padella agrees under the threat.*) Put it down, Torolino. And this learned cleric is to be honoured with equal courtesy.

PADELLA (*calling into the inn*) Spinetta. Spinetta! Where is that lazy girl? Spinetta!

SPINETTA (*she comes from behind the fountain, where she too has been having a nap*) Did someone call?

PADELLA See to our guests. The best rooms for the Captain and the Papal Nuncio and the stables for their servants. Quick about it.

TROPOLINO (*to Torolino*) I'll check the room.

Spinetta accompanies Tartaglia and Tropolino into the inn. Torolino puts the trunk down.

PADELLA It seems very heavy.

TOROLINO That's cos it is heavy. Always heavy isn't it?

BRIGHELLA Isn't what heavy?

TOROLINO What's in there.

ARLECCHINO Well, what's in there?

TOROLINO No, you don't catch me like that. If I told everybody what was in there, they might want to steal it, mightn't they? Mind you – as you guessed – it's a bit on the heavy side. Go on, try and lift it. (*Padella, Arlecchino and then Brighella try in turn, then together, but they can hardly lift a corner.*) So I can trust you three not to run off with it, can't I?

BRIGHELLA We wouldn't think of it, would we Padella?

PADELLA No – we wouldn't think of it would we, Arlecchino?

ARLECCHINO No, we wouldn't.

TOROLINO Wouldn't what?

ARLECCHINO What they said.

TOROLINO Right. And to open it, you'd need a key wouldn't you?
(*Torolino moves his pelvis forward and back*[158] *causing the key at his waist
to fly up and down. The eyes of the three Zanni are drawn to it.*) And I
keep the key right here.

TROPOLINO (*returning*) Right, take it up, Torolino – first door at the
top of the stairs.

Torolino carries the chest into the inn. Brighella draws Padella downstage.

BRIGHELLA (*sotto voce to Padella*) Get the key!

*Brighella returns to Pantalone's, and Padella to the inn. Arlecchino goes into
the Doctor's, and Tropolino takes up a military stance by the inn door.
Lupina opens the door of the 'convent'. She carries a saucer of milk and calls
for her cat, who is called Spiv. Finding no sign of it, she is going back in,
when she notices Tropolino standing there.*

LUPINA (*calling into the 'convent'*) I say girls, the military's back. That'll
cheer things up. (*To Tropolino.*) Coo-eee!

*She gives him an affectionate little wave, which he entirely ignores. She goes
into the 'convent'. Having deposited the trunk, Torolino reappears from the
inn.*

TOROLINO Tropolino, you know that key?

TROPOLINO What key?

TOROLINO The key that hangs from my belt. Well it doesn't.

TROPOLINO Doesn't what?

TOROLINO Hang from my belt. It's gone.

TROPOLINO Has it? Blimey, that was quick. Well, now we know what
sort of people we're dealing with – the kind of people who would
want to open the Captain's chest.

---

158. *Lazzi of 'The Policeman's Lot'*, No. 53, page 259

TOROLINO It's a good job it's the wrong key.

TROPOLINO They won't open the chest with that key. Right, Torolino, we pick up the Captain now and escort him into town.

They exit via the Entrance Gate.

Scene 8 – Brighella Confides

Brighella, Padella.

When they have gone, Brighella enters furtively from Pantalone's. He comes downstage centre to talk to the audience.

BRIGHELLA Well, how's it going? What do you think so far? You got to know your neighbours by now have you? Have you rumbled the 'convent' yet? 'The Little Sisters of Mercy'! I haven't had a butcher's of their 'Abbess' so far, but they say she's a bit of a looker and more upmarket than the other two scrubbers. And me? What d'yer think? No, honest – what would you say are the chances for a bright young chap like me of bettering himself, from the somewhat lowly station in which he finds himself? Two years I've worked for the old skinflint, Pantalone. And why? Why have I put up with him for so long? You may ask. Go on, ask. All right I'll tell you. (*He looks around to make sure they are not overheard.*) I think, no – I know for certain, that the old blighter has a hidden hoard somewhere. On one occasion I observed him through – no, not through the keyhole – through a knot in the wainscoting – hiding something – but when, the next time he was out, I took a look – he'd moved it! Oh, he's clever, very clever. But I'll find it yet. Or perhaps I won't need to – there is a new likelihood . . . Ah, you've spotted it – the Captain's trunk. Tricky, but there must be a way. Let's think about it. If you get any good ideas . . . You know me – I don't mind sharing; after all, what are friends for? (*Padella comes from the inn and shows the key to Brighella.*) There you are – fortune favours the . . . crafty. (*Noises of horses and the hunt returning.*) Blimey! They're back already?

Scene 9 – Return from the Hunt

Brighella, Arlecchino, Padella, Fritellino, Colombina, Pedrolino, Dr Graziano, Lelio, Pantalone, Isabella, Burattino, Franceschina.

More noises off of the returning hunt.

ARLECCHINO (*coming from the Doctor's*) What's that?

BRIGHELLA The hunt returning.

ARLECCHINO Not yet, it can't be. I haven't cleaned the bog! Graziano will beat me – he'll beat me.

PADELLA Burattino will beat me, I haven't mucked out the stables – he'll beat me.

An alarmed Arlecchino and Padella rush about to no purpose,[159] *while Brighella leans by the fountain. Fritellino, Colombina, and the mute Pedrolino enter. They stand together trying to suppress laughter.*

BRIGHELLA What happened? Was there no game?

COLOMBINA Oh yes – a right old game! (*More laughter.*)

FRITELLINO We had hardly gone over the first field when . . .

COLOMBINA . . . old Pantalone and the new Doctor started to . . .

FRITELLINO . . . set to.

ARLECCHINO What was it about?

COLOMBINA Something to do with Isabella marrying the Doctor's son.

PADELLA I didn't know she was going to marry the Doctor's son.

COLOMBINA She isn't. The old men couldn't agree on the marriage settlement. And when Dr Graziano demanded a dowry . . . (*Pedrolino mimes Pantalone attacking the Doctor.*)

FRITELLINO That's right, old Pantalone set about him with his horsewhip.

---

159. *Lazzo of 'Rushing About'*, No. 56, page 261

Pantalone and the Doctor ride in, followed by Isabella and Lelio. The two old men shake their fists at each other and ride apart. Pantalone and Isabella staying upstage, where they 'dismount'. Brighella and Colombina take the horses to the back of Pantalone's house as the Doctor and Lelio come forward. Pedrolino who has been getting in everyone's way, does the 'Gawping' Lazzo[160] during each of the short following scenes.

DR GRAZIANO (*to Lelio*) Now, you are not to speak to her again. Do you understand me?

LELIO Of course, Father. It was not my idea to marry the young woman. She seems rather disagreeable to me.

They move back and Arlecchino and Fritellino relieve them of their horses.

PANTALONE (*to Isabella*) In you go – and stay in your room, Miss. I will not be disobeyed.

ISABELLA I have not the slightest wish to disobey you, Father.

PANTALONE I'm glad to hear it, but I know your feminine wiles. I want no nonsense from you – you are not to speak to that youth.

ISABELLA You mean Lelio, Father?

PANTALONE Of course I mean Lelio, the goddamned Doctor's son.

ISABELLA I don't care a fig for him. He's stupid, overbearing, gauche, childish . . . (*Pantalone goes into his house. Isabella lingers a moment.*) And devilishly handsome.

LELIO (*as the Doctor exits*) Mind you, she has rather nice eyes.

Lelio and Isabella face each other across the piazza. She blows him a kiss.

Both exit to their homes. Burattino and Franceschina ride in on their horses. Pedrolino 'Gawps' between them.

FRANCESCHINA Did you see that?

BURATTINO See what?

FRANCESCHINA She blew him a kiss.

BURATTINO Nonsense! They don't even like each other.

160. *Lazzo of 'Gawping'*, No. 22, page 234

FRANCESCHINA That's why they're ideal for each other. Mark my words, they'll end up married.

BURATTINO Undoubtedly, but not to each other.

They exit round the back with their horses. Pedrolino 'Gawps'. Brighella enters, and then Padella.

PADELLA Psst! Brighella! (*Comes very close to Brighella, but Pedrolino comes right behind them sticking his face in between them.*) Listen. I've tried . . .

BRIGHELLA Never mind him – he can't say anything.

Pedrolino reacts to everything said: agreement, puzzlement, enthusiasm, doubt.

PADELLA I've tried the key. It doesn't fit the lock.

BRIGHELLA Never mind – option two.

PADELLA Option two?

BRIGHELLA Yes – brute force. (*They split up and exit.*)

Scene 10 – The Arrival of Spavento

Pedrolino, Captain Spavento, Tropolino, Abbess, and the full company (so far seen).

Pedrolino, now alone onstage stands on one leg and 'Gawps'.[161] *A slow smile lights up his face as we hear the sound of distant drums and trumpet. It gets louder as Rosa, soon to be joined by Lupina, appears at the door of the 'convent'. Pedrolino rushes off in the direction of the music. Franceschina appears at the inn window. Spinetta, Padella, Arlecchino, Fritellino, Burattino, Brighella and Colombina all come to see what's happening. The window of the 'convent' opens quietly to reveal the head of the Abbess. Pedrolino returns and mimes the approach of the Captain. Tropolino enters with a drum and takes up a stance. Torolino enters with a war-torn flag. Captain Spavento arrives. He looks around and for an instant makes eye contact with the Abbess, who half closes the shutters.*

SPAVENTO Captain Spavento dell Val Inferno – at your service. Known as Matamoros the Moor slayer – a very name to fright the souls of fearful adversaries, to strike terror into the hoards of Asia – a name

161. *Lazzo of 'Gawping'*, No. 22, page 234

used by nursemaids with which to threaten errant babes, or cause the white flag of surrender to fly above the siegéd garrison. But good people of . . . (*To Tropolino.*) Where the devil are we?

TROPOLINO Tribano, Captain.

SPAVENTO Good people of Tribano – whose name for friendliness, intelligence, and good looks is renowned throughout Italy – Good people, I come not in martial manner; I come to seek peace, rest, and tranquility among your fair valleys and wooded hills. I have had my share of the cannon's roar and the Saracen's blade. My bruiséd arms I intend to hang up for monuments, my marches change to delightful measures, to the accompaniment of a lady's lute. On winter nights I will sit by your fires and tell you tales of blood and thunder, of my exploits in the Valley of Death, and defeat of a thousand janissaries – of my ride through the Battlefield of Samanca. My escape from the Castle of Charon . . .

The crowd begin to lose interest and gradually disperse, leaving only Brighella and Padella, who applaud the Captain and exit.

TROPOLINO I think they've all gone Captain.

SPAVENTO Have they? (*He looks round and lastly, up at the 'convent' window. The Abbess closes it slowly.*) Was I a bit long-winded?

TROPOLINO Not at all, Captain. To quarters, Torolino.

SPAVENTO Tropolino, you know the campaign plans – strategy – tactics?

TROPOLINO Yes, Captain, by heart: spread rumours of your fame, honour, good looks – and the booty you have won.

They go into the inn. Torolino furls up the flag and follows them.

Scene 11 – *A Love Letter*

Fritellino, Dr Graziano, Pedrolino, Pantalone, Colombina, Arlecchino, Isabella.

Fritellino enters from the Doctor's with a small table, which he sets up just in front of the house and then exits. Pedrolino enters from Pantalone's with a small table which he sets up just in front of that house. He exits. The Doctor enters, followed by Fritellino carrying a chair. 'Chair' Lazzo[162] *during the following speech:*

DR GRAZIANO No, no, not in the shade. No, how can I read if there is no light on the page? I must be in the shade and my book in the sun.

FRITELLINO (*exiting*) Very well, Doctor. (*The Doctor settles to read.*)

Pantalone comes out of his house with Pedrolino carrying a chair.

PANTALONE Of course, bring it out. If you think I'm going to be put off my usual routine on a fine morning just because a certain unnameable person is also present, you are mistaken. Come on – my account book, pen and ink. (*Repeat 'Chair' Lazzo with Pedrolino.*)

Pedrolino brings them. Pantalone unlocks his account book. He mutters figures loudly – at which time the Doctor starts to read his Latin aloud. They play at ignoring each other.

Silent scene: Enter Lelio and Arlecchino. Lelio gives Arlecchino an envelope with instructions to deliver it to Isabella. Arlecchino tries to get past the Doctor and Pantalone during the Lazzo of 'Concealing the Letter'.[163]

PANTALONE (*to himself*) Seventy-five? That can't be right. I've paid that already. Where's the contract, eh? (*Ad lib.*) I'll have to go and look it up. (*He gets up and bumps into Colombina, who is carrying milk jugs.*) Now where are you going, girl?

COLOMBINA I've got to get the milk from the dairy haven't I? We're all out.

Columbina exits round the back of her house. Pantalone goes into his front door.

DR GRAZIANO That can't be right – 'Ergo si homines horum omnium tolarantes' . . . that must be a mistranslation from the Greek. I'll have to check it. Fritellino . . . oh never mind, he'd never find the right book. (*He goes into his house.*)

Arlecchino slips over to Pantalone's house and startles Colombina just as she is returning with the milk.

COLOMBINA Now look what you've done – made me spill my milk.

ARLECCHINO No use crying over spilt milk, my pretty maid.

162. *Lazzo of 'Placing the Chair'*, No. 52, page 258
163. *Lazzi of 'The Letter'*, No. 34, page 244

COLOMBINA Don't you 'my pretty maid' me – and stop staring at my jugs. A face like yours might turn my milk sour – off with you!

ARLECCHINO Colombina. (*Calling her back.*)

COLOMBINA Don't you call me that.

ARLECCHINO What shall I call you then?

COLOMBINA You needn't call me anything – for I have no intention of having further concourse with you!

ARLECCHINO Concourse? What does that mean?

COLOMBINA I dunno – but my mistress is always refusing to have it with people.

ARLECCHINO Come on, let's have a bit of concourse. Give us a kiss.

COLOMBINA Be quiet or you'll bring old Pantalone running.

ARLECCHINO Listen, I've got a letter for Donna Isabella.

COLOMBINA She doesn't want a letter from the likes of you.

ARLECCHINO It's not from me – it's from my master Lelio. See: 'To Donna Isabella.' (*He holds it so she can see.*)

COLOMBINA That doesn't say to Donna Isabella – It says 'Allabasi Annod ot'.

ARLECCHINO It doesn't say that, it says: (*Pretending to read.*) 'To Donna Isabella.'

COLOMBINA My mistress is learning me. It says; 'Allabasi Annod ot'. Though it's writ funny.

ISABELLA (*entering and taking the letter*) Very good – or it would be if you had it the right way up. 'To Donna Isabella.' I think that's me.[164]

She is about to go back into the house, but bumps into Pantalone coming out. She hides the letter behind her. Colombina and Arlecchino scatter. Pantalone returns to his chair.

---

164. There is a similar letter scene in Goldoni's *Servant of Two Masters* (Act II Scene 2).

Scene 12 – The Sussing

Burattino, Tartaglia, Arlecchino and the full company (so far seen).

Tartaglia enters from the inn, followed by Burattino. They come downstage centre.

BURATTINO On my knees, I beg Your Eminence's pardon.

TARTAGLIA But you're n-n-not.

BURATTINO Not what?

TARTAGLIA Not on your knees. (*Burattino kneels.*) And I hold you as much to b-b-blame as if you had committed the outr-r-rage. Your penance should be most severe. (*Looks it up in a pocket book.*) Adultery – Theft – Murder. F-f-farting on a Sunday, pur-pur-peeing in the washbasin. It must be here, somewhere. Offering violence to a priest – duemila lira. Ass-ass-assaulting a minor officer – tremilacinquecento. Ah, here – ass-ass-assaulting Papal Nuncio – when on a Papal errand – Ottomilaseicento.

BURATTINO Ottomilaseicento? Settle for trecento for cash?

Tartaglia holds up the collection box attached to his belt. Burattino puts in three coins. There is no bottom to the box so the coins drop into Tartaglia's other hand.

TARTAGLIA Bring me a bottle of your best wine – and a g-g-glass for yourself.

Tartaglia pays for the wine with one of the coins and sits at the end of the inn table while Burattino goes to fetch it. The Doctor returns to his chair, muttering about his translation. He calls over Burattino, who is carrying the wine for Tartaglia.

DR GRAZIANO Ah, my wine.

BURATTINO This is for our clerical guest.

DR GRAZIANO Well, bring me my usual, and a glass for yourself; I want to ask you something.

BURATTINO (*yelling out*) Spinetta, the Doctor's wine and two glasses.

*Burattino goes to Tartaglia and pours out the two glasses at that table.
Spavento enters with Tropolino. They parade up and down out of earshot of
the others, but occasionally nodding to them.*

SPAVENTO Anything?

TROPOLINO Not much so far. Your fame has been proclaimed in the
kitchen, and in the stables they are well informed on your valour.

SPAVENTO . . . and my wealth?

TROPOLINO And your wealth – and servants being what they are, it
will be all over the town in half an hour.

Spinetta enters with wine for the Doctor.

SPAVENTO And on the other fronts?

TROPOLINO No, not much. There's Dr Graziano and his son Lelio –
neither with money. Next, the 'convent' with its Sisters of Mercy –
nudge-nudge. (*They walk upstage.*)

TARTAGLIA (*to Burratino*) Now, perhaps you can help me if I explain
the pur-pur-purpose of my visit. (*Tête-à-tête as they drink.*)

Pantalone enters and returns to his chair.

TROPOLINO (*again downstage*) And there's Pantalone – that's the old
bird himself – lives like a pauper but is said to be worth a mint.
Daughter Isabella – quite a catch.

SPAVENTO Leave me here, and order some wine would you? (*He sits at
the other end of the inn table.*)

TROPOLINO (*to Burattino*) My master will take some wine. (*Exits.*)

BURATTINO (*calling*) Spinetta.

SPINETTA Yes Sir?

BURATTINO Wine for the Captain.

Pantalone motions Burattino over.

PANTALONE Burattino, who is the military man I see at your table?

BURATTINO A famous and victorious captain – possibly looking for a
wife.

PANTALONE Has he money?

BURATTINO I believe so. The servants talk of great booty.

SPAVENTO (*beckons Burattino*) Honoured host, oblige me by taking a glass of wine with me. (*Burattino comes to him and they drink.*) I am looking for a lady – a companion as it were. (*Burattino indicates the 'convent'.*) No – something a little more permanent; a wife in fact – but she must of course be of similar social and . . . er – er financial . . . you understand?

BURATTINO (*to Captain*) Perfectly, perfectly. A most valuable commodity has just come on the market. This morning it was under offer, but it's up again for the highest bidder. (*Burattino goes to Tartaglia.*)

TARTAGLIA (*to Burattino*) I am here on a most der-der-delicate mission. (*Burattino drinks and goes to the Doctor.*)

DR GRAZIANO (*to Burattino*) Who is the clerical gentleman? (*Burattino replies inaudibly, drinks, goes to Spavento.*)

SPAVENTO More wine Burattino, and . . . (*Whispered question.*)

BURATTINO (*to Captain*) . . . his name is Pantalone di Bisognose. (*Drinks and goes to Tartaglia.*)

TARTAGLIA (*to Burattino*) I'm looking for a w-w-woman. No, a special Lady . . . (*Burattino drinks and goes to the Doctor.*)

DR GRAZIANO (*to Burattino*) What's he here for?

BURATTINO I'm just about to find out. (*Drinks and is called by Pantalone. He answers Pantalone's question:*) A Papal Nuncio – his name is Tartaglia. (*Goes back to Tartaglia.*)

TARTAGLIA You see, during the previous Papacy the D-D-Duchess of Ferrara – who had been left in sole control of the estates, due to the demise of the Duke . . .

BURATTINO Demise of the d-d-dook . . . (*Getting a bit drunk.*)

SPAVENTO . . . Effect an introduction with this P-P-Pantalone . . .

BURATTINO (*to Tartaglia*) Duchess of . . . Duchess of . . . where did you say?

TARTAGLIA F-f-ferrara.

BURATTINO (*to Spavento*) Ferrara – I mean Pantalone de Bisognosi
(*Pantalone calls for Burattino.*) I'm not coming to your table, you've
nothing to drink! (*He goes to the Doctor, drinks, then goes to Tartaglia.*)

*The hubbub of the scene falls away suddenly, so that all attention is on
Tartaglia.*

TARTAGLIA Now, the Duchess was st-st-stripped of her titles.

BURATTINO St-st-stripped you say?

*The Doctor edges in to try to catch what is being said. Pantalone comes in
a bit and uses an ear trumpet. The Captain leans closer. Spinetta, Padella,
Fritellino, Franceschina, Brighella, Rosa and Lupina, Tropolino and
Torolino, all enter or appear at the windows to listen, ending with the entire
cast (so far seen) decorating the stage in listening attitudes.*

TARTAGLIA Stripped of her titles and possessions – some scandal or
other: orgies – even talk of b-b-black magic. Nocturnal meetings.
Radicalism, socialism, sodomism, liberalism. But now, due to the
mercy of Clement the Um-um-umpteenth, her case has been
looked into, and the charges found unsubstantiated. She is to be
par-par-par . . . let off.

BURATTINO But why does that concern us?

TARTAGLIA I nearly caught up with her some months ago but all things
point to the fact that she is either living here now, or about to arrive
here, in – incognito!

DR GRAZIANO You mean you don't know where she is?

TARTAGLIA No, not at the moment.

SPAVENTO You mean you've lost a Duchess?

TARTAGLIA Well, not so much l-lost as – m-m-mislaid!

*The cast freeze[165] in attitudes of amazement. Arlecchino comes forward and
talks to the audience.*

---

165. *Lazzi of 'Asides and Freezes'*, No. 1, page 211

ARLECCHINO A Duchess Mislaid. Well, there you have it! The title of
the play – bravo I say! Were we in a usual theatre, this would be the
moment for the curtain to fall and proclaim the end of the first act.
But we haven't got a curtain. Oh dear, oh dear! One way would be
for the actors to sneak off in a blackout. But that's not the *Commedia*
way. So I'm using that special quality with which this 'ere slapstick is
imbued, and that is its ability to freeze and unfreeze the actors. So,
with a small applause – small for we want to save the ovation for the
finale – you and the performers can be released for the interval,
whose imminence you have no doubt perceived.

*Arlecchino slaps his wand. Music is heard and the actors re-animate, bow to
the audience and exit.*

End of Act One.

Act Two

Scene 1 – The Siesta

Arlecchino, Dr Graziano, Brighella, Isabella, Pantalone, Lelio, Colombina, Padella.

Arlecchino strolls onto an empty stage and addresses the audience.

ARLECCHINO Well, here we are – Act Two! Quiet isn't it? (*Pause, looks round.*) Where's Pantalone, the Doctor, the Captain, Brighella? No, not even Pedrolino. You've guessed it. This is Italy, two o'clock. Siesta time – they're all asleep. No one would dream of being . . . (*The Doctor's door creaks open.*) Shush . . ! Wait a minute, perhaps they're not all asleep. (*Arlecchino conceals himself, as Graziano sneaks out of his door and furtively makes his way to the 'convent'. He knocks on the door, and slips quietly in.*) Looks as if he'll continue his siesta on a different mattress. And now what's this? (*Brighella carrying a hammer and jemmy, stealthily comes out from Pantalone's door, crosses towards the inn and is let in by Padella.*) They're up to something. I think you're getting to know what really happens during siesta time! Who'll it be next, I wonder? (*As he is saying this, Colombina creeps on, and to his surprise, goes into the 'convent'.*) Colombina going into the 'convent'? Well here's a pretty kettle of fish, and I was thinking of asking her to be my wife! Seems the rest are . . . No – let's watch this . . .

Lelio comes out of the Doctor's, looks around hoping to see Isabella. Disappointed he goes back in. Isabella come out of Pantalone's, looks around hoping to see Lelio. Pantalone has followed her out and eyes her suspiciously. She walks back, nonchalantly, into the house. Pantalone follows her, but turns suddenly to catch Lelio, again coming from the Doctor's. Pantalone shakes his fist. Lelio turns back. From the inn, Franceschina seductively beckons to Pantalone. At first he is doubtful but soon takes up the invitation. Lelio comes out again, and seeing that Pantalone is out of the way, creeps towards Pantalone's house. He stops and looks round to see the Doctor coming out of the 'convent'.

LELIO My Father! (*He hides round the side of Pantalone's house.*)

ARLECCHINO That was a quick one! (*The Doctor sneaks into his house.*)

COLOMBINA (*coming from the 'convent'*) Arlecchino, come here. (*He retreats further into hiding.*) I know you're there. I want you.

ARLECCHINO (*to audience*) I'm not sure I want to be wanted. (*She goes to him, takes him by the hand, and brings him downstage centre.*) I don't want any concourse with you. I saw you go into the whoreh . . . 'convent'.

COLOMBINA Don't be silly – they're just helping us with . . . And that's why Franceschina's trying to keep Pantalone away. Oh, never mind – we need you. (*She leads a puzzled and rather reluctant Arlecchino into the 'convent'.*)

Isabella again comes out. Lelio makes an attempt to grab her, but she slips out of his grasp and they play a lover's game of hide and chase. They come together centre stage.

Scene 2 – *The Lover's Knot*

Isabella, Lelio, Brighella, Pantalone, Dr Graziano.

LELIO You're smaller than I thought.

ISABELLA And you're bigger. A bigger oaf than I thought. Is that all you can say? You write me a charming letter – 'Tho' Cupid has oftimes assayed to wound my heart, yet have I still despised the foolish boy, and turned his arrows back again unwounded.'

LELIO You've learned it by heart?

ISABELLA And I now suspect you copied it word for word from 'The Golden Letter Writer'.

LELIO No, I wrote it from the depths of my true feelings.

ISABELLA Did you really? Well, say something nice now. Well, go on. I'm waiting.

LELIO Er – er – I don't know what . . . I'm . . . Now you're angry again.

ISABELLA Not in the least. I am quite indifferent.

LELIO You're not; you're frowning at me – Divinest Lady, shall all my endeavours to serve you fail? What must I do to restore the beneficent Rays of your Favour? Or must I suffer Shipwreck in the Quicksand of your inexorable Disdain?

Unobserved by the lovers, Brighella creeps from the inn to Pantalone's house.

ISABELLA That's from *The Amorous Gallant's Tongue*. I've read my father's copy.

LELIO (*he holds her*) And I read one message from your frowns and another from the soft touch of your sweet arms.

ISABELLA (*struggling to get free*) Give me my arm back.

LELIO We are bound by ties of love, which I am not strong enough to break.

He struggles as if he and Isabella were roped together. They are unaware that the Doctor is now observing them from his upstairs window. A moment later Pantalone is seen peering from the inn window. He darts back on seeing the Doctor, who also disappears.

ISABELLA Give me back my hand.

LELIO First, give me back my heart.

ISABELLA It's yours; I don't want it.

LELIO Then why do you not leave me?

ISABELLA I would, if you were not preventing me.

LELIO There, I release you.

He loosens his hold. She pulls a little away from him, but then comes back and they are about to embrace, when they are torn apart by Pantalone and the Doctor who have crept in from either side.

PANTALONE (*to Isabella*) How dare you disobey me?

DR GRAZIANO (*to Lelio*) What do you mean by this?

PANTALONE (*to Isabella*) To your room, Miss.

DR GRAZIANO (*to Lelio*) To your room, Sir.

PANTALONE (*to Graziano*) How dare you permit your son this outrage?

DR GRAZIANO (*to Pantalone*) Allow your daughter to entice . . .

PANTALONE Rascal!

DR GRAZIANO Villain!

They set about each other in a brief comic fight, until they are pulled apart by their children (duplicating the previous action by the parents). Brighella crosses back to the inn, this time with a larger hammer and jemmy. They all exit.

Scene 3 – A Father's Permission

Burattino, Captain Spavento, Pantalone, Isabella, Colombina.

Burattino enters with Captain Spavento from the inn.

SPAVENTO . . . And this Pantalone, has a marriageable daughter, you say?

BURATTINO Indeed and furthermore, having quarrelled with the Doctor, the coast is clear. I have intimated to the Signore that you are eager to meet him but have not presumed to give the reason. Await here, and I will fetch him right now.

He goes to Pantalone's house and returns with him.

BURATTINO At this moment, I, Burattino, put on a Classical Persona – that of Mercury in his capacity of go-between to the Gods, and it is my enviable duty to introduce Jupiter to Mars, Mars to Jupiter.

PANTALONE An honour, Signor Mars.

BURATTINO No, Mars, who in this earthly carnation, appears as Captain Spavento dell Val Inferno – known as Matamoros, the Moor Slayer. Spavento of Salamanca . . .

SPAVENTO . . . of Salamis, and Marathon, Arbela, Syracuse, Senlac, Hastings, Poitier, Crecy, Agincourt, Blenheim, Saratoga, Bannockburn.

BURATTINO Trafalgar, Waterloo, and all stations to Marston Moor.

SPAVENTO That's where I fought the Moors.

BURATTINO Captain Spavento. (*To Pantalone.*) Well, go on then.

PANTALONE I am honoured, Captain Spavento.

BURATTINO May I now present, the father of the gods, Jupiter, who descended from his heavenly throne to father our little community here. Magistrate, merchant and man of learning, Messer Pantalone di Bisognose.

SPAVENTO The honour, Messer Pantalone is all mine, all mine. Though a soldier, I am a great admirer of the arts of peace, learning . . . (*Aside.*) and money!

PANTALONE And I, of men of action . . . (*Aside.*) and money!

BURATTINO I am sure you gentlemen will wish to discuss matters of mutual interest. So I discard the role of Mercury and return to that of innkeeper. Ring if you need anything. (*Exits.*)

SPAVENTO Will you give me your arm, Signor Pantalone?

PANTALONE Give? I'm not sure about give, but you may have it on loan for a spell.

SPAVENTO (*they walk arm-in-arm*) Now, to the matter in hand. How shall I put it? Er . . . You have something of which I'm sure you are very fond.[166]

PANTALONE (*aside*) He must mean my money!

SPAVENTO (*aside*) I mean of course his daughter. (*Aloud.*) As it were, a treasure . . .

PANTALONE (*aside*) How can he know?

SPAVENTO . . . which has so far remained hidden from me . . .

PANTALONE (*aside*) He has learnt of my secret hoard. One of the servants has betrayed me.

SPAVENTO . . . and so I hear, a shining beauty – refined – pure . . .

PANTALONE (*half aside*) Gold. My gold!

SPAVENTO What did you say?

PANTALONE I said: 'My, isn't it cold?'

SPAVENTO As I was saying, pure in thought and deed. Virgo intacto.

166. This is the original version of the scene in *The Path of True Love* (See footnote, page 66).

PANTALONE Well, it has been through a few hands.

SPAVENTO But a time must come when the bird must fly the nest, and you must part with your treasure, and I am the one prepared to take it off your hands. (*Pantalone nearly faints.*) Eh? What do you say to that? (*Pantalone speechless.*) May I therefore formally ask for the hand of your daughter?

PANTALONE (*aside: understanding gradually*) Pure, and refined, and shining and . . . My treasure. My Daughter . . . My God . . . be praised, he doesn't know of my . . . g – goodness. Just what I wanted. Brighella says he has a great treasure with him. He may be very rich! (*To Captain.*) I suppose you've taken a lot of booty in your time. Have you acquired wealth from the enemies you vanquished?

SPAVENTO Oh indeed, many a fine castle and fair town have I sacked in my time, and put the treasures in my sack, and many a time have I wrung the secret hoarding place of a victim's gold, before I dispatched him to his Maker. To say nothing of the gifts showered on me by grateful kings, emperors, and potentates . . . !

PANTALONE Kings, emperors and potentates?

They repeat the phrase together ('Kings, emperors and potentates!') ad lib as a 'song and dance' Lazzo.[167] *As they complete this, Brighella, unobserved by Pantalone or Spavento, again makes his way to Pantalone's house.*

PANTALONE I'm sure my daughter would be delighted to receive a proposal from such a handsome, cultured, courageous man as your good self. May I soon be calling you son?

SPAVENTO Father! ('*Embracing' Lazzo.*[168])

PANTALONE Now I will go and tell the dear girl. She will be thrilled. She will want to make the best of herself, dress in all her finery, her hair – these women! But I will make sure she is here within the hour. Will that suit?

SPAVENTO Certainly – I go to prepare my proposal. (*Moves towards the inn door, then turns back.*) Signor Pantalone, just a moment. Shall we discuss the dowry now or . . . ?

167. *Lazzi of 'The Dance of Glee'*, No. 10, page 220
168. *Lazzi of 'Embracing'*, No. 15, page 225

PANTALONE The dowry?

SPAVENTO Yes, the dowry. (*Pantalone almost faints.*)

PANTALONE (*recovering*) It's that word. It's psychosomatic; like bill, account, and pay up – makes me feel ill.

SPAVENTO But we must discuss the dow . . .

PANTALONE Don't say it I beg you. Leave it till after the proposal. Then we will make all the arrangements. I will have to have my notary and a doctor present.

SPAVENTO Oh, very well, later then, and will you send out the fair er – er . . . ?

PANTALONE Isabella.

SPAVENTO Isabella.

PANTALONE Within the hour!

The Captain exits. Brighella just avoids him as he returns to the inn, with more equipment.[169]

PANTALONE (*calling*) Isabella, Isabella. (*Isabella enters accompanied by Colombina.*) Ah, there you are, my dear girl, my dear girl. I'm so happy for you, so happy.

ISABELLA Why are you happy for me, Father?

PANTALONE Why, your engagement. Splendid choice. Ah, of course, you haven't heard. I've chosen a husband for you!

ISABELLA A husband?

PANTALONE Yes, a Captain Spavento – a military man. Fine fellow, and doubtless very wealthy. When he sees how beautiful you are, I think – I hope – he will forget about the dowry. You are to be married this very day. What do you say to that, eh?

ISABELLA No – I will not.

PANTALONE Not what?

---

169. In the original production Brighella carried a modern chainsaw.

ISABELLA Not be married to that odious Captain Spavento. Not today, not tomorrow, not any day. Not ever. Never!

PANTALONE Nonsense. Colombina, tell her how lucky she is. And get her ready to meet the Captain. He is to propose within the hour. (*He exits.*)

ISABELLA Oh, Bina, what can I do? I will not marry that man. I love another.

COLOMBINA Yes, I think I know who the nother is. (*Isabella weeps tragically. To audience.*) Let her get through this. She does one at every performance. It's in her contract. (*Isabella goes into a 'Tirade' Lazzo.*[170]) There, there, that'll do. I'll think of something. You won't have to marry Spavento – and you'll get your Lelio – I promise. You know me. Have I ever let you down? It's all in hand.

ISABELLA In hand? Columbina, tell me what you mean?

COLOMBINA (*to audience*) Shush! Mum's the word. And listen – don't cross him – Pantalone – make out you're going along with it all. Off you go, I'll be with you in a minute. (*Isabella exits. To audience.*) So what's this all about? As you know it's traditionally required of us servants – the Zanni – to put things right in the love department – and today is no exception. It's a beaut. 'Course it could go wrong! Well, you saw . . . (*Indicates the 'convent'.*) Yes, the sisters are in on it. So keep your fingers crossed, and don't let on if you guess what's happening. (*She exits.*)

Scene 4 – Spavento Proposes

Captain Spavento, Tropolino, Sister Lupina.

The Captain enters, and calls for Tropolino.

TROPOLINO (*entering*) Yes, Captain? Can I get you something?

SPAVENTO No, not now, Tropolino. A great challenge now awaits me. A battle is about to be enjoined.

170. *Lazzi of 'Perquisites of the Role'*, No. 50, page 257 (and *Path of True Love*, page 72)

TROPOLINO A battle enjoined, Captain? Are there Turks here about, to be sought-out and slain?

SPAVENTO Wish it were Turks – know were you are with Turks – no, this time I have to face a woman.

TROPOLINO A woman – is she an Amazon?

SPAVENTO No. I am about to propose.

TROPOLINO Oh yes, the 'marriage' idea. Oh dear, we have come down in the world. Please don't put yourself out on my account, Captain. I know you owe me six months wages, but I can't bear the thought of you marrying.

SPAVENTO No, I must sacrifice myself.

TROPOLINO Who might the lady be?

SPAVENTO One Isabella, daughter of Pantalone.

TROPOLINO Oh well, if you must marry, it isn't such a bad choice – a very fine lady, in fact.

SPAVENTO A fine lady you say? I haven't set eyes on her yet. What's she like then, Trop?

TROPOLINO Well, I'd say she was tall . . . ish , fair . . . ish, and very elegant.

SPAVENTO I am to meet her here within the hour.

TROPOLINO Shall I stay to give you moral support?

SPAVENTO No, off with you. This battle I shall conduct 'Au Solitaire'.

Tropolino exits. The Captain waits. He rehearses bits of a proposal speech, doubtful of his abilities in this direction. Lupina, still looking for her cat, comes out of the 'convent' with the saucer of milk.

LUPINA Here Spiv . . . Spiv . . . Spiv . . . !

SPAVENTO (*aside*) My God it's her . . . Do I hear aright? – Spiv? – Can she mean Spav? And does she presume to summon me with such a diminutive?

LUPINA Spiv – Spiv – Spiv . . . !

SPAVENTO My God, my courage fails me. (*Trembles.*) Come on
Spavento, remember the Moors and the Hottentots. 'Au Battaile.'
'Courage mon brave.' (*He flings himself in front of Lupina.*) Madam –
I, by your beauty, thus struck . . . (*Lupina in terror throws the saucer
into the air, and runs for her life.*)

LUPINA Help, murder, assassins! (*The Captain chases her round the stage.*)

SPAVENTO Madam, pray pause.

They both stop for breath, then start off again.[171] *Tropolino enters.*

TROPOLINO What are you doing, Captain?

SPAVENTO Damn woman won't stop still. How can I propose to the
damn woman if she won't stop still? (*Off they go again.*)

TROPOLINO Captain, that's not Donna Isabella.

SPAVENTO Not Donna Isabella? Who the devil is it then?

TROPOLINO It's Sister Lupina, from the 'convent'.

SPAVENTO Good God. Save me Tropolino. (*He runs in opposite direction.*)

LUPINA Save me! Help! Murder!

Tropolino opens the door of the 'convent' so that Lupina can dash to safety.

TROPOLINO Oh dear, you do need looking after Captain. Donna
Isabella doesn't look like that. She's tallish, fairish, and very elegant-
ish. (*Mime description.*)

SPAVENTO I see, tall-ish, fair-ish, and elegant-ish. All right Lad, go back
to your meal. I'll cope. (*To himself.*) Tall-ish, fair-ish, elegant-ish.

TROPOLINO Wait! Listen! (*He goes and looks in the 'out of town' direction.*)
Captain, I think you have rivals. Look. (*The Captain joins him.*) They
appear to be two military men, perhaps officers of some outlandish
nation. (*They look into the distance.*) Are you going to challenge them,
Captain?

SPAVENTO I think not – strategy Tropolino, strategy. First observe.
(*They find a spot where they can observe without being seen.*)

---

171. *Lazzi of 'Chasing'* No. 6, page 216

Scene 5 – The Arrival of Fuomo and Fuoco

Captain Spavento, Fuomo, Fuoco, Tropolino, Spinetta, Padella, Burattino,

Captain Fuomo and Captain Fuoco appear. They are almost identical and move in unison. They knock at the inn door. Padella answers. They talk to him in a language ('Gibberish'[172]) he can't understand. He calls for Spinetta who can't make anything of it either. They get Burattino, who is equally at a loss. Tropolino comes from his hiding place and offers to help.

TROPOLINO (*translation, interspersed 'Gibberish' from Fuomo and Fuoco*)
Xxxxxx.[173]

They require two rooms.

Xxxxxxxxx.

Failing that –

Xxxxx xxx xxxxx.

One room with two beds.

Xxxxx xxx xxxx xx.

Or failing that, one bed with two pillows.

Xxxxxxxxxxxx xxxx xxx xxxx xxxxxx –

They are here in search of beautiful and rich wives.

Xxxxxx xxxxx xxxxxx.

They intend to offer themselves as they are so . . . ?

Xxxxx –

pretty?

Xxxxxx x xxxxx.

And one is a count and the other is a – baron.

Xxxxxx xxxxx xx xxxx.

No, that one is the baron, and that one is the count.

Xxxxxx xxxxxxx xxxxxxxxx xxxxxxxxx xxx.

---

172. *Lazzi of 'Gibberish'*, No. 24, page 235
173. Xxxxx = Improvised *'Gibberish'* from Fuomo and Fuoco

So would any wealthy women kindly queue up here in an hour's time . . .

Xxxxxx xxxxx xxxxxxx.

When they promise to interview them all personally?

Xxxxxx xxxxx xxxxx – xxx!

Goodbye, and a happy new year!

BURRATINO (*to Spinetta*) Put them in the cellar . . .

Fuoco and Fuomo go into the inn. All, except Tropolino, make appropriate exits. Captain Spavento comes out of hiding.

SPAVENTO Rivals! I'll have to get my skates on.

TROPOLINO Have you proposed yet, Captain?

SPAVENTO Haven't seen her yet.

TROPOLINO Remember Captain: tallish – but not too tallish – fairish and elegantish. (*He exits.*)

Scene 6 – Spavento Proposes Again

Captain Spavento, Spinetta, Sister Rosa, Abbess.

Spavento comes downstage muttering to himself ('Tallish, fairish and elegantish') and does not notice the partially dressed Sister Rosa entering from the 'convent'. She is looking in her purse. She finds a coin and makes her way over to the inn table. She rings the hand bell.

SPINETTA (*looking out*) The usual, Sister Rosa?

ROSA The usual, Spinetta.

Spinetta brings a pyramid of cream buns. Rosa sits eating them. Now aware of her, the Captain skirmishes round. She smiles at him.

SPAVENTO (*aside*) Short-ish? Fair-ish? Elegant – (*Rosa munches gluttonously.*) – ish! Well, I suppose, it might be her. (*He sits at the table near her. To Rosa.*) It would appear we're in for a fine day, Ma'am?

(*Rosa's replies are incomprehensible as her mouth is full, but the tone is sociable.*) I beg your pardon?

(*Eating noises.*) Oh yes, you could be right – probably rain later. Do you live hereabouts?

(*Rosa responds with a grunt and vague gesture. Aside.*) This can't be Isabella di Bisognose. I'll try the direct approach. (*To Rosa.*) May I be so bold as to enquire the name of the lady I'm addressing?

(*Her reply is still incomprehensible.*) What are you called, Madam?

ROSA (*clearing her mouth for a moment*) No, I'm not the Madam.

SPAVENTO What are you called?

ROSA Oh, I've been called all sorts of naughty things.

SPAVENTO What is your name please?

ROSA (*she has her mouth full again. She is trying to say:*) They call me Sister Rosa, but my real name is 'Ella'.

The Capain picks up the 'Ella', takes it for Isabella and launches into his proposal.

SPAVENTO Lady, I, by your beauty, thus struck, can do no other than name myself your slave, and beg that you consider my proposal in a kindly light.

ROSA Yes, of course dear, but I'll just finish my little treat first.

She is still tucking into the cakes. A sudden move of his pushes the cream in her face. She licks it up, and when she has completely cleared the plate, she rises and now is able to speak clearly.

Well, are you ready, Duckie?

SPAVENTO Ready, Ma'am?

ROSA (*she leads him towards the 'convent'*) And is that all right?

SPAVENTO Is what all right?

ROSA Fifty lire.

SPAVENTO Fifty lire?

ROSA For our little arrangement. Fifty lire in the collection box – for a private confessional with Little Sister Rosa.

SPAVENTO Oh dear, I think perhaps some other time.

ROSA Well I thought it was a bit early, but it was your idea.

The upper window of the 'convent' opens, and the imposing features of the Abbess appear. She calls down to Rosa.

ABBESS (*in holier-than-thou tones*) Sister Rosa – of the Inadequate Contraception. (*Rosa looks about her in dismay.*) Yes, it is the voice of your conscience.

ROSA Oh, it's you, Reverend Mother.

ABBESS Shame on you – going abroad without your habit! And cream buns again Sister?

ROSA No – er – well . . . Sorry.

ABBESS Are we truly sorry? Eight Hail Marys and scrub out the latrines. And who is the gentleman?

ROSA He's not a gentleman, he's a captain. He said he wanted me to give him a confessional, but now he's chickened out.

ABBESS To your devotions Sister. I will deal with the Captain. (*Rosa goes into the 'convent'.*)

Scene 7 – Spavento Meets his Match

Captain Spavento, Abbess.

SPAVENTO Pray do not trouble yourself, Madam. Er Ma'am . . . er . . . Mother – Reverend Mother. I was in error.

ABBESS Are we not all so?

SPAVENTO I mean, I did not recognise the lady as of your order. I mistook her for the lady I seek – a different lady.

ABBESS You seek a different lady; how different? This consultation needs greater proximity. Kindly wait a moment. (*She disappears from the window. The Captain hesitates, and starts to creep away. She appears at the 'convent' door.*) Oh, Captain, shame on you, you fly the field. Your much-vaunted courage fails you. (*She takes him gently by the arm and pulls him back. He mutters in protest.*) Is it the woman from whom you flee, or the representative of Mother Church?

SPAVENTO I assure you Ma'am, it is neither the one nor the other, for I have never known fear. (*He begins to roar.*) Oft in battle have I faced the Saracen Turk, and in the canon's mouth charged, my sabre whirling above . . .

ABBESS Peace, Captain. I heard you say your days of campaigning were over, and that you come to Tribano for retirement and tranquillity. (*He calms somewhat.*) There, that's better. We hardly want to broadcast our little tête-à-tête about the special woman you're looking for. (*She takes his arm affectionately, and they walk round together.*) Come, confess, have no fear.

SPAVENTO Fear! (*He explodes.*)

ABBESS Sorry, I was just about to say that the confessional is sacrosanct. Now, what are you looking for? Do you feel the need for a dominatrix?

SPAVENTO A what?

ABBESS A strict mistress.

SPAVENTO Certainly not!

ABBESS Don't be ashamed, perhaps . . . (*She whispers in his ear.*)

SPAVENTO Never . . . ! (*Inaudible to the audience she suggests various fetishes to which he responds first with protest and then with amusement.*) (*a*) Really Madam . . . (*b*) You can't mean it? (*c*) Are there such people? (*d*) Ha, ha, ha! (*Outright laughter.*) You have certainly enlightened me . . . and given me something to laugh about.

ABBESS Come on, Captain, be honest, what do you seek?

SPAVENTO Be honest, you say? And why should I be honest with you? That would contradict, conflict and confuse my entire modus vivendi. Honesty is not my forte; I specialise in deceit – I am an accomplished liar. I dissemble, I fabricate, I concoct, feign, pretend, perjure, play-act. And this you know, oh Reverend Mother of Mendacity, dear Sister in Sophistry. It takes a liar to know a liar.

ABBESS What can you mean?

SPAVENTO You are no Mother Superior, your abbey is naught but a brothel, and you, dear lady, are nothing but a whore!

ABBESS I object to that – whore, I accept. It's the 'nothing but' I would refute. (*The rest of the scene is played, closely and affectionately with erupting laughter between them. Their movements and body language almost of a love scene.*) And this lady you seek?

SPAVENTO Merely an heiress to recoup my depleted finances. There you have it – the truth.

ABBESS I bet you were never even at the wars.

SPAVENTO Indeed I was! I admit it was only as a quartermaster – in charge of the baggage train – but it was certainly at the front, sometimes even dangerous; you know the odd stray bullet or run-away horse. And when, exactly, did you become a bride of Christ?

ABBESS I'll have you know, a very respectable . . .

SPAVENTO Very respectable?

ABBESS . . . a very respectable brothel in Naples. (*Mock serious.*) Let us make a solemn pact and covenant. Our mutual confessions we will . . .

SPAVENTO Lock away in our hearts.

ABBESS . . . and throw away the key.

SPAVENTO It has been a pleasure to walk and talk with you, to feel your arm in mine, to know the perfume of your hair, and the sweetness of your breath. Farewell my sweet retribution; you have ruined my life. I am undone. I thought at some last day to confess my sins to a grey-headed friar, but instead I have received absolution from a whore in the masquerade of a Mother Superior.

ABBESS (*affectionately*) Farewell – quartermaster.

Scene 8 – *Spavento Doesn't Propose*

Captain Spavento, Isabella.

The Captain is sitting at the inn table. Pantalone pushes out Isabella, who enters spoiling for a fight. She sits next to the Captain, arms akimbo. Pause.

ISABELLA Well, get on with it then.

SPAVENTO 'Get on with it'?

ISABELLA That's what I said – get on with it.

SPAVENTO Forgive me for asking – but who are you?

ISABELLA Who do you think I am?

SPAVENTO You're not another Little Sister of Mercy?

ISABELLA No, I'm not, thank you very much. I am Isabella Aurelia Concordia Beatrice di Bisognose.

SPAVENTO Are you the real Isabella Aurelia Con . . . (*She helps him.*) cordia – Beatrice – di Bisognose?

ISABELLA I hope there are no bogus Isabella Aurelia Concordia Beatrice di Bisognoses running about!

SPAVENTO So, you are the genuine article. You're quite a pretty little thing aren't you? How old are you?

ISABELLA I'm twenty . . . er-er-um . . .

SPAVENTO Ah, you're twenty . . . er-er-um. Do you know how old I am?

ISABELLA I've no idea.

SPAVENTO Guess.

ISABELLA I suppose (*Aside.*) a hundred and . . . (*To him.*) forty er . . . er . . . um?

SPAVENTO I'm sixty er-er-ums. That makes approximately forty er-er-ums between us.

What I want to know is what you are doing accosting a poor old man of my age? Can't you pick on someone nearer your own, eh? Say twenty er-er-ums or thirty er-er-ums at the oldest.

ISABELLA Aren't you going to propose then?

SPAVENTO You wouldn't have me, would you?

ISABELLA No.

SPAVENTO I'm glad to hear it. I wouldn't have any respect for you if you'd sell yourself, just because your father's a mean old miser.

ISABELLA He's not. Well, he is – but I don't like anyone but me to say so. (*Pause.*) So you're not going to propose then?

SPAVENTO Certainly not. Be off with you. And remember, someone twenty or thirty er-er ums. Can you think of someone?

ISABELLA . . . Maybe I can.

He slumps into a chair. She comes behind him and kisses him on the pate.

Scene 9 – *The Arrival of the Mysterious Lady*

Colombina, Arlecchino, Padella, Burattino, Tartaglia, Dr Graziano, Tropolino, Captain Spavento.

Colombina enters from the 'convent' in male attire, checks to see there is no one about, and then addresses the audience:

COLOMBINA Roberto, page and trusted confident of Fiorinetta, Duchess of Ferrara – your servant. (*Bows.*) . . . No, it's me, Colombina. Well, at last I've got a breeches part. Sexy eh? Now, I told you we had to think up something to put paid to any ideas of that Captain Spavento marrying my sweet Isabella. Well – we've thought of something. Couldn't have done it without the help of the Abbess and her sisters of mercy. It may not work – but anyway here it is . . . (*The door of the 'convent' opens a little.*) Come on . . .

She drags on a rather reluctant cloaked and masked female figure. They confer in a whisper. 'The figure' keeps out of sight as Colombina walks jauntily to the inn and knocks on the door. It opens just wide enough for Padella to stick his head out.

PADELLA No vacancies. (*He slams the door. Colombina knocks again. No reply. She tries again. The door opens wide and she finds herself knocking on Padella's chest.*[174]) I told you there were no rooms.

COLOMBINA I am page to a lady of quality. Her carriage wheel broke outside the town. She needs rest and seclusion.

---

174. *Lazzo of 'Knocking'*, No. 32, page 242

PADELLA Still no rooms.

COLOMBINA I must speak to the manager.

BURATTINO (*coming out of the doorway and bringing the action downstage*) What's going on?

COLOMBINA I am page to a lady of quality, obliged to seek refuge till the wheel of her carriage can be repaired.

BURATTINO A lady of quality you say? What is her name?

COLOMBINA She is travelling – incognito.

BURATTINO Incognito, eh? (*Aside.*) The Duchess? (*To the cloaked figure.*) Your Grace . . . I mean Your Incognitoship . . . You are most welcome to my humble establishment. Of course we will find a room for Your . . . Ladyship, if you will come this way. How fortune . . . unfortunate that you are obliged to break your journey. Padella, show her Ladyship to the Penthouse suite.

PADELLA Penthouse suite?

BURATTINO (*sotto voce*) The attic. (*Padella ushers Colombina and the Mysterious Lady into the inn.*)

Tartaglia comes in via the Entrance Gate. Burattino goes to meet him.

She's arrived – it must be the lady you seek.

TARTAGLIA A wild goose chase – and I'm a goose for going – indications are she's here.

BURATTINO That's what I'm saying . . . (*Whispers.*)

TARTAGLIA I'll investigate. (*He goes into the inn.*)

The Doctor comes out of his house. Burattino rushes to him.

BURATTINO For your son, the ideal opportunity. The Duchess in disguise. Widowed, and once reinstated – rich beyond words!

They exit to their own houses. The Captain and Tropolino emerge from the inn and sit at the table.

TROPOLINO Still keen on the marriage malark, Captain?

SPAVENTO Not in the least, but I can't see any other way out. To be honest Tropolino, I've formed an attachment for a certain lady.

TROPOLINO That's good.

SPAVENTO That's bad. It's the Abbess of the 'convent'.

TROPOLINO That's bad. You can't marry a Madam, Sir. Besides, has she got any money?

SPAVENTO No, she seems to live from hand to mouth. Still, she's a fine lady and, in spite of everything, if I had the wherewithal I'd marry her. Still, ours is not to reason why, ours is . . . to marry where the money is.

TROPOLINO And apropos – a lady, incognito, arrived at the inn just now – the Duchess in disguise perhaps? Why not try your luck there?

SPAVENTO Suppose I must, suppose I must. Good lad.

TROPOLINO Here's your chance. (*He exits.*)

Scene 9 – *The Mysterious Lady Interviews Spavento*

Burattino, Arlecchino, Captain Spavento, Colombina.

During the following scene it will dawn on the audience (if it hasn't already) that the cloaked female figure is Arlecchino in drag. It is played in the Pantomime Dame tradition of obvious masculinity.[175] Now divested of the outer cloak, and using a veil or handheld domino to partially hide the comic mask of Arlecchino. He carries a devotional book, which he peruses when not otherwise involved, though it is clear he can't read. When he drinks he introduces various tricks of the 'Drinking' Lazzo.[176] He is ushered back onstage by a very obsequious Burratino.

BURATTINO Dear Lady, if you would be so kind as to honour our humble table here and this rustic seat with your honourable posterior, and partake of our local wine, her Ladyship's room will be prepared – I'm sure to her satisfaction.

ARLECCHINO (*in his 'Duchess' voice*) Certainly, my good man. But who . . . who is this person?

175. An even closer example would be in the style of *Charley's Aunt*.
176. *Lazzi of 'Drunkenness and Drinking'*, No. 13, page 223

BURATTINO This is the renowned Captain Spavento.

ARLECCHINO Spavento? Renowned, you say? Never 'eard of him.

SPAVENTO Captain Spavento dell Val Inferno, of Salamanca, of Salamis, Syracuse and Senlac.

ARLECCHINO (*to audience*) Ooh, he has been around.

SPAVENTO I am your servant – no, your slave. Believe me Ma'am, never on my travels through occident and orient have I beheld such elegance, such breeding.

ARLECCHINO Well yes, you see I was very high born . . . (*Aside.*) My mother had me on top of a haystack. She had my father on top of a haystack too . . . (*To the Captain.*) Go on.

SPAVENTO Call me a mad impetuous dog.

ARLECCHINO Very well: you're a mad impetuous dog – but I like you.

SPAVENTO A hound of war, brought to heel by your beauty.

ARLECCHINO (*aside*) Quite a one with the words, isn't he? Well, for a dog I mean.

SPAVENTO I fling myself at your feet.

ARLECCHINO Do be careful, you could do yourself a mischief.

SPAVENTO Be mine, I offer you my hand in marriage.

ARLECCHINO Oh, I don't know. You're very nice but . . . True, I am seeking a replacement for my dear departed, but you are not the only one. I tell you what . . . Now what was your name? Spavento. That's it, I won't forget. I'll put you on my list. (*Calls out.*) Roberto. Roberto. (*Colombina, still as the page, appears instantly.*) Please put the Captain on the List.

COLOMBINA (*holding up two pieces of paper*) The Short List or the Long List?

ARLECCHINO The Short I think. Thank you Captain, good day.

The Captain withdraws but finds a vantage point from which to observe. Colombina remains.

Scene 10 – The Mysterious Lady Interviews Fuomo and Fuoco

Arlecchino, Burattino, Fuomo, Fuoco, Colombina, Captain Spavento.

ARLECCHINO (*ringing the bell on the table and calling*) Burattino!

BURATTINO Yes, your Grace?

ARLECCHINO Burattino, who's next?

BURATTINO Who's next?

ARLECCHINO Who – is – the – next person who is going to propose to me?

BURATTINO Oh, yes, I see. (*A moment later.*) Captain Fuoco, Madam . . .

FUOMO (*turning on Burattino*) Fuomo!

BURATTINO Sorry – Fuomo. (*Burattino exits.*)

Fuomo now embarks on a passionate proposal to Arlecchino entirely in 'Gibberish'.

Arlecchino doesn't get a word in, merely looking alternately at Fuomo and the audience in amazement.[177] *Fuomo, on his knees before the supposed Duchess, finishes with a great flourish.*

ARLECCHINO (*to Colombina*) On the Long List, Roberto.

COLOMBINA (*adding name to Long List*) Captain Fuoco.

FUOMO (*aggressively to Colombina*) Fuomo!

COLOMBINA Sorry – Fuomo. (*Fuoco bursts in.*)

BURATTINO Captain Fuomo, your Grace.

FUOCO (*aggressively to Burattino*) Fuoco!

Fuoco thrusts Burattino aside. He has a drawn sword in his hands and he comes forward to attack Fuomo both verbally ('Gibberish' of course) and physically. Fuomo, who had remained kneeling, now rises, draws his sword and defends himself. They fight ferociously, with insults and threats flying. Eventually Fuomo gets the worst of it and is wounded. He stumbles about in comic agony.

177. *Lazzi of 'Clocking and Double Takes'*, No. 8, page 218

ARLECCHINO This way for the Doctor . . . (*Opens the door of the Doctor's house and Fuomo stumbles through it.*)

COLOMBINA Which list?

ARLECCHINO Neither. Even if he survives, he won't be much use to me.

Now Fuoco makes an approach with such passion that he frightens Arlecchino, who up-skirts and runs for his life. Comic chase[178] ending with an embrace from which Arlecchino can't extricate himself. From the shadows comes the Captain to the rescue. They duel, with the Captain eventually wounding Fuoco.

ARLECCHINO Why, Captain Spavento, how splendid. (*To Fuoco.*) This way for the Doctor. Roberto, put him at the top of the list. No, not Fuoco – Spavento of course!

Scene 11 – The Mysterious Lady Interviews Doctor Graziano

Fuoco, Dr Graziano, Lelio, Arlecchino, Colombina.

Fuoco is directed towards the Doctor's house, but bumps into the Doctor and Lelio just as they are coming out. During the following scene between the Doctor and his son, Arlecchino does a series of extravagant postures – draping himself on the chair and table as if posing for a glossy magazine.

DR GRAZIANO Oh good, business is picking up. (*To Fuoco.*) Shan't be long. Please go into the waiting room, and do try not to bleed on the new carpet. (*To Lelio.*) Now here's your chance boy, get stuck in.

LELIO Get stuck in, Father?

DR GRAZIANO Exactly – Quam hestitatum est perdutus.

LELIO But Father?

DR GRAZIANO Yes son?

LELIO She is obviously a lady of taste, refinement and learning – how much better if you were to press your suit. The Duchess is sure to appreciate your culture, learning and maturity.

178. *Lazzi of 'Chasing'*, No. 6, page 216

DR GRAZIANO I see your point. And it might be an opportunity for you to observe and learn. (*He goes to the table and rings the bell. Burattino appears.*) Burattino, announce me.

BURATTINO Doctor Graziano de Bologna. Doctor of Philosophy, Theology, Zoology.

ARLECCHINO Oh dear – so sorry, I got carried away. (*Finds bottle empty.*) And Burattino – more wine – being proposed to is very thirsty work. Who did you say this is . . . ?

DR GRAZIANO Doctor Graziano, graduate of Bologna University.

ARLECCHINO Proceed.

DR GRAZIANO Thrice you, by men of war, assailéd were,
With flashing arms and battle cries,
But you, your bastion defiant kept,
No flag of surrender offered you,
Nor portcullis raised, nor drawbridge lowered.

ARLECCHINO Watch it! Raising my port-whatever-it-is, and lowering me drawers, indeed!

DR GRAZIANO But where they fail, I, a man of peace and learning may succeed, for though you hide yourself under flounces and furbelows, I know your true identity! I know who you are!

ARLECCHINO (*aside*) Oh Gawd, we're rumbled!

DR GRAZIANO You are Diana – Goddess of the moon.

ARLECCHINO (*aside*) Saved – I thought the game was up. 'Ere mate, don't think these innuendos are getting you anywhere. Oh – put him on the Long List. We'll let you know. Next!

The Doctor, discomfited, returns to his house, accompanied by Lelio.

Scene 12 – *The Mysterious Lady Interviews Pantalone*

Arlecchino, Pantalone.

Pantalone appears and waves – in his coy vein.[179]

ARLECCHINO Oh, 'im! (*Burattino appears.*) It's all right, Burattino;
I know who this is. And Burattino, bring me another glass. (*To
audience.*) Look at him – love's young dream! Imagine that on your
pillow, girls.

PANTALONE Dear lady, had we but world enough and time, I would
with seemly delay woo you with flowers, dainty compliments,
tokens of esteem, admiration and love; but time's winged chariot
speeds apace . . .

ARLECCHINO (*to audience*) Not bad, eh?

PANTALONE . . . and I must declare my passion, and on my knees beg
your hand.

*He has great difficulty in lowering himself to his knees, and crashes to the
floor in the process.*

ARLECCHINO (*helping him up*) Oh dear, do get up. (*Aside.*) I hate to see
dumb animals suffer. (*To Pantalone.*) Never mind all that. Come and
sit beside me. (*Arlecchino puts two chairs side by side facing the audience.*)
There, that's better. Now I wonder, have you guessed who I really
am? I am not what I look. I'm warning you. (*Rude masculine gesture
not seen by Pantalone.*) I gather you want to marry me. Now, if I were
to accept, I would have to know more about you. (*In man's voice.*)
'Ave you, or 'ave you not, got any money? (*Back to Duchess voice.*)
Though my own wealth is substantial, I'm not going to marry a
pauper. I hear that you're very short of the readies – can't even
come up with a dowry for your daughter.

PANTALONE You need have no worries on that score. I have
considerable funds.

ARLECCHINO Where?

179. Pantalone normally veers between dignity and irritability, except as here, where
love is in the air.

PANTALONE Put by.

ARLECCHINO Put by where?

PANTALONE Never mind where, suffice they exist.

ARLECCHINO I would want your daughter to marry my godson.

PANTALONE Godson?

ARLECCHINO Yes, Lelio Graziano.

PANTALONE The goddamned Doctor's son, your godson?

ARLECCHINO Yes, and I insist upon it.

PANTALONE Very well, I agree – I will pay the dowry . . . (*Burattino and Colombina have come on and stand just behind them.*)

ARLECCHINO Witness! Did you hear that, Burattino and Roberto? We have witnesses that Pantalone has agreed to give a dowry for the marriage of Isabella to Lelio. (*To Pantalone.*) Very well, I'll marry you. Come on, give us a kiss.

Scene 13 – *The Dénouement*

Entire cast.

There is a series of very loud thudding noises from the inn – the sound of the trunk being dragged down the stairs.

BURATTINO What on earth is that? (*He rushes to investigate.*)

The cast, other than Tartaglia, appear from everywhere. Torolino and Tropolino enter.

Burattino appears holding Brighella by the ear, followed by Franceschina with Padella in a similar hold.

Fetch the Captain. I caught these two trying to steal his treasure. (*The Captain arrives.*) Captain, these rogues, one of them in my employ, have tried to rob you. Torolino, would you bring the chest?

Isabella and Lelio have entered and immediately embrace.

DR GRAZIANO What is this? Stop that, stop that!

PANTALONE Oh, leave them alone – I'll pay your blasted dowry. I'm going to marry a Duchess.

Torolino brings on the chest.

BURATTINO Yes, they've broken the lock – Captain I insist that you check to see if there is anything missing.

SPAVENTO No, that won't be necessary. Please don't bother . . .

BURATTINO I insist. (*Throws open the lid of the chest.*) What's this?

TROPOLINO (*stage whisper*) Tactical retreat, Captain?

The Captain, Tropolino and Torolino start to make a hasty exit.

BURATTINO Stop them! What is the meaning of this – there's nothing here but rags and old bricks!

SPAVENTO Quite true, a mere device to gain credit and kudos. It is strange that if you are seen to have wealth and affluence, people are most keen to give you more, and if you have none, they want to take what you haven't got away from you. (*The Abbess has entered and is standing next to him.*) This dear lady can tell you that I am nothing but a fraud, a liar, and a cheat – was this trunk truly filled with booty I would with great joy lay it all at her feet, for though only the Madam of the brothel of this small town, she is to me a most noble lady.

The Captain turns away in shame. Arlecchino, still in drag, has remained centre stage right opposite the Abbess who holds centre stage left. Tartaglia enters and stands between them.

TARTAGLIA What is all this? (*He sees the Abbess for the first time and starts to stutter violently and incomprehensibly, pointing at first to her and then to Arlecchino.*) Ger . . . jar werrr her-her her-ha n-n-not-nn-n-n-nev. G-g-g-g- by Joooo-vv-ee (*and so on, ending:*) Th-th-th-th-th-this (*Pointing to the Abbess.*) is the Duchess of Ferrara, rightful and legitimate holder of that title, now restored to her former rank and station. (*Tartaglia is apparently suddenly quite cured of his stammer.*) As for this creature – this is no Duchess. This is a fraudulent claimant and as such subject to the severest punishments of the state, of which I am the representative. Seize the creature!

The Captain

Tropolino and Torolino grab Arlecchino from either side and keep him in a tight hold.

ABBESS (*now Duchess of Ferrara, to Tartaglia and to the audience*) Wait! This is no fraudster – no false claimant to my titles. This is that renowned and greatly loved prankster – the Holy Fool, licensed to amuse, to lighten our journey through this vale of tears and to remind us that we are all but foolish children in the eyes of the Creator. Release him. Reveal yourself – Arlecchino.

Arlecchino leaps from his captors, who are left holding his drag costume. He prances about and bows to the audience.

And you, Tartaglia, are no Papal Nuncio, but a mere actor playing him so.
For this, dear friends, has been a play – of the Commedia dell'Arte.
All was pretend, all was a show, all was not necessarily so.
Are these true Lovers? – that we can't tell,

(*They embrace passionately.*) But you must agree they act it well.
Is he really a miser? (*Indicating Pantalone.*) Should you need to know,
See him in the bar – after the show.
And these maidens who seek your applause,
Are they also actors? – well, perhaps they are whores.
Brighella and Padella to jail can't go,
'Cos we'll need them for tomorrow's show.
There is but one exception, to all this deception,
Of me, it cannot be said
I am other than a Duchess – though I have been – misled.

Finis.

The Duchess of Ferrara

Part Two
THE LAZZI

A complicated *Lazzo* typical of the early eighteenth century

Introduction

The derivation of the word *Lazzi*[180] is uncertain and its usage variable. To be exact, in an historical sense, a *Lazzo* might be said to have been a piece of rehearsed comic business inserted into the improvised drama, usually at a moment when the audience's attention was flagging. It may have had nothing to do with the plot, nor have advanced the scene into which it was inserted.[181] The famous *Lazzo* of Harlequin 'Eating cherries',[182] or Pedrolino's *'Gawping'* in the *The Duchess Mislaid* (page 150) are examples of true *Lazzi* within this definition. Here, I use the term in a broader sense to mean any bit of stage business, from a single action or word, to a whole scene, which is devised and rehearsed beforehand and inserted into an improvised or scripted production, and usually called for by the dictates of the scenario. Not all here, have *Commedia dell'Arte* provenance,[183] though most are of considerable antiquity, coming down to us via pantomime, circus, music hall and silent film.

Most of them are suitable in themselves for workshop exercises; the students being divided into twos and threes to work on a *Lazzo*, with (or without) the help of the following descriptions. The devising and performing of such *Lazzi* are an essential skill of the *Commedia* player, and as such, should form at least one quarter of his/her training programme. The whole section can be profitably read through for an understanding of the nature of *Lazzi*, which contributes more to *Commedia* style than perhaps anything else. Alternatively, the appropriate descriptions can just be referred to, when applicable to a specific scene within a play.

The rehearsed business we call *Lazzi* are by their very nature, familiar, borrowed, stolen, appropriated, adapted and amended, so that the

---

180. Throughout this book a distinction is made between *Lazzi* (plural) and *Lazzo* (singular). Here, in the UK the word *Lazzi* is often used to indicate both forms. Though incorrect, it is convenient, and has become acceptable through usage.

181. See *Masks, Mimes and Miracles,* Allardyce Nicoll, Harrap, 1931 (page 219)

182. See *Playing Commedia*

183. It will be appreciated that many of the *Lazzi* mentioned in contemporary material are no more than a title which was of significance to the players of the time, but means little to us now. Others, on which we have more information, frequently prove distasteful, or unworkable for present day audiences.

original source can rarely be identified. They have been handed down from *Commedia* player to *Commedia* player – from clown to clown – from pantomime dame to panto horse – from music hall artiste to summer show comic; each taking that which was useful and adding something of their own. This is exactly what one must do when using a traditional *Lazzo*, always aiming to build on and adapt the original – and not merely making a lifeless copy.

For many of the following *Lazzi*, the *Commedia* actor or director has to think and work rather like a stage magician and although the aim is only occasionally to deceive the spectators, a similar application and thoroughness is needed, so that the end result – if not magic – is slick and precise enough to be entertaining in itself.

In the *Lazzi* that follow, the examples cited from British and American films, television, and occasionally theatre, are there to show that the traditions of *Commedia* are alive and can provide inspiration to today's and tomorrow's creative artistes. The understanding of a *Lazzo* is not dependent on familiarity with a particular reference.

Perhaps more characteristic of a *Lazzo* in the early days

The Lazzi of 'Asides and Freezes'

Although the *'aside'* in various forms and elaborations is frequently used in *Commedia*, the particular gesture familiar from Restoration Comedy, in which the actor 'speaks behind his hand' to indicate to the audience that the information is for its ears only, is rarely needed and untypical. It is part of *Commedia*'s earthy nature that nothing so affected and artificial is employed. The presence of the audience is so firmly acknowledged, that the actor has merely to turn the head to face them and speak the aside, usually in a slightly different tone than used in addressing other characters.

There are also several distinctive variations, particularly when it is combined with the *'freeze'*. Unless of the briefest duration, the *'aside'* usually creates a problem for the other characters present: what they are to do while one of their numbers is speaking to the audience. With *Commedia* we have a solution in the *'freeze'*, and that is for anyone else onstage to freeze their action for the duration of the *'aside'*; and the more frozen the poses the actors assume (mouth open ready to speak, a limb ready to move), the more acceptable will be the convention. The actor making the *'aside'* can even walk among the 'statues' and make comments about the situation at hand.

There is an entirely different approach to be used where possible, and that is to treat the *'aside'* as an audible 'subtext' expressing the character's inner thoughts. For example the scene from *The Duchess Mislaid* between Spavento and Pantalone (Act II Scene 3, page 182) is much more interesting if played in this way. Use the scene (starting with Spavento's line: 'Will you give me your arm?') as an acting exercise. Play the scene first as you would in Restoration Comedy – leaning away from your partner and speaking the *'asides'* behind one hand in the prescribed manner. Next, play it much more naturalistically, and don't say any of the *'asides'* – just think them intensely – in the character you are playing. Then repeat the scene, speaking the *'asides' sotto voce*, between gritted teeth. Do it this way several times, noticing how the moves – the coming together for the main lines and the slight turning away for the *'asides'* – develop naturally and organically. Finely project the *'asides'*, just enough to be heard by the audience, but don't alter the moves or the way they are said.

There are times when the *'freeze'* is not occasioned by an *'aside'*, but by another scene taking place in a different part of the stage, which requires the audience's attention; as in *The Path of True Love* (page 74). Here, all the performers not involved *'freeze'* their positions until the dialogue switches back to them.

2
The Lazzi of 'The Attitudes'

Some early nineteenth-century Harlequin *'Attitudes'*.

a. The Nineteenth Century

The *'Attitudes'* are an oddity – peculiar, unnatural and stylised in a way not consistent with the 'honesty' of *Commedia* tradition. The first mention of them appears in the early 1800s and seems to have gained ground with the publishing of the Penny Plain and Twopence Coloured sheets for model theatres. Around the same time, there was a shift from small intimate theatres to the vast auditoriums of the Regency and early Victorian periods. Harlequin and his fellows lost the intimacy they had enjoyed with the closely gathered spectators of the Piazzas and the audiences in the small court theatres. What had been suggested by subtle, even naturalistic, acting now had to be signalled with gestures readable at a distance. Many of these became stylised into something like semaphore. Some could be readily understood, but others, like semaphore itself, would require prior knowledge. They are contemporary with, and present the same problem as, the mime of classical ballet; where anyone can appreciate that a hand to the heart and then extended towards another means, 'I love you', but where other examples, like rolling the hands round each other above the head to signify, 'Shall we dance?' has to be known by the spectators, as well as the performers.

The '*Attitudes*' may have been derived from the distinctive gestures of individual Harlequins – things that impersonators could get hold of, like Tommy Cooper's hand movements and the funny walks of John Cleese in recent times. There are many illustrations of the Harlequin '*Attitudes*' from the early years of the nineteenth century, which can be copied when recreating a Victorian Harlequinade.

b. The Seventeenth Century

To evoke something of the dynamic quality which gave Arlecchino the power and popularity he enjoyed on the continent in the seventeenth century, one can study and simulate the poses from individual period paintings and engravings. These can be used to enliven and authenticate a performance. When required, as in the prologue to *The False Turk* (page 10), they can be strung together to create seventeenth- and eighteenth-century equivalents to the nineteenth-century '*Attitudes*'.

Some 'recreated' seventeenth-century *'Attitudes'*.

3

The Lazzi of 'The Bee, the Fly, and the Flea'

These are three *Commedia Lazzi*, which have been exploited by mime artistes the world over: they are so well known that they hardly need detailed description. The success of the *'Bee' Lazzo* depends heavily on the sound effects, usually provided by a musician with anything from a violin to a kazoo. This needs detailed rehearsal, or a highly sympathetic improvisational partnership. A very effective alternative is for the actor to provide his own sound, by 'buzzing' through near-closed lips` like a ventriloquist; the actor can then time the sound exactly to the moves. The *'Fly'*, is similar, with the added potential of 'swatting', in which the Zanni repeatedly hits and hurts himself. A traditional Arlecchino *Lazzo* ends with him catching and eating the 'fly'. With the *'Flea'*, we normally lose the sound effect, though a drum often accompanies the version used by circus clowns. We have the bonus of the 'scratching' and hectic searching, which can even include disrobing to find the invader. Again, the hungry Zanni can end by eating the 'flea'.

4

The Lazzo of 'Changing Places'

This happens most frequently when a pair of Zanni face a physical threat.

Pantalone is interrogating Brighella. Arlecchino is crouching behind Brighella. Pantalone's attention is momentarily distracted, and when he looks back again he sees that he is confronting Arlecchino. This must be achieved with great speed and economy of movement. Let's imagine that the three characters are in a line centrestage. Of the three, Brighella is centre, on his right Arlecchino and on his left Pantalone. Pantalone is facing stage right confronting Brighella, who is facing him. Arlecchino, close behind Brighella, also faces stage left. Pantalone looks briefly at the audience (See *'Clocking'*[184]), and Brighella takes two steps only: one very large one with his left foot diagonally backward, he then draws in the right foot and steps with it diagonally back and right so as to be behind Arlecchino, whom he shoves forward to be under Pantalone's threatening fist. The change over should be attained within three seconds.

The Captain also employs a similar move when faced with danger. He will push forward a Zanni, or even a maidservant if she is nearby.

5

The Lazzi of 'Charging'

The traditional *'Charging' Lazzo* is performed like this:

> *'Charging'* towards the left: Face front, the legs apart, then slowly raise the left leg, bent, and across you, with the toes turned up. At the same time, take the left arm across the body with the fist clenched, while raising the right arm to the side and a little behind you. Next, rise onto the ball of the right foot and pull up the body as if growing in height. Then at the climatic moment swing the left foot to the left side, turn the body to face left, and run toward the object of your passion, or wrath.

| 1 | 2 | 3 | 4 | The Target |

Pantalone demonstrates the *'charge'*

184. *Lazzi of 'Clocking and Double Takes,'* No. 8, page 218

This exact sequence of movements is often found in cartoon films. The early animators, especially from the Disney Studios, would employ comedians and dancers to demonstrate movements that were very accurately copied, and are useful where no record of the live performer remains.

6

The Lazzi of 'Chasing'

a. Pantomime 'Chases'

The chase is mostly the stuff of pantomime – by that, I mean corny and childish – but its very predictability can be amusing. The first thing to be considered is the character of the participants – in any case, it will always involve a remarkable degree of stupidity, in one or all of those involved.

On stage, the basic shape of the chase is a circle. 'A' chases 'B' in a clockwise direction, then they turn and 'B' chases 'A' in an anticlockwise direction for several rotations. There is usually a moment of deception, when 'A' stops, stands still, and adapts some kind of disguise, while 'B' continues circling round; in an early film, Chaplin puts a lampshade on his head to become a standard lamp. Sometimes even a disguise is unnecessary; the 'chased' has only to stop, take up an *'Heroic Pose'* to become a statue, which the 'chaser' ignores and continues on his way. Then the 'chaser' stops: 'That's funny! I don't remember seeing that statue before'. He goes back and examines it closely – gives it a kick perhaps. The 'statue' comes to life and the chase resumes. In a farce presented by the famous Piccolo Theatre of Milan, the 'statue' – being kicked – cried out 'clang' to prove it was made of brass.

In *The Haunting of Pantaloon* the chasing has a ritual quality that Clown and Harlequin enjoy reviving. Before the chase starts, Clown is given a sporting chance to get away, with a: 'One, two, three, off we go'. Halfway through they swap roles, so that Clown has a go at chasing Harlequin. In this example the chase is accompanied by blows from the slapstick, and there is a traditional step associated with it, which is known as the *'Hitchy-coo'*. The 'chased' leads by some four feet, his arms held high, so as to keep them away from the blows, hands waving

('Help!'). At approximately every eight counts, the 'chaser' strikes the 'chased' on the buttocks (a loud clap from the slapstick) and the 'chased' leaps into the air with a *'Hitchy-coo'*, holding his behind.

The *'Hitchy-coo'* is performed like this:

> Step on the left foot. Jump in the air with the right knee crossed in front of the left leg. Land by taking the right leg back behind the left and doing a 'ball change' – that is right foot, left foot – on the rhythm count of 'and one'. This is followed by six running steps and the *'Hitchy-coo'* repeated. The movement of the slapstick is based on sabre play, so the slash to the victim's right is taken with the knuckles down, and the blow to his left, knuckles up.

b. Adult 'Chases'

The 'Adult' chases, like the childish ones above, are equally good-natured. They are usually amatory, and most typically 'Un Vecchio' in pursuit of 'Una Servetta'. This is especially true of the earlier *Commedia dell'Arte*, with the small acting area of the trestle stages and private theatres conditioning the movement. There is a change during the eighteenth and nineteenth centuries, when much larger acting areas increased both the dramatic and comic possibilities.[185] Also, the introduction of the proscenium stage, for all its irreconcilability with the nature of *Commedia*, increased 'on/offstage' possibilities.[186] So we can get the Heroine in flight through the woods. She crosses the stage fleeing an invisible threat – she exits, and we see her pursuers, a band of desperate brigands. They have lost their quarry – they search and see her in the distance – they resume the chase and they exit. She crosses the stage again at a different angle. A style of scene typical of melodrama but originating in late eighteenth-century pantomime.

Back to the earlier and more typical amatory chasing as in *The Path of True Love* (page 59–60). Because of the space limitations the technique is one of rapid and sudden changes of direction, evasion, near catches, and the unnecessary surmounting of objects, like climbing over chairs, that one could easily go round.

185. Reaching an apex with the special freedom of the silent movies.
186. As in *Fools Gold* (page 98)

7

The Lazzo of 'Counting'

This infantile *Lazzo* delights the very youngest children, annoys those between nine and fourteen, and is looked on with tolerant amusement by adults. It is also given in *The Haunting of Pantaloon* (page 119) as part of the dialogue:

> *Harlequin, Columbine and Clown, stand in a line. Harlequin, starts by counting himself 'One'. He then walks behind Columbine, counting her as 'Two', then behind Clown counting 'Three'. He finds himself at the other end of the line and counts himself again 'Four'. 'That's not right' says Columbine. She stays in her position at the other end of the line, and pointing to each in turn, including herself, counts correctly: 'One, Two, Three'. Harlequin, starts again from his new position, himself one, Clown two, Columbine three, himself again four – the same conclusion as he had before. Clown says: 'I'll settle this', and goes to the front, facing the other two with his back to the audience. He points to Harlequin, 'One' and then to Columbine, 'Two'. 'Oh, dear, now there are only two of us'.*

Now you see why a five-year-old in the audience is made to feel so superior! [187]

8

The Lazzi of 'Clocking and Double Takes'

'Clocking' is a term for a full-face turn towards the audience indicating 'What did you think of that?', in reference to a line or action just taken by another. For a masterclass in this, watch Oliver Hardy in any of the Laurel and Hardy pictures.

The *'Double Take'* is an inattentive glance at another character, quickly followed by a second more attentive one. In the mouth of Adam

---

187. In *Room, Bed and Bath*, Buster Keaton gets away with a *'Counting' Lazzi* based on the confusion between 'Two' and 'Too'.

Trainsmith in *Comic Potential,*[188] Alan Ayckbourn gives an enlightening description:

> "Imagine you are reading a book, yes? You hear me come in to the room . . . You know it's me, so you don't look up at once. What you don't know is that I am covered in mud . . . from head to toe. You look up casually, you see me, register my presence, but your book is so interesting you quickly go back to it. Now as you look at your book again, the image of me suddenly registers on your brain . . . You look at me again. Quickly, sharply this time. Amazed."

He goes on to talk about Buster Keaton's quarter take, and the OTT *'Double Takes'* of James Finlayson of the Chaplin silent films. There is an even more extreme Arlecchino version, in which he takes the first look, then leaps into the air to face away. The realisation occurs mid-air and he lands back where he was, to give the second look.[189]

9
The Lazzi of 'Cross-Dressing'

When embarking on a scene calling for *'Cross-Dressing'*, it is advisable to distinguish between the various traditions available. Historically, the *Commedia dell'Arte* would largely have conformed to the 'convention', later typified by the Pantomime Dame, in which there is no wish to fool anyone that it is other than a man in a frock; and equally, the Principal Boy, where there is no wish that she be thought of as anything but a woman. Arlecchino's impersonation of a duchess in the second act of *The Duchess Mislaid* (pages 195-206) belongs to this tradition, but the too-professional mannerisms of the traditional dame should be avoided. An excellent example of this particular distinction is seen in the film of *Charley's Aunt,* in which Jack Benny (in spite of being rather too old for the casting) brilliantly portrays a college boy attempting to pass as a woman. In the man-as-woman tradition, there is also 'the protest element':

---

188. *Comic Potential,* Alan Ayckbourn, Faber & Faber, 1999
189. See *Playing Commedia*

'I want you to know, I'm really a bloke'. For example, the impersonator holds his pinkie up as he delicately sips from the wine glass, but when the company aren't looking he takes a great swig from the bottle. In *The Duchess Mislaid* when Arlecchino says in falsetto 'I would have to know more about you', but drops to an exaggeratedly deep and coarse man's voice for ' 'Ave you, or 'ave you not, got any money?' (page 202).

There are two other traditions which can be used where appropriate. The 'camp' version is exemplified in Danny La Rue and all the other good female impersonators. Then there is the version in which there is a serious attempt to 'become the woman'; like Dame Edna Everage and Robin Williams as Mrs Doubtfire, whose false bosoms would never be allowed to deflate.

The female-into-male transformation has a long history, gaining momentum from the date of the first actresses allowed to appear on the stage. Being a leader in this field, the extant scenarios of the *Commedia dell'Arte* give many opportunities for the leading actress to don male attire. These early examples, and the pictorial evidence from then until the end of the nineteenth century, show that the performer's female charms were accented rather than hidden. Late Victorian and Edwardian music hall brought forth a number of male impersonators who, without trying to totally deceive, were acclaimed for the delineation of stereotypical masculine characteristics. An idea of how they worked, can be seen in the film *Soldiers of the Queen* with Cicely Courtneidge.[190]

IO

The Lazzo of 'The Dance Of Glee'

This starts from a feeling of triumph or victory (not unlike the athlete's punch into the air), or joy at the success of one's plans (usually malevolent). The movements are not in the least elegant (more Bruegel than Watteau), betraying a peasant background from which even a supposed aristocrat like Pantalone is not entirely immune.

You can use most country-dance steps, performed in an emphatic manner – setting, skipping, step hopping, etc. – and where there are two

190. *Soldiers of the Queen* (1933)

or more players, arm links, doe-se-does, and shouldering, etc. Two particularly appropriate steps are *'Step-swishes'* and *'Knees-up'*:

'Step-swishes': Step side right, then swish left leg across, lifting it into the air with knee bent. Hop on right foot. Repeat to the left.

'Knees-up': Drop weight on to the left foot, raising the right knee high in front. Change onto the right leg, raising the left knee. Repeat ad lib (Habitués of London pubs will be familiar with *Knees up Mother Brown*).

Similar steps can be employed by a character (especially Pantalone and Pulcinella), in a slower, cod-sentimental mode.

II

The Lazzi of 'Disguises and Role Swapping'

Beloved by Shakespeare and every scenario deviser of the *Commedia dell'Arte*, this is the very stuff of our theatre. As far as *Commedia dell'Arte* is concerned, it became particularly prevalent during the last years of the seventeenth century when both Arlecchino and Colombina took on various identities (often expressed in the title of the play on offer: *Arlecchino, Thief, Copper and Judge* and, *Colombina, Lawyer for the Prosecution and for the Defence*).

The main factor in all such disguisings, is that they are rarely, if ever, complete. By convention, however slight the camouflage may be, it is sufficient to fool the intended members of the cast, but no one else – least of all the audience. We also see this in the closely allied *'Costume Change' Lazzi,* where part of Arlecchino's distinctive garment is always seen beneath his attempted disguise. This convention we can refer to as a *'Token Change'*; it requires that beards and moustaches be patently false, wigs and hats ill fitting, and items of dress clearly made for someone of another size and shape. Cross-dressing in a lady's bonnet is made ridiculous by facial hair,[191] false bosoms are expected to slip to unnatural locations, and of course the joy of the 'breeches part' is the obvious femininity of the impersonator.[192]

Some of Arlecchino's more outlandish disguises
through which his own costume is seen

As described in the *Lazzi of 'Exchanging Clothes'*,[193] onstage changes need to be rapid – where possible, instantaneous. Trick costumes have to be devised, and individual ingenuity can augment traditional solutions. Trick-changes of this type belong to the later *Commedia* of the eighteenth century, and were almost a required element of the pantomimes, operas and ballets of the early nineteenth century. The apex of the art, was to be found in the 'Quick-change Artiste' of Victorian music hall, who would play all the roles in a dramatic sketch. There are a few continental acts still practising it,[194] though its survival is usually in the form of a parody.[195] An important consideration is whether or not the costume has to be seen from the back. If not, one can use Alice bands, bicycle clips, and steel springs to clip round the neck, waist, knee, or ankle – old clock springs were often used in the past. Don't let any misguided sense of historical accuracy stop you using Velcro; if the *Commedia* players had known of it, they would have used it!

191. Kenny Everett in almost every television programme he made.
192. See also *Lazzi of 'Cross-Dressing'*, No. 9, page 219
193. *Lazzi of 'Exchanging Clothes'*, No. 17, page 227
194. Notably Antarnio Brachette at the Mogador, Paris.
195. Tommy Cooper's much loved 'Hat' routine.

Onstage disguising can be in view or hidden – that is, behind a screen, curtains, or bits of scenery. A traditional onstage effect is made by several of the cast getting round to obscure the audience's view of the change.[196] In this case the usual tolerance of '*Token Change*' is less acceptable, and the greater and more complete the transformation the better.

12

The Lazzi of 'Dismemberment!'

The horrors of contemporary medicine seem to have held a particular fascination for *Commedia dell'Arte*; although the Doctor was not principally a physician, he was often called upon for that highlight of seventeenth century, the enema, and numerous excuses were found for illusions of dismemberment. The comedy operation is done behind a screen – usually with the 'surgeon's' head and shoulders seen above, and the patient's feet sticking out to one side. During the operation he calls for the surgical instruments: knife, scalpel, forceps, swab, saw, hammer, screwdriver, whiskey (which he drinks), drill, spanner – and finally, needle and thread. Body parts are handed out and thrown into a bucket, others, including intestines, flung into the air. Legs which have been kicking are held down and then 'sawn off'. The sequence ends with sewing up of the patient, and presenting him with the bill.

A version of greater refinement is the shadowgraph: translucent screen, lamp, similar props to the above, chosen to look good in silhouette. Don't embark on this unless you have plenty of time to devote to planning and rehearsal.

13

The Lazzi of 'Drunkenness and Drinking'

Surprisingly, there is little reference to drunkenness in either the *Commedia dell'Arte* scenarios or the known *Lazzi*. We have to wait until the

---

196. Some may remember seeing this to startling effect when Katherine Dunham made costume changes while momentarily obscured by her dancers.

Victorian and Edwardian music hall for a full exploitation of the comic possibilities: the top-hat-and-tailed Jimmy James, deposited from a hansom cab within a few yards of his front door, and giving a highly physical *Lazzo* of his attempts to get there; his encounter with a lamppost, his attempts to light a cigarette (and find his mouth), his search for the key – and then the search for the keyhole.

In the plays here present, both instances of '*Drunkenness and Drinking*' occur in *The Duchess Mislaid*; Burattino serving two masters (Act I Scene 12, page 173) need only be slightly tipsy – with disbalance and quick recovery – as he swiftly moves from one table to another. Arlecchino as the Duchess hardly gets drunk at all; he merely demonstrates the difference between the feminine and masculine approach to drinking.

14
The Lazzo of 'Either End'

This is where the Zanni puts his hand over his mouth to stop any sound or breath coming out . . . and then puts his hand over his bum, to make sure no sound escapes from there either. The moves need to be made firmly and swiftly. It is famously part of the longer *Lazzo* of Arlecchino's attempt at suicide; he decides he'll kill himself by holding his breath. He wriggles about with his hand over his nose and mouth, until some wind escapes from the other end.[197]

197. See *Playing Commedia*

15

The Lazzi of 'Embracing'

The embracing *Lazzi* are preponderantly male with male: at meeting, parting, or on mutual agreement. In the traditional *'tre volte'* (three times):

> The actors face each other some four or five feet apart. They hold their arms out to the side and slightly forward. They then take a few steps backward away from each other, in mutual appreciation. They both slightly raise their right arms and lower their left into a diagonal position. They then walk towards one another until their chests are in contact. Both have their right foot forward and their left foot back. As they embrace their arms go round their partner affectionately patting him on the back. They now part, by lunging backwards onto the left leg. (still facing each other). They change the arms by raising the left and lowering the right. They then re-engage in the new hold. Repeat affectionate patting. Repeat on the first side to complete the *'tre volte'*. To express greater exuberance at the embrace, the back leg may be raised coyly in the air.

There is a highly energetic version to express exceptional delight at meeting. The recognition occurs at a distance and the meeting is done at a full run. The mechanics of the arm movements are the same as above, but on contact instead of the back-slapping, one player lifts the other into the air, so that his feet leave the ground and are raised behind him. They part, and change arm positions, and it is the other player's turn to be lifted. They part again this time to a greater distance. One runs and jumps up with his legs round his partner's waist, and is spun wildly round.

16

The Lazzi of 'The Emperor's Props'

This term has been recently coined, but is apposite and convenient, as *'The Emperor's Props'*, like *The Emperor's New Clothes*, are simply not there at all! They are the precursors of *'Illusory mime'* – all those invisible walls, staircases, umbrellas in the wind, dogs on leads – but here requiring a slightly different emphasis. *Commedia* mime needs to be vigorous, as near as would be the handling of the actual object, consistent with clear 'readability' by the audience. The mannerisms or affectation often seen in the French school of mime, where there is a tendency to slow up the action with a flowing – in itself beautiful, but here, inappropriate – grace should be avoided.

Generally speaking, when an object has been created by one character, its existence and exact properties of weight and bulk (and its last location), must continue to be observed by all the others. There are exceptions as in *Fool's Gold* (page 78) where Zan Mortadella fulfils the function of the little boy who couldn't see the Emperor's new clothes.

In *Commedia* the creation of the object is usually helped by the spoken word:

LELIO You see this letter? (*Mimes holding 'Invisible' letter. Arlecchino looks puzzled.*) This letter (*Shaking it.*)

ARLECCHINO (*pointing to letter*) Ah! That letter!

LELIO Yes, this letter. What does it say on the envelope? (*Holds 'letter' up for Arlecchino to read.*)

ARLECCHINO I don't know. I can't read.

LELIO It says: 'To the fair Lady Isabella, at the House of Signor Pantalone, Piazza Bisognia'.

ARLECCHINO (*reading hesitantly*) . . . 'the fair Lady Isabella, at the House of Signor Pantalone, Piazza Bisognia . . .'

LELIO Do you know the Piazza Bisognia? (*Arlecchino nods his head.*)[198]

---

198. This *Lazzo* – of mimed responses – is to be found in almost all the Marx Brother's films, when Chico questions Harpo.

Do you know Signor Pantalone? (*Arlecchino nods but pulls a face.*) Do you know where he lives (*Nods.*) Do you know the Lady Isabella? (*Nods with big smile.*) Then take this letter to her (*Hands letter to Arlecchino. Arlecchino starts off.*) and give her this rose. (*Lelio mimes caressing a rose lovingly then hands it to Arlecchino.*)

ARLECCHINO This rose (*Holds up letter.*) and this letter. (*Holds up rose.*)

LELIO (*physically correcting Arlecchino*) No, this rose and this letter.

ARLECCHINO (*starts off. Stops. Looks on floor*) I've dropped the rose.

LELIO No, you fool, you've dropped the letter. (*Arlecchino goes. He returns later in the scene.*)

ARLECCHINO I've got a reply from the Lady Isabella.

LELIO Give it to me then . . .

ARLECCHINO I've lost it! (*Arlecchino starts searching in his pockets, in his belt – down his trousers.*) No, I remember, I put it my . . . (*Takes off his hat, pulls out the 'invisible' mimed letter and hands it to Lelio.*)

'*Emperor's Props*' can expand to include '*Emperor's Sets*'; sumptuous palaces, dark forests, raging seas and when required, 'the vasty fields of France' . . . all invisible of course.

17

The Lazzi of 'Exchanging Clothes'

An exchange of roles is frequently demanded by the plot. This, of course, can take place on or offstage, and when onstage, the change can be 'straight' or 'comic'.

a. The 'Straight Exchange'

The '*Straight Exchange*' (as distinct from intentionally comic) itself can present a problem, because even a '*Token Change*' (symbolic or incomplete) can cause an unacceptable stage hiatus.

If we take Act II Scene 1 (page 74) from *The Path of True Love* we see that the 'token' costume exchange could be limited to Franceschina's cap and apron, with Isabella's headdress and fan. This needs to be achieved as rapidly as possible, and this is the kind of stage business that cannot be left to improvisation; it will mean experimenting with the props and then thorough rehearsal.

The following describes how it was performed in a recent production. It appears complex and possibly difficult to follow, and your own logically worked out blocking could work as well. It is included as an example of the detailed approach often needed:

> Isabella is to stage right of Franceschina. Both actors then turn to face stage left. Isabella undoes Franceschina's apron and holds onto it by the apron strings (the apron remaining in front of the maid). She then raises her left arm to make it easier for Franceschina to duck under it and make a half circle round to get behind her mistress, and thus able to tie the apron on her. They then face each other to exchange head-dresses. It only then remains for Isabella to take the fan looped to her wrist and hand it to Franceschina. The exchange should be completed within 10 seconds.

b. The 'Comic Change'

For a deliberately comic sequence, there are a number of traditional bits of business that start with the consideration of the clothing involved, and then very thorough rehearsal. The movements must first be learnt in slow motion. A basic version is as follows. The coat (or jacket) has to be loose with wide sleeves, and the lining can be in a bright contrasting colour to make the move effective.

> 'B' is wearing the coat. 'A' stands to his right. They hold hands 'B's' right in 'A's' left. 'A' reaches across and grabs the right lapel of the coat, and starts to pull it off 'B's' shoulder. Both take a few steps, ('B' to downstage right of 'A'. 'A' to upstage left of 'B') ending back to back. 'A' releases hold of the lapel and pulls the left sleeve (inside out) onto his left arm, then grabs 'B's' left hand with his right. They continue the clockwise turn as 'A' pulls the right sleeve onto the left arm, pulling the coat to his shoulder. 'A' is now wearing coat (inside out!). [199]

199. Thanks to Tweedy of Gifford's Circus for taking me through this.

c. The 'Screen Change'

Another version is the *'Half On/Half Off'*[200] costume change. It is most effective where two characters need to change – either with each other, or into two entirely different costumes. The goal is to make sure that the stage is not left empty for more than a few seconds. There needs to be a freestanding screen, large enough to conceal both the actors, and with access from either side.[201]

ARLECCHINO I shall pretend to be the Doctor.

BRIGHELLA How will you do that?

ARLECCHINO I know where he keeps his Sunday best. I shall put that on and no one will know me. Don't go away. (*Goes behind screen.*)

BRIGHELLA (*to audience*) . . . And I will disguise myself as Pantalone. He doesn't have a Sunday suit, but I think I can find an old one. (*Goes back behind the other side of screen.*)

ARLECCHINO (*comes out wearing the Doctor's hat*) I've found his hat! (*Dives back behind the screen.*)

BRIGHELLA (*returning*) I've found his shoes. (*Shuffles round in Pantalone's slippers, muttering like the old man, then exits behind left side of screen.*)

Arlecchino comes from the right side wearing the full Doctor's costume. Then Brighella returns with more of Pantalone's costume; he bumps into Arlecchino.

BRIGHELLA I know who you are.

ARLECCHINO Of course you know me, I'm Doctor Graziano. (*He does an impression.*)

BRIGHELLA No you're not – you're Arlecchino.

ARLECCHINO How did you know?

BRIGHELLA Your trousers are showing. (*Arlecchino makes a quick exit behind the screen. To audience.*) He would never fool me! (*Goes behind the screen and returns immediately with Pantalone's jacket into which he struggles while onstage.*) Hat! I need his hat! (*Looks behind screen without*

200. *Lazzi of 'Half On/Half Off'*, No. 27, page 237
201. It is possible to work this from either wing where the stage is fairly small.

success, then exits into the wings to search for it.)

ARLECCHINO (*comes from behind the screen, now more or less fully disguised as the Doctor*) He won't know me now. Now, where has he gone? (*Also exits offstage.*)

Brighella re-enters as Pantalone and from another direction the real Doctor arrives (typical Commedia!).

GRAZIANO Ah, Signor Pantalone, I have been looking everywhere for you. There is a most important matter I wish to discuss.

BRIGHELLA Ha, ha – very good but you can't fool me!

Brighella snatches off the Doctor's hat and pulls at the poor man's beard. Fake Doctor enters. Usual realisation and chase.

d. The 'Hoop Change'

The quickest of all costume changes is still occasionally seen in the circus: here the clown starts to run and a colleague holds a paper hoop in front of him. The Clown bursts through the hoop instantly assuming a new costume – often a dame's dress and hat, which has been strategically pinned to the back of the hoop.

18

The Lazzi of 'Extra Limbs'

These are *Lazzi* with a number of variations, which can be classified by the positional relationship of the partners, with either one – or both – standing, sitting, or lying.

The most familiar is when one person stands close behind another, replacing that person's hands and arms with his own. In the popular workshop exercise, he tries to match appropriate movements to his partner's improvised speech. A similar relationship, with more movement than verbal possibilities, is:

> 'B's' legs, rather than arms, replace those of 'A'. 'B' lies on a rostrum, perhaps illustrating a bed, with his legs from the knees down hanging over, facing audience. 'A' then stands over 'B' (facing the audience of course), the 'join' being

covered by a sheet or long costume. The result is a very tall creature made up from 'B's' legs, 'A's' arms, head and torso – who performs an on the spot dance routine.[202]

The above are 'agreed' *Lazzi*. 'Non-agreed' *Lazzi* are where 'A' is supposed to be unaware of 'B's' presence: Pedrolino's partner in Act I Scene 1 of *The Duchess Mislaid* is the dead body (page 150). The exact routine is dependent on the structure of the set. Here, he can be lying on his side facing the audience, or on his back propped slightly against the doorpost. Pedrolino, in either case must sit very close to, or ideally on, the body – if he is not too heavy. This routine belongs to a group of 'scary' *Lazzi*, where the extra limbs may not necessarily be human. They are often those of a Gorilla or other large ape (an actor in a 'skin'), but it might occasionally be, for example, a snake or an elephant's trunk (an arm or a puppet simulating the creature) – or most frequently the 'ghost' (an actor in costume or a skeleton puppet). The best of the *'Extra Limbs'* *Lazzi* contain some element of danger for the protagonist.

19

The Lazzi of 'Fainting'

With corsets and tight lacing, came ladies fainting – and to do so gracefully was frequently required of the company's Innamorata. It was to become more popular in the Victorian melodrama, but was nonetheless a useful defensive ploy from the late seventeenth century onwards. There are distinctive disadvantages in fainting to the floor: once down, one would be out of view of the audience (except in the rare venue with tiered seating); and of course there was always the

202. This was used to great effect in the Krazy Kat Theatre production of *Grimaldi's Pantomime* tour, 2000.

likelihood of spoiling the gown that you had provided, at so much expense to yourself.[203] So unless there is a bed or chaise longue within tottering distance, the goal is to strategically arrange to fall into someone's arms, preferably those of the beloved. The *'Tottering'* becomes an important preliminary to the actual fall, and can consist of a series of backward staggers, or an elaborate 'Dying Swan' *pas de bourrée*.

One of the *Lazzo* forms is to make several sudden changes of direction, which force the attentive hero to chase his adored, so that she may safely wilt into his arms.

Another is the *'Multiple Faint'* where she recovers and faints again, usually into another character's grasp. This can be repeated, ad lib. The important factor here is that no indication is given as to where she will land next. This example includes a couple of points about the technique:

> Suppose the fall is to be made towards the left then the supporter must stand slightly to the left and behind the one about to 'faint'. She must fall directly to the left side, bending the knees slightly but keeping the torso rigid. As she falls, the supporter must take his left arm round her waist and lunge firmly onto his left leg. The right arm may also go round her, his hands clasped together if the maiden needs the extra support. The position is similar to the famous Tango position.

This being *Commedia*, there is no guarantee that the one fainting is the Innamorata. The variations are limitless: Hero into Heroine's arms; Arlecchino in drag (or otherwise) into Pantalone's; the Captain (from fear) into his Zanni's; the Doctor at the sight of blood; and so on.

20

The Lazzi of 'Forbidding'

This is a speciality of Pantalone's, who is very keen on forbidding things, but can be used by any of the other 'Masters'. The routine will vary from a simple hand movement to quite an elaborate routine.

---

203. The extent of an actor's wardrobe was often more helpful in getting engagements than their acting ability. Even until the 1960s one was expected to supply all costumes, other than historic or exotic ones.

When it is a refusal to a single person, a servant or his daughter, a single hand movement is enough:

> Traditionally, this movement starts with the arm crossed in front of the body, the fingers spread out and the palm down. The arm is flung out sideways in an imperious gesture to accompany the 'No', 'Never', or similar expression of rejection.

When it is time to break up the lovers, there is the two-arm version:

> The errant couple are physically parted by Pantalone coming between them, and tearing their embrace apart. Both his arms are then held in front of his chest and struck outward as he says: 'I forbid it!' The lovers then, with appropriate gestures of anguish and despair, cast out (as in country dancing), perhaps to make a half circle to meet again and embrace further upstage.

In *The False Turk* (page 12) a second pair are also to be parted, and it works like this:

> The above moves having been completed with Lelio and Isabella ending upstage, Pantalone centre stage, Arlecchino and Franceschina now come together downstage centre. Pantalone says, 'And I forbid that.' He separates them (as he did the lovers), and they cast out. Walking upstage, Pantalone again confronts and separates the lovers. This can be repeated, ad lib.

21

The Lazzi of 'Fragmented Sentences'

These are word *Lazzi* in which sentences, even words, are taken over by one character from another.[204] Unlike most *Lazzi*, this technique can be improvised, and occasionally – to the joy of all concerned – it can come out of an entirely improvised scene. However, it takes experience, confidence in one's partner and a rather rare natural ability. Learning the scripted version can help develop this skill, or create the illusion of spontaneity – an example is to be found in *The Duchess Mislaid* (Act I Scene 6, page 159). Other similar games and *Lazzi* can be found in *Playing Commedia*.[205]

---

204. The technique was frequently exploited by Ronnie Barker in the television series *The Two Ronnies*.

205. See *Playing Commedia*

22

The Lazzo of 'Gawping'

The *'Gawping' Lazzo* belongs almost exclusively to Pedrolino; that is, to the stupid Pedrolino, precursor of Pierrot, as we find him in *The Duchess Mislaid* (page 150). *'Gawping'* is what I call a 'concurring' *Lazzo*, in that it takes place while other scenes are in progress. It requires no time, and very little space. It is not directly involved – but often provides a sort of commentary on – the scene that is proceeding. Pedrolino *'Gawps'* at people from afar, and an inch or two from their faces – physically for the most part keeping very still and moving slowly. He will take up awkward poses and maintain them without movement, as when he remains on one leg at the beginning of Act I Scene 10. When he *'Gawps'*, he is, for the most part, completely ignored by those playing the main scene.

23

The Lazzi of 'Getting Nowhere'

This is where one character prevents another from getting away by holding him in his grasp. It is usual that the grasp is to some item of dress, and so the hold depends on the type of costume worn. The one wanting to escape is usually of lower status, frequently Arlecchino:

> Burattino, in his innkeeper role, has an unpleasant task for Arlecchino, who starts to creep away stealthily, but finds himself firmly grasped by the collar. The comic element of this *Lazzo* is in Arlecchino's continuing to take the steps without making any progress. As he does so, he leans further and further back to try to get away, but ends up walking on the

spot. A version can also be performed at a run, where the hold is usually at the belt.

With the example in Act I Scene 4, of *The Duchess Mislaid* (page 153), Arlecchino is over-eager and he starts off at a run. Burattino holds him by the belt, as he runs at full tilt on the spot for several lines of dialogue. A 'towards' rather than 'away' variation, is where one individual rushes aggressively towards another, and is stopped by an outstretched arm to the chest or forehead. The aggressor continues to run on the spot, at full tilt.

When a higher-status Mask like the Doctor or Pantalone is held the result is typically a change of direction:

> The Doctor enters upstage right, his nose buried in a book as he walks. His intended direction is towards his house – downstage left. He is totally oblivious to the fact that Brighella has taken him by the end of his cloak, causing him to make a full U-turn and continue off in the direction from which he had come.

Another occasion is when a character, moving in one direction, is lifted bodily from under the armpits by two others, and carried in a new one, though he continues the walking or running movements with his legs in the air.

24
The Lazzi of 'Gibberish'

'*Gibberish*' (also known as 'Gobbledegook' and 'Grummelot') is a valuable workshop exercise (see *Playing Commedia*), but was used extensively in *Commedia dell'Arte* performances. It can normally be improvised (in sounds reminiscent of an appropriate country or region). In the case of Fuomo and Fuoco, in the second act of *The Duchess Mislaid* (pages 188 and 199), it is most effective if, for much of the time, they speak in unison. This may require the '*Gibberish*' to be written out and learnt.

25

The Lazzo of 'Going Backwards'

This is a *Lazzo* I devised first for a science fiction play and then included as part of the '*Passeggiata*' *Lazzo* in *Pantalone Goes A-Wooing* (page 46). I am not aware of it being done elsewhere, but I may be wrong; I often think I have entirely invented a *Lazzo*, only to discover it years later, in an old movie. The section to be reversed has to be rehearsed precisely, and then the moves worked out one at a time in reverse. The most showy one is walking backwards, and the most difficult, rising from a fall – and of course it should all be done as fast as possible. Some of the moves may prove to be impossible, so go back and modify the forward sequence.

26

The Lazzo of 'Grimaldi's Laugh'

a   b   c   d   e

This is an example of a *Lazzo* reconstructed by examination of prints or pictures, and analysed and compared with the nearest known movement. There is no certainty that this is exactly how the movements were made, but in all such cases they have proved practical in workshop and effective in performance, and are true to the style in general.[206] With that caveat the '*Grimaldi's Laugh*' is as follows:

206. Compare *Lazzi of 'Attitudes'*, No. 2, page 212

The Clown stands facing front, his feet turned in and his knees knocking, his arms on his hips (a). Then, while one arm remains there, the other is raised into a point towards the object of his ridicule. There is a bend in the elbow and the hand is in the 'polite' upside-down point with the palm uppermost, fingers bent, except the index finger which is extended. The knees now turn out and the feet change to first position. Retaining that position, he rhythmically pumps his shoulders up (b) and down (c) for four counts in a stylised portrayal of laughter, followed by four tips of the head right (d) and left (e) like a funfair automata. Repeat as required. His mouth is open and his face fixed in an expression of manic hilarity.

Note: The move is all mimed – silent.

27

The Lazzi of 'Half On/Half Off'

Plot development can take place on or offstage (Shakespearean battle scenes for example), but in *Commedia* there is a special category; the *'Half On/Half Off'*. Although a stage wing is convenient, anything large enough for an actor to hide behind, like a screen, curtain, prop rock or tree, can provide the *'Off'*. Sometimes, as in *Fool's Gold* (pages 93-94), a character will describe by mime or narration, what is going on offstage.

Scaramouche

The Scaramouche Lazzo

A frequently mentioned *Lazzo* of the great Scaramouche of Tiberio Fiorilli is a good example and actually illustrated in *The New and Curious School of Theatrical Dancing*.[207] Fleshed out with likely business from similar traditions, it might work like this:

207. Gregorio Lambrazi, Nuremburg, 1716

Scaramouche puts his head out from the wing on stage left, and then withdraws it. He comes half way out, then disappears again. He puts his right leg out from the wing for a moment, then just his hand (the right one, palm forward) and withdraws it. He makes a lot of noise as he runs round backstage, hitting the backcloth or curtain as he goes, so we know just where he is. He now repeats the previous actions from the right wing – as before – head, half body, left leg, left hand. He runs back to the original side hitting the backcloth as he goes, but much quicker this time. He puts his head round from the original wing, and comes a few feet onstage, where he does a bit of a dance – facing the audience and kicking his legs to the side. He then exits (off left). His hand comes out from that wing again – waves, withdraws. Immediately, his hand comes out from the opposite wing (stage right) and disappears again: Then a leg from the left wing; doing a kicking movement. It vanishes, and immediately appears from the right wing, etc. (Yes, there's a double).

Scaramouche splits himself in two

This was the opening of Fiorilli's Scaramouche routine, that featured (among other spectacular and eccentric effects): walking on his haunches so that the hem of his jacket touched the floor, giving an image of a strange dwarf-like figure; and *'Strides'*, which were a series of splits descending to the floor and then pulling up on a straight front leg, and repeating on the other, to cross the stage in about four moves. The Nicholas Brothers were two of the very few dancers who could do this, in more recent times.[208]

28
The Lazzo of 'Here, here, then here'

This is where a question, though perfectly well understood, is met with an alternative, or too-literal response. In *Pantalone Goes A-Wooing* (page 38) Pantalone's question: 'Where have you been?', is answered by Arlecchino with: 'I was here', indicating where he was only a second ago. 'And before that I was here', moving and pointing to a spot only a few feet away. ' And then I was at the door . . . ' etc. Zanni, much to Pantalone's annoyance, repeats the *Lazzo*. This is one of those *Lazzi* that seems very silly, but works well in performance.

29
The Lazzo of 'He's Behind You!'

A favourite of British pantomime, which it inherited from the *Commedia dell'Arte*, which inherited it from . . . Well, it was probably a popular joke in Neolithic times: 'Look out, Ugg, there's a sabre-tooth behind you!'. Even now, a predatory animal is often the threat; two good examples, are those of Laurel and Hardy with the ape on the rope bridge in *Swiss Miss* and Chaplin with a bear in *The Gold Rush*. In this last example, there is a subtle variation in that the innocent 'little tramp' never does see the bear – only we know of his danger. This highlights an important element in an otherwise childish and banal tradition, and that is, that it

---

208. *Down Argentine Way* (1940) and *Stormy Weather* (1943).

always works best where the audience's sympathy, interest and involvement is with the innocent – the stalked, rather than the stalker.

One need hardly describe the mechanisms. The threat creeps up on our hero. The audience warns: 'He's behind you'. The hero asks 'Where?'. It is just a matter of wherever he looks, the deceiver moves out of his view. If he looks to the right diagonal front, the deceiver will move to the left behind him. If he walks round, the threat follows closely behind, and so on.

30
The Lazzi of 'Hunger'

One of the main characteristics of the early Arlecchino was his insatiable hunger. And the 'sign' would have been based on popular street gestures; but what these would have been, we can only guess. A modern Italian one is to hold up the hand – the fingers straight, bunched together and pointing towards the wide-open mouth – then the hand is moved closer and further from the mouth in a rhythmic movement. And this will serve well for any of the Zanni Masks. The well-known theatrical gesture of rubbing the tummy with a circular movement was used by Grimaldi, and might have originated with him. It is useful where the indications are primarily comic.

Some of the original seventeenth-century 'Hunger' Lazzi are unlikely to be acceptable to modern sensibilities, seeming to us crude in the extreme; notably one, in which Arlecchino[209] bashes out his brains and proceeds

---

209. When the former Arlecchino became the too-elegant Harlequin, most of the coarser comic *Lazzi* were taken over by Grimaldi's Clown. Conversely today, the business known to have belonged to Grimaldi, may be appropriated by the actor playing the early Arlecchino.

to eat the results with relish. There are others, not quite so revolting, that can be reworked, including those that can be based on eating food in an unprepared condition:

> Zanni, left alone, indicates that he is hungry. Opens his knap-sack – turns it inside out – nothing! Sits and thinks. Scratches his head – thinks –scratches his head again – finds a flea – eats that. Still hungry – catches a passing beetle – eats that. Sits and gets an idea! Finds a bit of string and a stick (both actual, not mimed). Improvises a fishing rod. Starts to fish. Thinks he has caught something. Finds he has an old boot (a real prop) attached to his line. He tries to eat that, but it is too tough. Throws it back. At last catches a fish. Takes it off the hook and swallows it still wriggling, head first. It all disappears except the tailfin, which is sticking out of Arlecchino's mouth. He gets hiccups and has a job to swallow it. To conclude, he is surprised by another character and just manages to make the final swallow in time!

This *Lazzo,* if it is to be performed, requires a great deal of devising, making and rehearsing, from actor, director, and prop-maker. The 'fishing' is best achieved when Arlecchino is on a raised rostrum, so that the line can disappear behind it and the boot, and later the fish, can be attached by a stage hand. There are various possibilities with trick comestibles; from paper, which is crushed in the mouth (and spat out later) to occasions when things can be made of jelly, which can be swallowed fairly easily.

31

The Lazzi of 'Interjections'

Rather than a specific action or routine, *'Interjections'* is a term for a type of *Lazzo* performed by two actors; the principal one, delivering a mono-logue to the audience, is interrupted, qualified or rejected by the other. It flows from the characters, and the situation in which they find themselves.

The first actor may be flattering, socially mendacious; the other may expose it in a truthful, sarcastic or possibly obscene way.[210]

At it's best, it can come about spontaneously in improvisation, and in *Playing Commedia*[211] there are a number of word games to stimulate this possibility. However it is useful to have a few memorised sequences, and examples can be found in *Pantalone Goes A-Wooing* (pages 45 and 48-49).

32
The Lazzo of 'Knocking'

The *'Knocking' Lazzo* is reserved for 'Emperor's doors' – a frequently used item of invisible scenery. The actual knocking is done by raising the arm and rapping with the knuckles, using a stylish action of the wrist. The variations, for a synchronised sound, are: (a) an off stage sound effect; (b) a stamping of the actor's foot; or (c) saying the words 'knock – knock – knock' on each action of the wrist (sounding the 'K' to make it more onomatopoeic). In the sequence from *Pantalone Goes A-Wooing* (page 47) each of the Masks use a different rhythm as they knock on the door of Donna Lucia. Pantalone: ' Knock – Knock – Knock – Knock'. Arlecchino: 'Knock – Knock – Knockety – Knock'. Zanni: 'Knockety – Knockety – Knock – Knock – Knock'.

33
The Lazzi of 'Ladders'

A ladder is a frequently used prop in *Commedia*, essential for clandestine assignations, hurried exits and of course for rescuing heroines. They are needed for wooing at maiden's windows, with a Zanni securing the base and acting as a Cyrano for the tongue-tied hero; for the lecherous Pantalone or Graziano, teetering on the ladder, to glimpse the disrobing Fiorinetta (until she sends him flying when she flings open the window);

210. Rowan Atkinson as the aide to the President in the television series *Not the Nine O'Clock News*.

211. See *Playing Commedia*

as an aid to the spying, thieving, and even assassinations by Brighella and his henchman; and quite innocently by a couple of none-too-competent Zanni to perform the odd job for their master. This Zanni pair survive as the 'Broker's Men' of British pantomime.

The following traditional pantomime ladder routine, set to music, requires some knowledge of eccentric dancing but can be adapted to the abilities of the performers:

Two workmen enter from stage left carrying a short ladder (6ft long). Workman 'A' leads, workman 'B' follows holding the other end of the ladder, which rests on their right shoulders, and is supported with their right arms. They start with the left foot, taking seven large steps (onto the the heels with the toes turned up, keeping the knees straight, known as *'Johnny Walkers'*) and one step back. They then do three *'Johnny Walkers'*, and one step back. Repeat three *'Johnny Walkers'*, and take three steps back.

Three *'Johnny Walkers'* forward, pause for one beat. Repeat three *'Johnny Walkers'*. *'Heel swivels'* (weight on the heels, toes turned up) left and right. Workman 'B' does an extra *'heel swivel'* and changes the ladder onto his left shoulder, supporting it with his left arm, so that the workmen are facing in opposite directions. Workman 'A' takes a step backwards left and joins the right foot to it leaning forwards at he does this. He then takes four small steps – left, right, left, right. At the same time Workman 'B' makes the same steps but on the other foot and in the opposite direction, so they both end up leaning back and pulling the ladder between them. They stop, face front and lift the ladder over their heads so that it ends up held in front of them. Both do a *'Clown Slide'* (raise one leg, and slide along the floor sideways on the other) to the right, but with the impression that workman 'A' is pulling the ladder in that direction. They now do the '*Clown Slide*' to the left with workman 'B' doing the pulling. There is a pause after each '*Clown Slide*' for each workman to protest that they should be going in his direction. The speed now catches up into a full '*Clown Slide*' sequence, which goes like this: four '*Clown Slides*' (right, left, right, left). Double right, double left. Repeat.

There is an optional climax to the routine, which requires special props (three ladders of different lengths) and can only be done where there is a proscenium stage with the standard wing arrangement. It works like this:

Their routine completed, the workmen go toward the wing downstage right. One of the men exits, but the second man delays his exit by walking on the spot a few feet from the wing. While he is there, the first man enters from one wing further upstage, still carrying the front of the ladder (the ladder looks as if it must have bent in the middle). He enters some eight feet or so before the other is finally pulled off, to re-enter at the back of a now much longer ladder. They circle the stage and the first workman exits by the same wing as before (downstage right.) but this time the leader reappears at an opposite wing. So we have one workman entering stage left as the other exits stage right. The entering partner makes excuses to delay as if the second were pulling back, while he now has the chance to run round the back of the set, to appear holding the end of a very short ladder. In addition to the three versions of the ladder, the assistance of a couple of stage hands is required!

34
The Lazzi of 'The Letter'

The letter is a time-honoured device of the Italianate plot, and frequently found in the *Commedia* scenarios – forged, stolen, mislaid, misdirected – and, as in *The Haunting of Pantaloon*, intercepted (page 123). In this play, being intended for children, the *Lazzo* can take on a juvenile perspective:

'Concealing the Letter'

Pantaloon, walking slightly ahead of his daughter Columbine, doesn't see Clown hand her the letter, but he is suspicious and wants to know what is going on between them. 'Nothing!' they mime. Columbine and Clown are now standing shoulder-to-shoulder facing the audience; Clown being stage right of Columbine. Behind her back, she passes the letter to Clown, and she shows her empty hands. 'And you?' demands Pantaloon of Clown, who passes the letter back to Columbine, and

shows *his* empty hands. Pantaloon starts to walk round them clockwise to see behind their backs. The pair, still shoulder-to-shoulder, shuffle round in a half-circle, also clockwise, so that they are still facing Pantaloon but will have their backs to the audience. Columbine has the letter in her right hand, still behind her, and now clearly seen by the audience. She shows her left hand to her father. She changes – passing the letter to her left hand and showing him her right. She then passes it to Clown and shows both hands. Clown now has it in his right hand and shows *his* left. Then changes the letter over to show his right. With his left hand he tucks it between his knees, so that all four palms are held out to Pantaloon, who next moves round to the front again. Columbine and Clown shuffle back, Clown trying to keep the letter between his knees, at the last moment it drops to the floor. Clown tries to hide it by standing on it, but it is seen by Pantaloon, who picks it up and reads it out loud – to Columbine's discomfort.

35
The Lazzi of 'Listing'

'Listing' Lazzi can be monologue or duologue. The traditional ones are mainly about food, where the Zanni enumerate all the foods they could buy if they had the money – and then imagine eating them, with such relish that they feel first satiated, and then sick! Another example is where Zanni 'A' suggests the menu for a coming banquet, and Zanni 'B' keeps pressing the merits of 'Sausages'.[212] Others not concerned with food are where a list is ended with a non sequitur. For example, the magician recalling the first time he sawed a women in half: 'the lights, the music, the hushed spectators, the blood!'. There are those made comic by the inclusion of unexpected and inappropriate items – as in the request for surgical instruments in *The Lazzi of 'Dismemberment'*.[213] From this it can be seen that sometimes the items will need to be practical props. This is true of the pantomime 'Laundry List' where the items are visually comic: Widow Twanky calls out the list as Idle Jack hangs the washing on the line.

A list of a different kind is the enumeration of all the hurt to be done to a rival; a brief and none too vicious example, is to be found in *The Haunting of Pantaloon* (page 124).[214] Another – a duologue – starts with: 'What shall we do, then?' This might be followed by: 'We could go for a walk, but where would we go?' The possibilities are then listed and en-acted (mimed out in anticipation) till the couple get very tired. The tag is: 'I must say I'm glad we didn't go for a walk. What shall we do, then?'

36
The Lazzi of 'Looking'

Usually, this is a check to see if the action about to be taken might be observed by somebody else. Here is another opportunity to remind the

---

212. See *Playing Commedia*

213. *Lazzi of 'Dismemberment'*, No. 12 , page 223

214. See an example of a 'Threat listing' in the *Lazzi of 'Threats'*, No. 62, page 264

reader that a whole scale, raging from the subtle and naturalistic, to the most OTT and stylised, is within the choice of the actor. So a *'Looking'* *Lazzo* could vary from a quick glance to either side, to a choreographed sequence of steps, lunges, head and arm movements. A traditional action is to make a lunge to the right, with the head indicating the *'Looking'* direction, and to counter-balance it by holding the arms across the body in the opposite direction. The head then swivels or scoops from one direction to the other. The movement can then be repeated starting with a lunge to the left. [215] These more stylised versions are more justified when there is more than one person doing them, and in that case the movements should be accurately synchronised. [216]

37
The Lazzi of 'Lust'

These are usually male-mimed *'Asides'* to the audience indicating: 'I fancy this one!', and mostly in the provenance of the older Masks. Their version is to turn the head to the audience, and pant like a dog with the tongue hanging out, or darting in and out, and at the same time pawing the ground like a bull, and/or wiping the feet alternately against the floor. This is often followed by the *'Charge'* *Lazzo*.[217] A macho version, also used by Brighella and other younger roles, is to extend the arms towards the desired female, and wriggle the fingers lasciviously, while standing on one leg with the other raised with the foot flexed, shaking the leg in and out.

In the female version, which is more a 'come and get me', the hands go to the waist, and the character either dips up and down, or swings the hips. The eyebrows raise and lower. It is more likely to be followed by flight from, rather than charge towards.[218]

---

215. See *Playing Commedia* pages 119-122 for the details of this movement, and also pages 45-50 for lunges and a *'Looking'* routine.

216. See also *Lazzo of 'Searching'*, No. 57, page 262

217. *Lazzi of 'Charging'*, No. 5, page 215

218. But of course there is nothing to stop you from breaking with the tradition.

38

The Lazzi of 'Making do with'

This group of *Lazzi* includes all those moments where something easily to hand is made to stand in for something else, usually something of greater value or importance. A dustbin lid becomes the shield of Perseus; a chair stands in for the mighty steed Bucephalus; a cabbage does for the head of John the Baptist. This substitution of the mundane for the significant is very dear to the heart of the *Commedia* player, for here we have evidence of his origins – his proletarian challenge to his betters by putting a saucepan on his head and arming himself with a garden hoe, to ridicule their manners and trappings (a little of the early *frisson* he caused, might be felt in my suggestion that a cabbage might substitute for the head of the saint). In the same way that Picasso was able to take parts of a bicycle and transform them into the skull of a stag, so in this *Lazzo* the rough substitute has more to say than the most finely crafted stage property. Perhaps the greatest exponent of these *Lazzi* of substitution, was Joseph Grimaldi: from three coalscuttles he made himself the uniform of a hussar; from vegetables, an animated companion; from a tin bath and a ladle, the big bass drum.

An example from the present plays is the making of the ghost in *The Haunting of Pantaloon* (page 125). Here the audience can enjoy Harlequin's ingenuity in creating the 'ghost' from the objects presented to him. These naturally have to be customised to some degree: a hook is fixed just under the head of the mop. From this are hung the hanger with the flowing nightshirt, and also the tin plate for the face (tin, so that a hole can be drilled through it, to receive the hook). A fresh piece of paper may be stuck to the plate so that the face can be drawn on it with a marker pen for each performance. A thread may be attached to the end of one sleeve of the nightshirt, to increase the 'ghost's' animation.

39

The Lazzo of 'Mime Drawing'

Instead of miming an object (or even a person) by demonstrating their dimensions, weight, and characteristics, this mime delineates the object, or the physical peculiarities of the person, by drawing an outline in the 'air' – as if on a pane of glass between him and the audience. The following is a typically elegant Pierrot *Lazzo*:

> Pierrot rolls up his sleeves, and raises one finger: 'Now, watch this!' He puts the finger in his mouth to wet it, and then starting from low left draws the doorjamb to the top, then the cross piece and continues down the right jamb. Next, he draws the door handle. He then tries to open the door, by turning the handle, but it won't move. After several tries, he draws the letterbox, which he pushes open and peers through sadly. Next, he gets an idea, and draws a keyhole. He searches about him and finds a small key. He tries this in the keyhole. The key turns. He tries the door handle and this time it turns, and he opens and creeps through the door.

40

The Lazzi of 'Mimicking'

I should say that there are two forms – one of them being to make fun of another character, and the other to describe him or her. In the first case, the victim is usually present though unaware, and in the second, more usually absent. In both cases there is some caricature and exaggeration.

a. 'Mimicking' to identify

Sometimes the character is named, but usually just referred to by a 'nudge-nudge, you know who!', supported by a visual identification; 'taking on' the stance, or gait of the character to be described, and sometimes including *'Mime Drawing'*[219] of characteristics or apparel. *'Mime Drawing'* might include indicating the aquiline nose of Pantalone, the Captain's moustache, the heroine's waist and bust, the Doctor's hat, or Pulcinella's large belly.

---

219. *Lazzo of 'Mime Drawing'*, No. 39, page 248

b. 'Mimicking' to 'take the mickey'

These are various, but all depend on the victim being unaware that he is being mocked. They could include: (a) Walking behind someone copying their walk and other movement mannerisms; (b) Mouthing words as the other speaks – particularly when they are expected to be a tedious repetition of familiar phrases; (c) Reacting to emotional contact with exaggerated empathy – an example being the modern one of crying mock tears, or miming playing a violin whilst a 'sad' story is being told. A typical *Commedia dell'Arte* version is made during the Captain's enumeration of one of his tales of courage. Zanni can ridicule him by either taking ridiculously exaggerated poses of valour, or the reverse, i.e. miming actions depicting the Captain's cowardice.

41
The Lazzi of 'The Misdirected Embrace'

There are a number of variations on *'The Misdirected Embrace'*, but they all have a common pattern: the would-be embracer's attempts to unite with the object of his affections, all end up with someone – or even something – quite other than the one he desires in his arms. The mechanics of the 'change' are helped by an excess of passion or *'Lust'* on the part of the initiator of the action.

Example One:

> *Captain Spavento and the fair Isabella stand centre stage. Spavento stage left, Isabella stage right, some five paces apart. They face each other.[220] Spavento's weight is on his right foot, the knee bent, his left leg extended and pointed behind him. He leans forward, his pose suggesting eager desire. Isabella's weight is on her left foot, her right behind her. Her pose expressing distaste and alarm. Behind Isabella, that is to say to her right, is her maid, Franceschina. Spavento moves a hand towards Isabella.*

CAPTAIN Oft have I beheld your beauty from afar.

> *She turns from him, changing her weight, to face Franceschina, miming*

---

220. *Lazzi of 'Lust'*, No. 37, page 247

'What shall I do?' He turns away, changing weight, to consult a bit of paper on which he has a speech prepared. They face each other again getting a little closer.

CAPTAIN But now I behold you in such proximity.

They turn from each other again, and back.

CAPTAIN I can no longer hold my ardour in check.

He turns away once more, this time as a preparation for his embrace. He then makes a grab for what he expects to be Isabella, but in the meantime she has ducked out of harm's way and her place taken by her maid.

Example Two:

> Doctor Graziano interrupts the maid Spinetta with his amorous advances as she attempts to mop the floor. He chases her about the stage,[221] offers her a coin.[222] He traps her against a wall so she can't escape. He turns away to draw breath (or communicate his intention to the audience). He turns back and makes a grab for her. Spinetta is too quick for him and Doctor Graziano finds himself kissing her mop, with his foot caught in her water bucket.

The lovers' embraces are not *Lazzi* – not stylised, not comic. They are for real, tender or passionate, as the scenario demands.

42
The Lazzi of 'Money'

Some traditional mimes are:

'Money':

> Elbows remain close to the torso, lower arms raised and held slightly wide. Palms up. The thumb makes little rubbing movements against the first and second fingers, which are held together.

221. *Lazzi of 'Lust,'* No. 37, page 247
222. *Lazzi of 'Money',* No. 42, page 251

'Give me some money':

Hold out the palm of the left hand and with the right hand, 'thumb' several mimed coins into it to indicate money. Then close the left hand to the waist and hold the right palm out to receive the coin (which may be mimed or actual). A covert version starts by looking right and left, to check that one is not observed before thumbing the coins as before, but secretively, close to the chest – the performer then turns away from his partner and holds out his right palm behind him. The arm is straight and the wrist turned inwards.

'Much Money':

Used to indicate that a character, not present, is wealthy. The palm of one hand is again held forth. Above it the other hand mimes a growing pile of gold coins by wriggling the fingers (pointed down) and gradually raising the hand.

'Hiding Money':

Starts with any of the above, followed by a hiding mime suitable to the situation: throwing it into a safe and turning the key; hiding it about one's person and then holding the empty hands out to show you have nothing; digging a hole, putting a casket in it and covering it with earth. This last example is probably the one used by Arlecchino in Act I Scene 5 of *The Duchess Mislaid* (page 158). All such mimes must be done at considerable speed.

'No Money':

As we all know, this is indicated by putting the hands in the pockets and pulling out the lining. This can be 'actual', but as the gesture is so well known it can be mimed.

The 'Bribe':

The purse (in *Commedia* usually actual, not mimed) is taken from the belt and held up and shaken meaningfully. Alternatively, a coin can be taken from the purse and held aloft temptingly.

43
The Lazzi of 'Moving a Body'

Perhaps the best of all recent body-moving sequences is to be seen in the episode of *Fawlty Towers* where a hotel guest inconveniently dies on Basil. There are two such Lazzi in *The Duchess Mislaid*, each requiring a slightly different approach. The first (Act I Scene 2, page 152) is principally confined to lifting the body, and disagreeing about which direction to take it – pulling apart, doubling up, spinning round. Pedrolino is scared and unwilling, so perhaps Brighella has to end up by dragging the body himself from one doorway to another.

The next version (Act I Scene 3, page 155), by Burattino, Padella and Spinetta, might show a sort of apparent professional competence, with the body refusing to behave itself – it won't keep its arms tucked in, sticks a rigid leg into the air and when the leg is pushed down, the body sits up. If 'the Body' is something of an acrobat, there are some effective possibilities, showing *Commedia* at its most idiomatic. Once the body is placed in the wheelbarrow, legs bent over the front and each side of the wheel, the handles of the barrow being raised, the body spills forward and does a forward roll ending full-length.

This *Lazzo* exemplifies once more, the intensive rehearsal required in performing such a piece of comic business.

44
The Lazzi of 'Muttering and Mumbling'

Closely related to *'Gibberish'* it is a substitute for comprehensible language; but while *'Gibberish'* is intended to be understood (like the Englishman abroad, the speaker thinks that if he speaks loud enough, the foreigner is bound to understand), *'Mutterings'* are private affairs and *'Mumblings'* apologetic, vague. One advantage for theatre use is that odd words and phrases of English can come out of the general rumble of sounds to express the thoughts, emotions and character of the mutterer. So Pantalone will *'Mutter'* irritably:

'Muttermutter mutter mutter mutter if he thinks he's going to mutter muttermutter mutter get what's coming muttermutter mutter.'

Or the Doctor:

'Muttermutter entomologically and attamorphically mutter mutter ipso facto mutter caucus belly mutter, anyway hypothetical if not darn right hyperbolic mutter mutter.'

One might make a distinction between the two by saying *'Muttering'* is in monologue and *'Mumbling'*, dialogue. Both were brilliantly used in *Whistle and I'll Come to You*, an adaption of a P.D. James story directed for television by Jonathan Miller, and starring Michael Horden.

45
The Lazzi of 'Names'

This can include the devising of any play on names. The most frequent is accidental or intentional misnaming and mispronouncing: 'Big Conk Nosey' for 'Bisognosi',[223] and the substitution of antonymous names, i.e. 'Jack' for Jill (male for female); 'Susan' for Bert (female for male); 'Hercules' for someone small and weak; and 'Sweet Thing' to an ugly and irritable old woman.[224]

Harlequin's objection to being called 'Jackanapes', sparks off a whole scene of *'Names' Lazzi*. The sequence with the audience is played thus:

Harlequin asks a child in the audience for her name. She answers, say, 'Sharon'. Harlequin then shakes her warmly by the hand and says: 'Very nice to meet you, William.' She protests. Harlequin then repeats this with another child. He then turns to Clown: 'There you are – they don't like being called by the wrong name – and I don't like it either. My name is Harlequin'. etc.

The *'Watt's my name?' Lazzo* is from music hall, and can be seen in the Abbott and Costello film *Hold that Ghost* (1941).

223. See *Fool's Gold*, page 94
224. See *Home from the Wars*, page 126

46
The Lazzi of 'Nothing will stop me'

The *Lazzi* where a character will continue sweeping, mopping, scrubbing – and all such household chores or repetitive tasks, such as digging, hammering, fly swatting or butterfly catching – regardless of who gets in the way, tries to stop it, dies, commits murder or enacts a love scene. He/she goes on sweeping, or hammering, or whatever, and any other character onstage must fit his actions to the relentless goal of the perpetrator. Like other *'Concurring' Lazzi*[225] the aim should be to retain as much improvisation as possible.

47
The Lazzo of ' Nudge-nudge, wink-wink.'

Both *'Nudge-nudge'* and *'Wink-wink'* are examples of a fairly small number of instinctive gestures that are agreed among most races and may be of even prehistoric origin. *'Nudge-nudge'* involves close proximity, being an elbow action only to be communicated to the person immediately next to you, and its purpose is to draw attention to a third person or his actions. It has a certain crudity and could be translated as 'cop that, mate'. Similarly, *'Wink-wink'* (a double eyewink) is intended to be covert, and means: 'You agree, yes?' For theatrical purposes – like the stage whisper – the actions have to be exaggerated so as to be observable by the audience.

48
The Lazzi of 'Parting'

These are more usually and correctly called *Uscite* or exits, and were memorised speeches – often rhymed couplets – inserted into the improvised performance and are the rightful fare of the Innamorati. Of the two or three occurring in the plays given, all are made part of the script, which should make their nature clear. They are performed in

225. See *Lazzi of 'Gawping'*, No. 22, page 234

exaggeratedly heroic (or by the Innamorata, tearful) vein, preceded by a series of ostentatious strides towards the wings, the striking of a flamboyant pose, followed by a showy exit.

49
The Lazzi of 'The Passeggiata'

This is a journey enacted on the stage, most frequently a walk, but could be by any other form of transport: riding on horseback, driving a car, or a horse and cart (as in the stage version of *The Woman in Black*).

It is normally performed side-on to the audience, and like Marcel Marceau's famous 'Walk of Life', remains on the spot, by using the accepted 'mime walk' or the *Commedia* 'tapis walk'.[226]

Whichever is chosen, the important factor is that the attention is drawn away from the movement of the feet, by the actions of the upper body and the head. The incidents of the journey, small and large, are mimed or commented upon: passers-by are acknowledged, buildings and views admired, obstacles surmounted, traffic avoided, temperature and weather are expressed by body language. *'The Passeggiata'* in *Pantalone Goes A-Wooing*[227] gives an example of how such a *Lazzo* can be developed.

Though a spectacular set piece for modern physical theatre, *'The Passeggiata'* has its antecedence in the early years of the nineteenth

226. See *Playing Commedia* ('Mime and Movement Games' page 56).
227. Scene 3, page 46

century. Especially in Paris, and later in London, the public demanded more and more in the way of scenic novelty, and the Panorama was introduced. The actors walked or ran against a moving backcloth operated by giant rollers on each side of the stage. The more affluent theatres were also able to install a 'Tapis' or trackway moving in the opposite direction of the actors. The culmination was a race with live horses and their jockeys, towards the winning post.[228]

50
The Lazzi of 'Perquisites of the Role'

These may be included here, but properly belong to a separate class of prepared material like *Uscite* and *Chiusette* (closing and exiting rhymed couplets) that does not have the comic nature of the *Lazzi*. They are featured solo moments (like the aria in opera) which were expected from each of the 'master' characters. Typically, the Innamorata would have her *'Tirade'*;[229] The Innamorato his *'Lament'*;[230] the Captain his *'Rodomontade'* and the Doctor his *'Disquisition'*.

In Polonius's speech to Laertes (*Hamlet*, Act I Scene 3) we have a perfect example of the *'Consiglio'*, or counsel, expected from Pantalone.

Perquisite of the Innamorata: the *'Tirade'*

228. *The Derby Winner* (Drury Lane, 1894)
229. See *The Path of True Love*, Act II Scene 1, page 72
230. See *The Path of True Love*, Act I Scene 4, page 63

51

The Lazzi of 'Picking pockets, removing keys, etc.'

'Picking pockets', along with the surreptitious removal of keys, documents, and letters, is a skill in which most Zanni, male and female, are highly proficient. The nature of the action will depend, to an extent, on the costumes worn by the characters, and the period in which the piece is set. Pantalone, who is so frequently the victim, is more likely to have a purse hanging from his belt, than the modern concept of coat or trouser pocket. In the eighteenth century, 'cutpurse' was the more usual sobriquet for this criminal specialisation. However, the method is not dissimilar. The technique used by the stage magician and also by the street pickpocket, is to distract the victim by various body contacts: shaking hands repeatedly, pats on the back, etc. An affectionate or passionate embrace is often employed to mask the theft. Colombina will remove a purse, key, or letter by love games: caressing, tickling, finger prodding, needling.

The Doctor and Pantalone are not above a little mutual pocket picking – a character trait that can embellish the *'Embracing' Lazzo*.[231] The lower hand is seen groping about for a purse or pocket, usually to ascertain whether the partner has money, rather than to steal it.[232]

52

The Lazzo of 'Placing the Chair'

The Zanni holds the chair ready to place it where his master requires. The *Lazzo* is created by the indecision of his master, who looks as if he is going to sit but suddenly switches to another spot, confusing the Zanni – so he is not there when the master finally 'sits' and falls backwards onto the floor. Development of this depends on the acrobatic skill of the actor playing the master: for example the fall might be followed by a backward roll which ends standing, with the Zanni just in time to place the chair for his master to sit – to almost invariable applause.

231. *Lazzi of 'Embracing'*, No. 15, page 225
232. See Astaire and Crosby in *Blue Skies* (1946)

53
The Lazzo of 'The Policeman's Lot'

This is one of a comparatively small number of *Lazzi* that are part of the public consciousness and known to almost everyone. Version 1 consists of merely placing the heels of the feet together and turning out the toes (Ballet first position), clasping the hands behind one's back, and bending up and down at the knees fairly slowly, accompanied by a phrase such as 'Oi, Oi, Oi!' (one bend and straighten). 'What's goin' on 'ere?' (second bend and straighten).

A slightly more energetic version (Version 2), also used by other uniformed personnel, is to start with the legs straight, feet turned out as before, and to lift the heels, by suddenly bending knees, *without* raising the height of the body, and sharply returning the knees to straight. This is used by Torolino in *The Duchess Mislaid*, Act I Scene 3, with the addition of a forward movement of the pelvis causing the key to move up and down somewhat suggestively.

The way in which an actor can personalise such a *Lazzo* is shown by Fulton Mackay as Mr Mackay in the television series *Porridge*. He varies version two by adding a very slight rise, and holding his chin rather higher than natural in the manner of a small man attempting to exert his authority. The name of the *Lazzo* is taken from an Edwardian comic song, *The Policeman's Lot is not a Happy One*.

54
The Lazzi of 'Proposing'

To fulfil its definition as a comic *Lazzo*, the proposal will usually be unwanted – and one of the comic possibilities is the unwillingness of the heroine being proposed to. No sooner has the elderly Pantalone, Doctor, or Captain managed to get down onto his knees in the prescribed manner, than she has removed herself to another location, and the poor man must make another attempt. A sequence of pursuit and evasion around, over and under stage furniture can be choreographed, limited only by the skill and agility of the actors.

In *The Path of True Love* (page 80) Captain Spavento finds that he has proposed to the servant, Franceschina; he is turned towards her on his right, and is kneeling on his left knee. Behind him, to stage left, stands the heroine Isabella. Discovering his mistake, he has only to switch onto his right knee without rising, to be facing her and immediately repeat the proposal word for word.

Other variations of the proposal rely on the character traits of those involved, especially that of the proposer: the Captain full of bombast and blunder; the Doctor with pedantry and pomposity; and Pantalone stressing his youthful vigour and virility in a piping treble.

Servant proposals are likely to take place at an awkward moment, during some other activity. For example: Colombina is busy cooking as Arlecchino proposes, and he is distracted from completing his mission by his greed for the food around him.

We have said that *Lazzi* are not properly in the provenance of the lovers, but the great moment of the desired proposal is not usually devoid of humour. Perhaps the Innamorato might have neglected to abase himself in the traditional posture and the Innamorata indicates that she expects it: Joan Greenwood as Gwendolyn needs only a downward glance to bring the would-be Ernest to his knees.[233] Or she may take charge of the event in a 'Shavian' manner ('There is no need for such nonsense, of course I'll marry you, you silly boy').

55
The Lazzi of 'Relay & Relate'

This is a device to communicate events that are supposed to be happening offstage, and is eminently suited to *Commedia* with its willingness to speak directly to the audience.

233. Film version of *The Importance of Being Earnest,* Oscar Wilde (1952)

We are familiar with Shakespeare and other writers' use of the chorus, or narrator to tell us things that have happened, to compress time that might otherwise span hours, or months, or years. The *'Relay & Relate'* *Lazzo* also compresses space, so that it would be possible to describe a distant battle taking place, or the approach of a caravan across a vast desert. This is easiest with a proscenium stage and wings but is possible elsewhere. As an example, one might imagine a stage version of *The Wizard of Oz* – Dorothy, with the Lion, the Tin Man, and the Scarecrow approaching the Emerald City. They come to the edge of the stage, their eyes fixed on a distant horizon just beyond the last row of spectators. They do an on-the-spot walking *Lazzo*, describing to each other or to the audience the vision they are approaching.

There are two examples in the present plays. There is a very useful one in *Fool's Gold* (page 93) that avoids the necessity of faking in some way the digging of the hole, and Pedrolino's mime in *The Duchess Mislaid* is used to build up the Captain's entrance (page 169).

56

The Lazzo of 'Rushing About'

The *'Rushing About' Lazzo* (also known as a 'Havoc') is just what it says, the main feature being that it is totally pointless (or would be in the real world). Anything that needs to be done is never more than half-done and generally hardly started. Buckets are taken to the well to be filled, and left there to fetch a broom. Sweeping is started and the buckets are remembered. They are then carried to the stables – at a run of course – but halfway there, it is realised they haven't been filled. Three or four Zanni are engaged in similar activities, getting in each other's way, un-doing anything someone has managed to complete, knocking into people and sending things flying; with all sorts of opportunities to include choreographed tumbling, catching and juggling. A most perfect example, was to be seen some years ago in a production by *The Piccolo Theatre of Milan* where the Arlecchino of Marcello Moretti performed amazing feats of tumbling and juggling in order to fulfil his duties as *The Servant of Two Masters*, in Goldoni's play.

57

The Lazzo of 'Searching'

This is where a person, or more usually an object is searched for, similar to the police searching for drugs, or a gang for the microfilm. Here is an imagined scenario:

> Pantalone has lost his left shoe. He looks for it himself and then calls for his servants Brighella and Arlecchino to help him. 'What shoe is it, Master?' 'Like this one, you fools.' He takes off the right one and shakes it at them. They start the search sensibly, looking in likely places – under the bed, behind the curtains. Pantalone has put down the right shoe. Brighella finds it. 'Here it is, Master! Right here all the time.' Pantalone joyfully puts it on, then: 'That's the right one. No, it's the wrong one. The right one is the left one. Oh, get on with it or I will be late for my appointment.' The Zanni restart the search, which now becomes surrealist, looking in more and more unlikely places – about Pantalone's person, and on each other (like a custom's search), in each other's ears, and up each other's noses. The left shoe – so far undiscovered – is shall we say by his bed, half hidden by bedclothes. Pantalone, stomping with one shoe on, manages to put the other foot straight into the left shoe – possible, because he traditionally wears a kind of open Turkish slipper. Now he has a shoe on each foot. All go on searching, including Pantalone himself. Then discovery! Sudden slowing up of the frantic action. They look at each other puzzled. Then a synchronised group *'Clocking'* of the audience. The *Lazzo* should either be accompanied by music, or lots of noise, swearing and exclamations.

58

The Lazzo of 'Startling each other'

We have said that the *Lazzi* can be anything from a single action to a whole scene. *'Startling each other'* is one of the briefest, where character

'B' comes suddenly into 'A's' proximity, causing him to cry out and nearly jump out of his skin. There is also the *Double Startle* when 'A's' reaction causes 'B' to get a fright. Often a third character, 'C', will startle either 'A' or 'B', and it can be used as a running gag throughout the scene.

59

The Lazzi of 'The Surprise Embrace'

It is usually the 'embracer' rather than the 'embracee' who is the more surprised. The embracer is invariably a male character, aroused by what he presumes to be the back or posterior of a familiar female. He makes clear his lewd intentions to the audience,[234] and rushes upon the object of his desire. She turns just in time to halt the demonstration of unwanted affection. Or, turns to prove that it is someone quite other than the one he had expected: repellent, austere, high status, or most frequently another man.[235]

60

The Lazzi of 'Tedium'

This belongs to that group of *Lazzi* in which there is a covert communication with the audience – a sort of silent aside. It could range from a single expression of doubt, contempt or amazement, to a whole sequence of reactions to the scene in progress. This often takes the form of a protest against the inordinate length and tedium of a speech or action.

A perfect example of this is seen in Laurel and Hardy's *The Fixer Uppers*, where Stan is the recipient of a long held kiss from the beautiful and elegant Mea Busch. Oliver starts with the briefest of glances to camera but soon develops it, with heavy gasps, loosening of his neckband, consulting his wristwatch and putting it to his ear to check if it is still going. For *Commedia*, the watch would be an anachronism; a

234. See *Lazzi of 'Lust'*, No. 37, page 247

235. In an episode of *Open All Hours,* a character (male) makes a grab for the 'milk girl' and finds a male substitute in his grasp.

traditional *Lazzo* is the miming of lathering the face and shaving, the implication being that there has been time to grow a beard.

61
The Lazzi of 'Thinking'

This is done by making a series of deliberate pacing steps. They must be made on a rhythm, which should be repeated. For example six steps in one direction and a pause for two beats. Turn and repeat in the other direction. Reduce to three steps and pause for one beat. Repeat in the other direction. The walks are accompanied by any stereotypical posture of *'Thinking'* – hand to chin, finger tapping lips, or fist to forehead like Rodin's *Thinker*. The pauses usually represent a possible solution, and the continuation, a rejection of that idea. Face front for the final 'Eureka!'.

It is also often used by two persons, in which case, they start by walking away from each other in opposite directions. If there is a third, he can walk up and downstage. They meet in the centre to consider progress. As in all this type of *Lazzi,* the walking needs to be synchronised. The postures, reactions and expressions are not varying with the characters and situation in which they find themselves.

There is an example of this *Lazzo* in the Marx Brother's film *At The Circus* during the zoo scene. It ends with a rather nice verbal gag:

GROUCHO We must think again.

CHICO We've tried it – I'll go home and think. Come and wake me in a couple of hours.

62
The Lazzi of 'Threats'

Here we are talking the threat of physical violence. These definitions and classifications are useful, for once we specify a particular form – as in this case of *'Threats'* – we become aware of other possibilities that might in themselves be useful. There could be 'Threats' with a gun, with a knife, or non-corporal; subtle hints of exposure; emotional or financial blackmail. But the *Commedia* threat is traditionally physical, and of the 'fisticuff' variety. As this is a threat and not the actual moment of GBH, it will take the form of a demonstration.

There is an excellent example of just this in the early Chaplin short *Easy Street*.[236] Charlie, the novice policeman is patrolling the no-go area of Easy Street when he sees the local heavy, Eric Campbell (the strong man of the early Chaplin days), approaching threateningly. He attempts to call for reinforcements from the phone that is attached to a lamppost at the corner of the street. As Campbell approaches, Chaplin fools about with the mouthpiece, looking into it as if it were a telescope. Campbell grabs it from him and looks into it. Charlie takes the opportunity to give him a mighty blow

Cosimo threatens

with his truncheon, which the big man hardly feels, but sufficient to arouse his anger, starting with a demonstration of his strength. He stretches out his arms: 'See how wide I am?' He rolls up each sleeve slowly and elegantly, and proceeds to bend the lamppost in two. At this point, Charlie manages to get Campbell's head in the lamp and turn on the gas. Interestingly, the bending lamppost appears in the *Commedia* section of the Stewart Granger film *Scaramouche*.[237]

The exact nature of the reaction to the threat depends on the character of the recipient. In the usual form, the 'Heavy', having being provoked to anger, gives a demonstration of his strength (as in the Chaplin example), without causing any actual harm to his adversary. At this magnificent display of testosterone, the intended victim takes the defence of bringing forward his feminine side; he shrinks in size, opens

236. *Easy Street* (1916)
237. *Scaramouche* (1952)

wide his eyes, all innocence and vulnerability and coy smiles. He kisses the proffered fist and measures the biceps admiringly. The villain, momentarily confused, drops his guard – only to receive a painful kick to the source of his masculinity, while his victim makes a lightning getaway or employs further tactics of brain over brawn.

In the case of Cosimo's threat to Pulcinella in *Home from the Wars* (page 28), Pulcinella's reaction is more likely to be one of surly defeat, having little in the way of brains and certainly no feminine side.

63
The Lazzi of 'Token Conspiring'

'Token conspiring' is called so because the 'onstage' time taken, is a fraction of what it would be in real life. The participants are nearly always the Zanni (male and female) and their intent is always benign; it usually represents the means by which the servants are able to help the lovers in their efforts to unite.

If it takes place between two characters, they face in towards each other and slightly upstage – with the impression of turning their backs on the rest of the cast and the audience. They speak voraciously to each other in stage-whispered gobbledegook. They use rapid gestures of debate: heads nod, fingers shake and bottoms wag. A plot of some complexity is proposed and resolved on within, say, ten seconds. When there are three or more involved they get into a sort of rugby scrum. The content is similar, though the addition of several sudden freezes in the action can be effective.

64
The Lazzo of '. . . Two Bits'

No claim that this is of any great antiquity, though no doubt there was something similar to predate it. The full phrase from which the *Lazzo* takes its title is: '*Shave and a haircut – two bits*', deriving from American Vaudeville. The required movement consists of a '*Ball change*', (i.e. ball of the right foot behind the left, step flat on the left) and a drop forward onto the right foot, the left being raised behind, and the palm of the right hand held uppermost to the audience in a request for applause. The timing is . . . *and one, two!* The verbal equivalent to complete a none-too-funny gag is the 'Boom-boom' of TV's Basil Brush.

65

The Lazzi of 'The Umbrella Gag'

For the greater span of *Commedia dell'Arte*'s history, umbrellas would be anachronistic, but it would be a pity to lose the generic title from music hall for all those occasions when an object is planted on another without his (only occasionally her) knowledge – a sort of reversal of the pick pocket *Lazzo*. In the original music hall version, one character accidentally takes – or is asked to hold – another's umbrella. He gives it back to the owner, only to find he has it on his arm again a moment later. The umbrella is very suitable for hooking on the arm, coat collar, etc., but a means can be found to attach many other articles: hat, bag, purse, letter, weapon, item of clothing, and even a notice saying 'Don't trust this person', which can be pinned to the victim's back. Also, with the collaboration of the actor playing the recipient, small objects can be palmed:

Arlecchino is being told off for eating one of Pantalone's apples. He keeps on taking bites out of it as the old man berates him, shaking his fist into his face.

PANTALONE Give it to me at once. (*Arlecchino takes two quick bites and then hides it behind his back.*) Hold out your hands.

Arlecchino proffers the empty left hand, then the right. Pantalone turns Arlecchino round, to look at his back but doesn't find his apple. Again, he shakes his fist at Arlecchino, who taps him gently on the clenched fist. Pantalone opens his hand, to find he is grasping the remains of the apple core. A chase ensues!

66

The Lazzi of "Vanishing and Invisibility"

The concept belongs principally to the Harlequin of those great panto-mimes seen in the last years of the nineteenth century at Drury Lane and other major theatres throughout the provinces; Harlequin, the bespangled dancer-magician whose enchanted baton is no longer the slapstick of comedy, but a wand that initiates the great transformation scenes. With it, he taps the kitchen mangle and it changes into a ship to transport the Principal Girl to the Kingdom of Neptune. He waves it at the drab cottage wall and it vanishes, to be replaced by a glittering undersea cavern. However, if we look back to the European *Commedia dell'Arte* – to the Italians, and to Molière – there is the 'fourberie'. This is the scam in which the 'gentilhomme', Pantalone, might be sold a wondrous ring that bestows invisibility on whoever wears it.

SCAPIN Well, would you like to try it? But . . . I will have to have the five hundred francs before you do – after all, when you're invisible, you might run away. Ha, ha, ha! (*Pantalone pays up and then puts on the ring.*) There you are – well, I think you are. I can't see you. Say something, so I know where you are.

PANTALONE I'm here – right here.

SCAPIN Where? (*Purposely bumping into Pantalone.*) I'm so sorry . . . But it's your fault – you'll have to be very careful when you're wearing the ring. You might get run over by a horse and cart.

TRIVELIN (*who is in on the scam and pretending not to see Pantalone*) Have you seen Pantalone anywhere? He owes my master some money, and has sent me to look for him.

SCAPIN No, I haven't seen him. He's not around here.

PANTALONE Ha, ha! This ring's worth every cent. Now my creditors will never find me.

Scapin and Trivelin vanish – PDQ!

67

The Lazzi of 'The Zanni Duo'

These are the 'Brokers Men' of pantomime, the double act of music hall, the original of all comic double acts, and their *Lazzi* are nearly all based on the idea of duplication. Sometimes the pair are clones, as with Fuoco and Fuomo in *The Duchess Mislaid,* but more frequently we have the smart Zanni 'A' and the stupid Zanni 'B' – Abbot and Costello, Laurel and Hardy – and as we see the smart Zanni is not always that bright. The stupid Zanni always wants to copy everything his smart brother does. If Zanni 'A' takes big strides, Zanni 'B' will copy them, almost simultaneously, but not quite. If Zanni 'A' shakes his fist at someone, so will 'B', but with a little less conviction. Zanni 'B' will copy everything his partner says, but gets it wrong. His attempts to duplicate his partner's actions end in disaster, as when Pedrolino tries to copy Brighella in Act I Scene 2 of *The Duchess Mislaid* (page 151). Brighella throws a stone up at Pantalone's shuttered window to wake him – then Pedrolino throws horse droppings, which hit Pantalone full in the face.

Lazzo or
Improvisation?

Appendix 1: Stage Fights

As always, the primary consideration is safety, and that means choreography and rehearsal – this is one place where improvisation is not to be encouraged. In fact, fights have much in common with *Lazzi*; they need to be rehearsed business, ready to be included into the improvised or scripted scene. It is typical of *Commedia* that they can be used in other plays, with only minor adaptation.

Where swordplay is concerned, a decision has to be made as to whether 'real' swords or wooden ones will be used. Wooden ones are good because that's 'poor' theatre, and 'poor' theatre is good *Commedia*! If you miss the sound of clashing steel, use 'mouth sounds', or by striking tin cans on or offstage. When the intention is wholly comic, a third choice is to substitute slapsticks for swords, which provide excellent sound effects. If you decide on steel swords, make sure the points are padded with insulating tape. Always point the blades above or below the level of your partner's face; a third party can easily bump into you and cause an accident, however careful you are being. The amount of actual swordplay can be augmented by 'Errol Flynn' antics: tables overturned, chests leapt upon, and curtains slashed. Unarmed fights give excellent comic possibilities, including blows that don't land home – or blows resulting in acrobatic falls, rolls and flips inspired by the martial arts.

Appendix 2: Onstage Locations

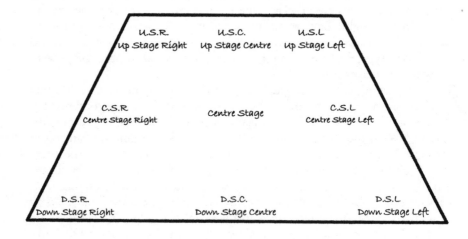